Music as Cognition

MUSIC AS COGNITION

The Development of Thought in Sound

Mary Louise Serafine

Columbia University Press
New York   1988

Library of Congress Cataloging-in-Publication Data

Serafine, Mary Louise.
  Music as cognition.

  Bibliography: p.
  Includes index.
  1. Music—Psychology. 2. Cognition. I. Title.
ML3838.S48 1987   781'.15   87–5122
ISBN 0–231–05742–3

c 10 9 8 7 6 5 4 3 2

Columbia University Press
New York   Guildford, Surrey
Copyright © 1988 Columbia University Press
All rights reserved
Printed in the United States of America

Contents

Preface ix

1. **The Problem: Whence Music Comes** 1
   Facts about Music 1
   Theories about Music 7

2. **The Idea of Music as Cognition** 29
   Preliminary Concepts 29
   Case Study: The Formal Western Tradition 42
   Psychological Research in Music 52

3. **Some Processes** 69
   Defining Music Cognition 69
   Temporal Processes 74
   Nontemporal Processes 79
   Aims of a Developmental Approach 88

4. **The Development of Temporal Processes in the Child** 95
   General Introduction to the Studies 95
   Temporality: Understanding the Successive Dimension 107
   Temporality: Understanding Simultaneity 134

5. **The Development of Nontemporal Processes in the Child** 157
   Tonal Closure: Understanding Endedness 157
   Transformations: Understanding Similarity and Difference 171
   Abstraction: Recognizing Parts in New Contexts 196
   Hierarchic Levels: Understanding Musical Structure 213

6. **Conclusions** 223
   Developmental Trends 224
   The Role of Formal Training and Pitch Discrimination 228

Temporal and Nontemporal Processes   231
Conclusion   233

References   237

Index   243

Preface

This book had its beginning in 1971 when, as a graduate student, I began to give piano lessons to a number of able learners, mainly children. The critical moment occurred during a lesson in which, inexcusably short on good sense, I was teaching a child how to use the metronome. Even after repeated explanation and demonstration, she insisted that the metronome followed the beat of the music that I was playing, instead of vice versa. When the rhythms got faster, she said, so did the clicks. And how, she wondered, leaning over to peer at the back of the metronome, can a machine know what the piano is doing?

A subsequent study bore out the conclusion that the meter perceived by children is not that marvel of regularity indicated by our notational system or readily imposed by adults on all manner of rhythms, however variable (Serafine 1979). Instead, children perceive a "meter," if at all, that is not separable from ongoing rhythm. This raised to my mind the possibility that what the child more generally hears of music is not at all like that heard by the adult. And if the perception of a thing so varies across the life span, I wondered, where then does the thing reside?

This book is an attempt to determine where music resides, or put otherwise, what it is. I conclude that various implicit definitions of music, such as music-as-notation, music-as-emotion, and even music-as-sound are at best in need of repair; I propose the idea of music as cognition for their replacement. Chapters 1, 2, and 3 set out my proposal and describe some specific cognitive processes that give rise to the artform as we know it. Chapters 4 and 5 describe the route of the development of those processes in the child, from the age of 5 to early adolescence and adulthood. Finally, I draw conclusions about musical development and the distinction between temporal and nontemporal processes. The reader will see that, throughout the book, my commitment to developmental psychology as an approach to epistemology remains firm.

This work was undertaken during the years 1979–83, while I was a postdoctoral fellow at Yale. The list of debts I incurred there is long, principally because of what I learned from William Kessen, Irvin Child, and Robert Crowder, in psychology, and from Allen Forte in music theory. To the degree that the book is successful in treading among the issues of development, cross-cultural aesthetics, cognition, and music analysis, it is owing to their insight, criticism, and the accumulated wisdom of their own programs of research. I am especially grateful that my thinking about history, music, and human development benefited from the influence of my postdoctoral sponsor, Bill Kessen.

I am also indebted to the able research assistance of Beth Stevenson, Stacy Anderson, Gail Spear, Lisa Barca-Hall, Margaret Ebin, Herta Flor, John Stevenson, and Sara K. Schneider, all of whom worked on the project at Yale, and to Stacy Smith and Diane Bednarski, who later worked with me at Vassar. Beth Stevenson must be singled out for conducting the data collection and for performing innumerable miracles during her two years with the project. She administered hundreds of tasks to even recalcitrant preschoolers, and did so with experimental wisdom and good musical sense. I would also like to thank Lee Rothfarb, who composed all of the music for the research. Quite possibly there are better designed experiments than those reported here, but I am certain none sound as good. (See especially the Hierarchic Levels task, item 4.) I am also grateful to Deborah Stein for providing the reductions referred to in chapter 3.

Subjects for the study were drawn primarily from the Spring Glen Elementary School of Hamden, Connecticut, where the generosity of the teachers and staff was outdone only by the good will of their students. For the same reasons we were fortunate to have the participation of the Neighborhood Music School of New Haven, Connecticut, the New Haven Suzuki Violin School, and the Arlington Elementary School of Poughkeepsie, New York.

The book owes much to Penelope Britton, who drew the musical examples, and to Mildred Tubby, who blessedly typed instead of word-processed the manuscript. I am grateful to United Feature Syndicate for permission to reproduce the cartoon shown in chapter 1, and to the journal *Cognition* for permission to use sections of my article "Cognition in Music" in chapters 2 and 3.

Finally, I am grateful to the Spencer Foundation for their support of the project since its inception.

Music as Cognition

The Problem:
Whence Music Comes

FACTS ABOUT MUSIC

Because it is so ubiquitous and universal a phenomenon, whose existence remains unexplained by any apparent practical purpose, and more so because its very nature is elusive, music has been boggling the minds of scholars for well over three thousand years. Not that the difficulties have limited the number of theories put forth about what music is, or, as I prefer to say, where music resides or whence it comes. Traditional conceptions have emphasized, among other things, that music springs from need of emotional communication, or from inherent mathematical order, or from the pleasure of beautiful sounds. But many and even more recent views fail to accommodate four facts which I take to be the starting point for any theory of music and which, in my view, give rise to the thesis of music as cognition. These facts are, first, that all cultures possess music and all persons have knowledge of it to a considerable degree; second, that there are many and vastly different types of music, even within a single culture; third, that music changes; and fourth, that the young of a culture come eventually to adopt the general tastes of their parents. Below I review these facts—music's universality, diversity, change, and acquisition—before describing some of the traditional conceptions of music that contrast with the one proposed here.

Universality

There are two senses in which music is universal: No culture exists without it and all persons have knowledge of it to a considerable degree. Whether cultures are defined by geographic region, social class, or age group, each has its music; Cajun, classical, and "heavy metal" are species of music associated respectively with such cultures.

Most readers will have no difficulty agreeing that music exists in all cultures, but what may be more controversial is the claim that all persons have knowledge of it to a consequential degree. Yet the probable abilities of the average, even musically untutored adult reveal impressive (if intuitive) understandings. On the simplest level such a person can easily distinguish music from other sounds and can discriminate his own from foreign music. He can identify a musical style as folk, classical, or jazz (perhaps also making finer distinctions) and undoubtedly prefers one of these. He can certainly recognize a familiar melody no matter what the particular accompaniment (the appearance of "Going Home" in Dvořák's *New World Symphony* would be a case in point), and several strands of melody are likely to be stored in his memory. On a more advanced level the person can tell whether two pieces of music are similar or different in global features such as mood, loudness, meter or beat, tempo, timbre, rhythmic character, and relative number of instruments, and probably can also judge more specific melodic-structural characteristics. (For example, everyone I've asked has verified after a moment's reflection that the melodies of "Twinkle, Twinkle Little Star" and "Baa, Baa Black Sheep" are identical.) It is likely that the person detects the similarity between a theme and its variation. While listening to a piece of music the person knows, at least intuitively, whether the phrase he is hearing is fully in progress, is possibly about to end, or is definitely now ending. On hearing repetitions, such as the recurring refrain of a song, he perceives them as familiar and not as new music each time; in fact, he probably comes to expect the refrain at appropriate points. If asked, the person could tell whether a particular melody "makes sense," or "sounds good," or could be easily sung, and so on.

Such abilities represent significant understandings and intuitions about music, and there are other, more specific ones that might be listed depending on the particular musical style(s) with which the person is assumed to be familiar. These understandings and intuitions constitute the musical knowledge shared by virtually all members of a culture. The cartoon shown in figure 1.1 is an example of humor that capitalizes on how widespread such knowledge is. The cartoon's effect depends only in part on the reader's familiarity with the sequence of words and tones in the song itself. More importantly it depends on the reader's intuitive

© 1977 Newspaper Enterprise Association, Inc.

Figure 1.1

knowledge that an unresolved approach to the tonic, with its consequent feeling of incompleteness, is set up by the tones on "le-et free-dom." The humor lies in sympathizing with the gentleman's annoyance at the delay in resolution, which he accomplishes himself on "ring." Note that more is involved here than simply an interruption followed by continuation. Rather, the reader intuitively knows (to put it in technical terms) that a descending approach to the tonic that stops on the supertonic ("—dom") *must* eventually continue. Consequently, had a supposedly humorous interruption occurred elsewhere in the song, it would not have been so successful.

One task of a theory of music is to contend with how widespread such musical knowledge is, to address not only the obvious skill of the few (such as that possessed by trained musicians), as has traditionally been the case, but also the subtler skill of the many.

Diversity

It is common to speak of "music" as though it were a single entity and all of a piece, but more properly speaking there are many and diverse musics. These take the form of different types or styles, and a large number of them may coexist within a single culture. The evidence for multiple styles is the almost endless list of labels that describe them; baroque, impressionist, twelve-tone, big band, blues, gospel, and Dixieland are but a few examples. Such styles are in large measure distinct entities, each with its own compositional practices (typical melodic structures, harmonies, and so forth), a group of composers and performers who work rather exclusively in that style, and a body of listeners who understand and habitually listen to it.

One of the tasks of a general theory of music is to contend with such multiple, diverse, and co-existing musics.

Change

The more difficult challenge for a general theory, however, is the fact that musical styles continuously change, evolving over time into new styles and themselves becoming obsolete. The evidence for this is very clear over long spans of time (historically, every style of composition has become extinct) and in some cases over short spans, such as within the lifetime of a single composer. The works of Beethoven, representing as they do a shift from classical to more romantic style, provide an example. The symptom of style change is the incessant writing of new music. Every ten years American composers alone add one million *copyrighted* new works to the stock of compositions already extant, but the actual number written, performed, and heard—including those uncopyrighted—is undoubtedly much larger.[1]

The facts of style diversity and style change have been the major stumbling blocks for psychological theories of music because, as we shall see, it has been difficult to conceptualize psychological processes that apply beyond the tonal, European style written between 1650 and 1900. Still, no theory of music can afford to ignore musical change.

Acquisition

What is amazing about the acquisition of music by the young is not that they eventually play instruments and pieces on which they have been instructed by their elders, but rather that they know subtler things which no one has told them about: what counts as order in music, what features of it should be attended to, what makes melodies similar and different, what properly makes a tune end, and so forth.

A general theory of music must address the question, how does the understanding of music come to be? In so doing, it must mark the route of development from the child's conception of music to the adult's.

In summary, music's universality, diversity, change, and acquisition are facts that must be accommodated by a general theory of what music is and where it comes from. The central claim of this book is that music is a form of thought and that it develops over the life span much as other forms of thought develop, principally those such as language, mathematical reasoning, and ideas about the physical world. This view is elaborated in subsequent chapters, but a number of special assumptions and claims can be made explicit at this point.

[1]The number copyrighted includes both serious and popular works. (From "Copyright Registration, by Subject Matter: 1970 to 1982," U.S. Bureau of the Census, Statistical Abstract of the United States, 104th ed., Washington, D.C., 1983.) There are now at least 72,000 composers in the United States who have published and/or recorded at least one piece of music and who are members of ASCAP or BMI, although the number of composers who are actively engaged in music yet are not members of these organizations is certainly much higher.

The first is that the principal transaction in a musical enterprise is assumed to be that between a person—composer, performer, or listener—and a piece of music. More specifically, the critical interaction is not that between composer and listener, or performer and listener, or composer and performer, but rather that between one of those actors and a piece of music. This means that the idea of musical communication among composing, performing, and listening parties is not, in the present view, central to the conduct of the artform.

The second claim is that music arises from a core set of cognitive processes common to all three activities, composing, performing, and listening. This is not to say that such activities are cognitively identical in all respects; on the contrary, each employs processes unique to it. But composing, performing, and listening share *some* overlapping cognitive processes, or the artform could not exist for very long. This means that some of the music cognitions of composers must also be the music cognitions of listeners and vice versa, although this does not necessarily imply a communicative function. As a result, musical-cognitive processes are both "in the head" and evidenced "in the music." Two corollaries follow:

(1) The patterns, relationships, and organizations that we claim to see "in the music" must also be apprehended by listeners, or they do not count as evidence of "real" music cognitions.
(2) The processes that we claim to have discovered "in the head" (chiefly through perception experiments) must also be evidenced in how music actually *is,* now and in other eras.

Thus, the disciplines of music theory and history, whose task it is to pinpoint the structure and evolution of music, and the disciplines of behavioral science, whose business it is to identify human processes, are parallel routes of attack on the problem of music cognition. Ultimately they must come to the same destination.

The third claim is that two types of cognitive processes occur in music—what I refer to as *style-specific* and *generic* processes—and that the distinction between them must not be overlooked. Style-specific processes are those relevant to a single musical style; for example, the feeling of stasis or completion that one experiences on hearing a dominant-to-tonic harmonic progression results from style-specific knowledge appropriate to the so-called tonal style or idiom of the West. Generic processes, on the other hand, are by definition universal and occur in all styles. The understanding of closure or completion *in general,* however it might be accomplished in a particular style, is an example of a generic process. Generic processes in music are difficult to identify, but I argue that they are central to a psychological theory of music.

The fourth claim is that cognition in music—in listening as well as in composing and performing—is an active, constructive process. The position I advance must be called "strong" cognitivism because it goes somewhat beyond the assertion that perception and memory are not necessarily veridical. Rather, the position questions whether musical properties can be said to preexist in pieces of music. We return to this point later.

A related claim concerns the constituent elements of music. Traditionally, the elements of music are assumed to be tones and assemblages of tones called chords. Such a view critically determines how we conceive composition and perception. For example, tones may be considered the material with which a composer works, by arranging and conglomerating them, or tones may be considered the basic units processed by the listener. The present view, however, holds that tones and chords cannot in any meaningful and especially psychological way be considered the elements of music. Rather, tones and chords are viewed as the inevitable by-product of musical writing and analysis, and as such are useful, even necessary analytic tools with minimal cognitive reality.

In summary, I put forth here a particular view of music as cognition, and in so doing propose a group of generic processes that meet two conditions: applicability across a range of styles and (probable) employment in both composition and listening. A major portion of the book is given over to describing studies of how these processes develop from childhood to adulthood. The view of music as cognition that I espouse here contrasts with several traditional views of music's nature: that music springs forth from an individual trait; that it is a form of communication; that it is a cluster of learned behaviors; that it is a special feature of nature; and that it is an object or stimulus composed of sound. I treat each of these alternatives below.

THEORIES ABOUT MUSIC

Music as Trait

Historically, one of the most influential theories of music has been the theory of music as trait. Some proclivity called musicality or musical talent, aptitude, ability, or intelligence is held to exist inside a person as a central core or germ and to be responsible for the person's activity in music. The proclivity is thought to exist in some persons more than in others, its source may be either environmental or innate, and the amount of it one has is thought to be relatively stable over time, at least after early childhood. An implicit but nevertheless central assumption of this view is that music arises by virtue of the existence of this trait, particularly in the very talented, such as composers and *virtuosi*.

The trait theory of music owes much to Francis Galton (1822–1911). It was Galton who made a critical addition to Darwin's theory that the natural selection of inherited *physical* differences among individuals was responsible for change in a species. Namely, Galton assumed that there were also inherited *psychological* differences among individuals (traits inside people), that such traits were responsible for eminent achievement, and that in principle they could be measured. Galton's special contributions to the trait theory of music were two. First, he tried to show systematically, through lineage tracing in families such as the Bachs, that musicality was inherited. Second, he worked indefatigably to devise tests for another trait, namely intelligence, and his tests later served as models for tests of musicality. In particular Galton's assumption that sensory acuity was tantamount to intelligence had a determining influence on music tests. On both of these counts—inherited musicality and sensory-physical measures of intelligence—it must be said that Galton, like many great figures who have influenced our thinking, failed utterly in the particulars, meanwhile succeeding brilliantly in the general outlines. For in assuming that parent/child similarities must indicate an inherited trait, Galton failed to consider that families share not only inheritance but environment, and thus he downplayed the influence of the latter. Moreover, Galton's tests were not good measures of intelligence. Still, his influence was profound, and within a few decades after his death dozens of tests of musical ability were developed with the goal of separating the musical wheat from the chaff. In large part this goal was thought to be accomplished by measuring, as Galton proposed, sensory acuity.

A proper chronology of the music-testing movement begins with Seashore's *Measures of Musical Talents,* first published in 1919. The test required subjects to tell whether the second of two oscillator-generated tones was higher or lower (pitch), stronger or weaker (loudness), longer or shorter (time), or same or different (timbre). Some 200 pairs of tones would be compared in this way. Kwalwasser and Dykema followed with a similar test published in 1930, except that subjects compared not only single tones but also short piano melodies and various instruments. In addition they were tested on which of two possibilities better completes a melody. Wing, in England, offered a test that same year in which subjects were asked to determine how many tones there were in a given chord and whether two melodies were the same or different in terms of preferable rhythm, harmony, loudness, and phrasing. Later, Wing offered a combined test of musical ability and appreciation (1948). Also in England, Mainwaring (1931) developed a test in which subjects were asked such questions as: Which two of the following three or four tones are the same? In which pair of intervals are the two tones further apart? And, ten seconds after hearing a tune, did the last two tones go up or down or were they the same? Drake's test appeared in 1934 and required but two tasks: determining whether a second melody was the same as the first or whether it was different in key, time, or tones; and counting at the same rate as metronome beats, then, when told to stop, indicating the number of beats counted thus far. In 1942 Gaston offered a test with tasks similar to some of those already described, and in addition his subjects were asked to determine whether, given a single tone followed by a chord, the former was contained in the latter. Lundin followed with yet another ability test in 1949.

These are but a handful of the widely known, moderately well-researched tests that were published (and revised and reissued) in the period from 1920 to 1960. In addition, countless more tests were developed and used but were not commercially available. During the 1960s, three additional tests were developed which remain the standard for tests of their type. These were, in the United States, Gordon's test of musical *aptitude,* Colwell's of *achievement,* and in Britain, Bentley's test of musical *ability.* Compared to earlier tests, these were superior in sound quality, reliability, and data bases for norms. In addition they employed more complex and legitimately musical stimuli, although perception remained the central task. Gordon asked his subjects whether, given two tunes, the second is a melodic variation of the first, or is in the same tempo, or meter, or has the better phrasing, or ending, or style. Colwell's two-hour battery included pitch, interval, meter, and major/minor discrimination, as well as tasks such as the following: A piano melody is heard followed by a three-part string setting of the same melody; the subject indicates which part has the melody. Bentley asked his subjects to determine, among other things, how many tones there were in a chord and whether two melodies were the same or different (and in the latter case which tone had changed).

Tests such as these—which made perceptual ability the measure of musicality as a trait—had a profound effect on music-psychological research in the half-century after Seashore's contribution of 1919. A large part of the musical research on adults and nearly all of that on children was conducted with the use of such tests (see reviews by Shuter 1968; Shuter-Dyson and Gabriel 1981). The resulting literature is sizeable, although a number of issues were never resolved (see Serafine 1986). The one most relevant to us here is whether musicality as a trait truly exists, and this necessarily turns on whether it can be objectively measured. Three facts seem to challenge a positive answer. First, experts in the field have historically been unable to agree on what musicality is, what its components are, and how it should be measured—whether through perception tests alone or through additional measures involving manual dexterity, interest in music, and so forth. A case in point is the long-standing Seashore-Mursell controversy, dating from the 1920s and '30s, in which bitter disagreement ensued over the importance of perceptual acuity, methods of test validation, and other issues (see Seashore 1938; Mursell 1937). Dispute among psychologists on the theoretical nature of a trait has never impeded its measurement, however much it may give way to cynicism. But in the case of musicality two additional facts have raised doubts about the concept. First, correlations among the various tests are low, giving little support to the notion that a single trait is being measured. Even isolated subtests designed to measure the same capacity (for example, pitch perception or time perception) are not highly intercorrelated. Second, the predictive validity of the tests has turned out to be marginal. Thus, measurement difficulties, as well as theoretical ones, have made trouble for the assertion that musicality exists as a trait. Perhaps equally troublesome is the logic that seems to underlie the concept itself. It is basically as follows:

(1) *Observation*: People vary in the degree to which they engage in music; some are musicians and some are not.
(2) *Assumptions*: (a) Behavior is caused (or even made inevitable) by the possession of relevant traits.
    (b) People possess different traits, to varying degrees.
(3) *Conclusion*: Variation in musical behavior is caused by variation in a trait such as "musicality" or "musical talent."

Such logic is implicit in much talk about music. To cite a recent example, Smith (1984) gives an informal report on a new measure of cerebral dominance and the left/right differences that he found between professional musicians and the general population. His conclusions, however, are framed exclusively in terms of the measure "and its relation to musical talent" even though no measure of talent was administered. That is, something called "musical talent" was presumed to reside in the musicians, to power their behavior, and to be absent in the nonmusician public. Note that one is assumed to be a musician *as a result* of being talented, not the other way around.

A closer look at the argument spelled out above reveals that, while Observation (1) is undeniable, Conclusion (3) and the Assumptions at (2) are questionable. That is, there seems to be reason for doubting that a trait, particularly a single trait, can be the *cause* of a particular behavior. In the case of music tests that borrowed Galton's perceptual emphasis, there is even more reason to doubt that perceptual acuity alone is a cause of musical behavior. Small wonder that such tests fared poorly when it came to the prediction of actual musicianship.

On the other hand, defenders of trait-testing generally make two replies: (1) that although musical talent may consist of several components, measuring a single component of it (perceptual acuity) nevertheless estimates the whole constellation; and (2) that perceptual acuity may be a necessary even if not sufficient condition for musical behavior. Each of these replies has some obvious difficulties. The first is untrue to the degree that the component measured differs in substance from the other (unmeasured) ones. The second leaves unexplained why *degrees* of perceptual acuity should predict *degrees* of musical talent and behavior. That is, it would seem that the perceptual acuity necessary for musical activity would be a threshold, all-or-nothing affair: You either have the capacity to sing and play in tune or you do not, and it seems unlikely that increasingly fine degrees of acuity are evidence of increasingly fine degrees of musicianship. In particular the detection of differences smaller than a few cents or milliseconds would not seem to offer much musical advantage.

In summary, both theoretical and measurement problems have threatened the concept of musicality or musical talent—as a trait within persons—and it has been especially difficult to substantiate perceptual acuity as its criterion. Still, talent has remained one of the most ubiquitous psychological constructs put to use in explaining music.

For the present purposes it is worth noting how this approach addresses the four characteristics of music mentioned earlier. In the case of universality, the trait theory generally allows that persons of talent are to be found in all cultures, but it holds that the endowment for musical capacity is unevenly distributed across the population. The view does not assume that significant musical knowledge is universally present across individuals. On the issues of music's diversity and continuous change, the trait approach has little to say; it simply does not take these two facts to be starting points for the theory. And on the issue of acquisition, trait approaches are concerned with how individuals come to be in possession of musical talent (e.g., through innate endowment or experience) and whether the trait is stable over the life span. On such questions trait approaches contrast with that taken here in their focus on the differences rather than similarities across individuals that influence acquisition.

Music as Communication

A view that is older and perhaps even more widely held than trait theory is the view that music arises principally from human communication: A composer or performer transmits some *message* more or less directly to a receptive listener. There are several variants of the music-as-communication theory, but nearly all agree that the message is an emotional one. Further, they agree that it is this emotional communication—*not* merely pleasing the senses, as an older, hedonistic esthetic once held—that is the principal purpose of the artform. Beyond this agreement, variants of the theory differ greatly on the nature of the emotions communicated and where they reside (in the music? composer? listener?). For example, consider briefly three theories, one from the nineteenth century and two contemporary ones.

Tolstoy's (1898/1955) view, the quintessential romantic conception, consists of these elements:

(1) The composer is possessed of a feeling or emotion.
(2) He seeks to communicate it to others, that is, to evoke in them the same feeling.
(3) Since words are inadequate to the purpose, he uses music (or art, poetry, etc.)..
(4) In hearing the music, the listener is seized by the same feelings the composer had felt.

Thus Tolstoy envisions a direct chain of emotional contagion from the composer (via the performer) through the work to the listener. In such a vision the criterion for goodness is clear: the sincerity of the composer's emotion matters most. In true romantic spirit, this leads Tolstoy to a critics-be-damned attitude that elevates peasant and folk music above that of "professionals" and that claims a social-humanitarian role for the arts: Art reduces our natural savagery and binds us together in community.

At first glance Tolstoy's view has some elements that recommend it. It rightly holds that the aim of music is not mere pleasure, and what it substitutes for pleasure is a wholesome, socially useful sort of communication that is certainly admirable to espouse. Who can argue with shared emotion and the creation of bonds among men? Still, it is clear that Tolstoy's view is not only incapable of being substantiated by any form of evidence (how could we show it were true?), but also that what little evidence there is seems to contradict it entirely. For composers are not themselves *in a state of* anger, sorrow, or love while they work on a piece, and listeners do not attend concerts with the aim of being infected with sundry emotional states as they move from piece to piece on the program. Indeed, listeners are notoriously at odds with one another in attempting to pinpoint *specific* emotions represented in a piece, although they may concur on global characterizations ("gay," "somber," etc.) for some clear-cut cases.

It is on two counts, then, that we find fault with Tolstoy: (1) the highly specific message that he hopes will be communicated is at best only a global characterization and even then occurs only in some instances; and (2) Tolstoy's listener is a passive one whose emotions come not from within but are stimulated entirely from the outside. Such a view is generally in conflict with what we know to be true about emotion, although I will not detail the point further here.

A more recent approach to music as communication is Kivy's (1980), which is briefly the following:

(1) Music is indeed *expressive of* particular emotions and moods (e.g., anger, sadness).

(2) This does not imply, however, that the composer or performer is *expressing* emotion. The players are not angry while playing and the audience does not prepare for fight or flight. No contagious arousal of feeling occurs.

(3) Rather, music affects us because it reminds us of certain emotions

(my term), or, in Kivy's terms, because we *understand* the music to be expressive of particular states.

(4) Music does this by *resembling* other types of emotional expression. A melody or tempo may resemble the characteristics of speech and gesture (such as pitch and speed) that are associated with specific emotions. For example, the voice falls and is quieter in grief and sad music does so as well.

It is on this last point that Kivy's view diverges from Suzanne Langer's (1953), with which it otherwise has some in common. Both theorists agree that music does not directly *express* but rather is *expressive of* certain emotions. Langer holds, however, that music is only generally expressive: It represents the general *form* of our feeling life, the ebb and flow and coming and going of various passions, sadnesses, and joys, but it does not represent specific emotions. Kivy, on the other hand, holds that music is quite specific. He goes so far as to cite contrasting examples of "exuberant joy" as opposed to "confident but more subdued joy" in a comparison of the "Pleni sunt coeli" of Bach's *Mass in B minor* with "I know that my redeemer liveth" from Handel's *Messiah* (p. 53). My own opinion is that Kivy is fighting a losing battle on the issue of emotional specifics. Nevertheless, of the musical expression theorists he gives the most plausible account of those pieces of music likely to fall clearly into categories such as sad or joyous, and he is the most thorough in providing real evidence from the musical repertory. What his theory does not accommodate are all the other pieces of music—and there are far too many of them—that are not clear candidates for stock, stereotypic emotions or moods.

An emotional communication theory that potentially accommodates all music is Leonard Meyer's (1956, 1967, 1973). The theory is unique in positing the communication of emotional meanings, meanwhile resisting outright referentialism, for in this view music's emotional punches are packed inside the music itself. No symbolization or resemblance takes place that allows something in the music to refer to or represent something else outside, such as grief or love. Briefly, Meyer's main points are these:

(1) *Definition of emotion*: "Emotion or affect is aroused when a tendency to respond is arrested or inhibited" (1956:14). In other words, when we feel that we are about to act or respond in a certain way, yet are prevented from doing so, then the resulting arousal is emotion. I reach for the habitual cigarette, find there is none, and the result is emotion.

(2) As we listen to music we become aware of *tendencies* in the tonal

events and patterns, which give rise to *expectations* (whether conscious or not) about what tonal events will come next. Examples are the following: After a dominant chord, I expect resolution to tonic; after a rising sequence of tones, I expect descent; after wide melodic skips, I expect stepwise filling in.

(3) Our emotional experience of music arises from the variable ways in which such musical tendencies, and our resulting expectations, are in fact handled by the composer. Over the course of a piece of music, our expectations may be met, prolonged, or denied, and the play upon them constitutes emotional experience.

(4) Thus, musical meaning is entirely intramusical and is tantamount to expectation. A particular dominant chord has meaning for me because of the expectation it gives rise to; and once the chord has been resolved, prolonged, or otherwise dealt with by the events that follow it, its meaning may be said to change relative to the expectation I originally had for it.

Meyer's theory is in some ways similar to the cognitive thesis I propose here because it emphasizes the internal mental processes of the human subject and not, for example, stable, personal traits or forces external to humans such as those that I take up later. But Meyer's theory is different from the approach I take here in the following way: it leads to a concern with processes—however internal or cognitive—that pertain to particular, individual *styles* of music; that is, it leads us to ask what sort of something-or-other in baroque or twelve-tone or Indian music causes such-and-so expectation to occur in listeners. Indeed, the very idea of style is one of Meyer's central theoretical pillars. By contrast, the approach I take here seeks to distinguish those (cognitive) processes that are style-specific from those that may be pan-stylistic or universal; it then purports to study only the latter. If Meyer's theory can be said to embody a process that is pan-stylistic in the sense I propose it, the sole candidate for such a process would be expectation itself, since presumably tendencies, and therefore expectations, occur in all styles.

The contrast between Meyer's concern with style and my own with pan-stylistic cognitions is nowhere more apparent than on the issue of how the human organism comes to acquire the cognitions in question. Meyer assumes that "learning" and even "habit" play important roles in understanding music, undoubtedly because his theory concerns the sorts of stylistic effects that vary from culture to culture. By contrast, my own view emphasizes *development,* because I am concerned with the generic processes that might be expected to hold across cultures and individuals.

But to return to the more general notion of music as communication. Most such theories posit a more or less direct line of transmission from the composer or performer through the work to the listener, thus the critical determiner of the listener's experience is *perception,* and not other processes such as, for example, cognition. I hope it will become clear in later chapters why I believe musical experience is more a matter of cognition than perception, but for now I want to press only this point: It is not clear that the demands of either descriptive accuracy or theoretical necessity compel us to posit a *communicative* process in music, even if perception were granted as the principal mode of musical experience. Communication, in the sense that we ordinarily mean it, is simply not suggested necessarily by the facts about music that we observe to be true: that people engage in and understand it, that it is diverse and changing, that the young acquire it, and so forth. If I may be permitted to reason by analogy, music is perhaps more like literature than like language, and the latter, not the former, has communication as its *raison d'être.*

Music as Behavior

When a thorough history of twentieth-century psychology is one day written, it will certainly be remarked that the philosophy of behaviorism, which did a thriving business in every other area of psychology, did not sell well in the field of music. Indeed, nearly everyone has made the antibehaviorist assumption that music involves something inherently and unavoidably internal, such as talent, emotion, or cognition. Consequently, behaviorism has been occasionally criticized but more often ignored as an approach to music, with only a few exceptions. Some scholars in the field of music education (see Madsen et al. 1975; Madsen and Kuhn 1978) and a few psychologists such as Lundin (1967) have made implicit assumptions of a behaviorist sort, although a full-blown elaboration of the view has never been worked out. The main points would seem to be the following:

(1) Musical activity is best regarded as a series of overt, observable behaviors. Thus we may speak of composing behavior (e.g., holding a pencil, putting marks on paper), performing behavior (holding the

instrument, placing the fingers, drawing the bow), and listening behavior (e.g., selecting music, attending, etc.).

(2) The positing of internal mental functions is either unnecessary to an
adequate theory of music or is simply an error.

(3) Rather, the causes of musical behavior are the consequences (especially rewards) that follow upon a relevant behavior.

(4) Implicit conclusion: Music exists and persists because people find it
rewarding to compose, perform, and listen to it; adults knowingly or
unknowingly arrange for rewarding consequences for children when
they engage in music.

I do not attempt a thoroughgoing challenge to musical behaviorism
here. Mounting such a challenge would be a formidable task because
certain aspects of the system are theoretically appealing (e.g., the resis-
tance to positing what cannot be observed), and because some forms of
musical activity seem especially amenable to behaviorist interpretation.
Playing an instrument—which is the clearest, most salient evidence we
have of human music-doing—is, at least in part, a sequence of arbitrary
motor behaviors learned through successive approximation and reinforcement. Nevertheless, musical behaviorism can be expected to have the
same logical difficulties that the more general behaviorist theory has (see
recent discussions by Lowry 1982; Flanagan 1984), and the theory seems
to take a ludicrously simplistic view of composition and listening. Indeed,
there is no way of accounting for those two activities without recourse to
hard-core mentalism.

It is precisely on the grounds of the antimentalism represented in
point 2 above that behaviorism founders the most in the case of music.
The difficulty is that, although many facts about music can be fitted into
the framework of behaviorism—for example, acquisition is explained by
approximation and reinforcement; stylistic diversity is explained by composers' different reinforcement histories—the claim of antimentalism re-
fuses to square with the fact of continuous musical change. For the
invention and acceptance of new works or styles cannot be reasonably
construed as *reinforced behaviors,* which by definition must have already
occurred.

Few theories contrast more sharply with a cognitive approach to music
than the theory of music-as-behavior. Points of overlap virtually do not
exist.

Music as Nature

Perhaps the sole candidate for a more extreme anticognitive stance is the theory that music's genesis is non*human,* not just nonmental. I refer to this as the theory of music as nature because its assumption is that music arises from some force or quality that is part and parcel of nature itself, and not from specifically human activity and propensity. There are several variants of this theory: (1) music as divine inspiration; (2) music as the elaboration of preexisting structures and processes; and (3) music as a reflection of inherent mathematical order. I consider each of these only briefly here and return to them later, since the latter two have surfaced in some of the cognitive approaches to music now current.

The notion that music is the doing of the gods, executed through the ineffable inspiration of composers, is an ancient one that I assume warrants little counterargument here. What is important about this notion, however, is that its presence in our intellectual history and folk wisdom probably eases the acceptance of other, nonreligious music as nature theories that similarly rest on the extrahuman and supernatural.

One such theory is the view that music is influenced by special structures and processes—such as intervals, scales, and evolutionary forces—that are independent of human origin. To a considerable degree the assumptions in such views are not explicitly fleshed out but rather remain implicit. The principal assumptions regarding intervals, for example, as I glean them from contemporary textbooks in music theory and acoustics, seem to be the following:

(1) Musically, the octave, perfect fifth, and major third are "special" intervals.
   That is, the octave frames the musical scale, "sounds like" the same note, is responsible for chord inversions, etc.; the perfect fifth allows for v7 to 1 cadences and thus modulation, is a "consonant" interval (?), etc.; the major third forms, with the other two intervals, the major triad, and so on.

(2) Acoustically, the octave, perfect fifth, and major third are "special" intervals.
   That is, in each case the ratios of the frequencies of their component tones are perfect whole number ratios (2:1 for the octave, 3:2 for the fifth, 5:4 for the third). Also, the octave, fifth, and third appear early in the overtone series.

(3) Implicit conclusion: The octave, perfect fifth, and major third are

musically special *because* they are acoustically special. That is, how they are used in our music is a direct consequence of their numerologic or acoustic characteristics.

One difficulty with this view is that no mechanism is posited whereby the numerical ratios or early overtones are eventually translated into the octave usages, root movements by a fifth, or other characteristics found in real music. By what causal chain of events does a composer come to use these intervals in the prescribed way? To the degree that the view posits no special mechanism for effecting the translation, it is a species of the divine inspiration theory: God or Nature or Somebody set up the numbers and the music so that they turned out that way. But to the degree that the view assumes the mechanism to be human cognition, it rests on this assumption: that the mind *prefers* and *selects* whole-number ratios; or, put more specifically, that what the mind (or ear) hears early in the overtone series it prefers to use harmonically in the bass line. This is, admittedly, an extreme charcterization of the view, but I push it to the extreme because it seems to me, in its basic assumption, preposterous. It is unable to give an acceptable account of where the intervals came from to begin with or how they came to influence our music as is so strongly supposed. Ultimately this view boils down to the assumption that the intervals were always there, that they preexisted before even the earliest acts of composition, and that their presence inexplicably influenced how music actually turned out.

Similar claims have been made for the diatonic, major/minor scale. A summary of them follows:

(1) The diatonic scale is *musically* significant:
   a. It is the raw material from which music is generated; that is, composers rearrange its tones in order to make music.
   b. The scale causes variety and interest to inhere in music because it contains a variety of intervals (seven) of different types (major, minor, perfect).
   c. The scale is responsible for the structure, organization, and coherence found in scale-based music because of points 2 and/or 3 below.
(2) The diatonic scale is specially adapted to the innate qualities of human perception.
   a. The scale contains seven tones, which is the number of items known to be readily perceived and remembered on a short-term basis (Miller 1956).

b. The scale matches the ear's frequency-filtering properties, since the various sensitivities of the basilar membrane approximate the diatonic scale.

c. The scale reflects (perhaps perceptually innate) similarity relations that are unrelated to mere frequency proximity. For example, in the key of C major the tone most similar to C is not D, the closest in frequency, but rather C an octave away. The next most similar tone is G, then E, and so forth.

(3) The diatonic scale is given acoustically:

a. Its tones are given in the overtone series.

b. It is universal because other scales, while dissimilar in surface features, are in fact variants of the diatonic scale.

(4) Implicit Conclusion: The diatonic scale is given in nature and preexists.

That is, *either*:

(a) The diatonic scale is musically significant (and consequently perception-adapted) because of its acoustic origin; thus, the scale must physically preexist in nature;

or:

(b) The diatonic scale is musically significant because human perceptual apparatus developed from it; thus, the scale must be a sort of innate idea; it preexists in the mind or ear.

In later chapters I try to convince the reader that the above assertions are in error, not only the conclusion that the do-re-mi scale may preexist in mind or physical reality but the preceding assertions as well. With regard to point 1, for example, I argue that the act of composition cannot be construed as the arrangement of tones from a fixed universe, that the scale is not the raw material, alphabet, or elemental building blocks of music. Rather, the scale is a theoretical artifact, the by-product of music analysis. It results from reflection on music *after* rather than before the act of composition has taken place. On this view the scale is largely irrelevant to a description of music perception, and it cannot be responsible for the variety, structure, and coherence we find in music. This is not to say that the rules of harmony and counterpoint, which describe the Western tonal idiom and of which the scale is a central part, are irrelevant to a description of the perception of that idiom. But the scale itself is an artifact of analysis, not the universe of elements out of which music is organized. Thus the difficulty with assertions such as those subsumed under point 2 is that they direct our attention to scale-perception, meanwhile leaving entirely unexplained how one gets from the perceptual convenience presumably embodied in the scale to the tonal complexity of real music. All well and good that the scale has seven items, but real music has millions of tones shifting across multiple scales, sometimes even in short periods of time. Perception theories based on the scale are inadequate because they do not specify the relation between scales and music, or between perceiving the scale and perceiving music.

Point 3—that the scale is acoustically given in the overtone series—is neither incontestably true nor even a strictly empirical question. An answer to it depends on how far one is willing to go in accepting as evidence for the theory overtone frequencies that only *approximate* scale tone frequencies (as they do), and what sorts of adjustments for tuning systems one is willing to assume. A loose interpretation of the overtone series would allow one to see the diatonic scale therein (at least more or less) plus, it must be conceded, some other scales as well. On the contrary a strict interpretation that disavows approximations and insists that overtone frequencies must exactly mirror the relations in the diatonic scale would not be so generous to the theory. Additionally, one of the critical problems in the overtones-as-source-of-the-scale theory is that it fails to give an account of how the particular relationships represented by overtone frequencies wind up appearing in real music. Consider the theory's implicit claim: that the *generally inaudible* overtones emanating from a single tone form a scale, which composers are then disposed to use as raw material in making music. But by what mechanism might this be accomplished? Possibly the relationships among frequencies in the overtone series are absorbed by the unconscious mind and are later drawn upon in composition. This is somewhat far-fetched, however, and in any case an inadequate explanation.

There are other arguments against the overtone hypothesis, and the glorification of scales generally, that I take up later. Among these are the historical recency of the diatonic scale, the absence of its use in modern music, and the multiplicity of scales found in nonwestern cultures. But here I want to emphasize only that the view of scales as preexisting in nature—whether in mind, ear, or physical reality—is a species of faith.

Such a view asserts that the scale was given to humankind by some force or entity outside ourselves, that we did not create the scale of our own means.

Where, then, do scales come from? The view put forth here is that scales are mundane, man-made things that arose from the development of musical writing, from the demands of music pedagogy, and from the scholarly tradition of music analysis that bore on both of these. Put otherwise, it was the historical attempt on the part of scholars to analyze music's nature, to write music down, and to transmit a musical tradition to novices that resulted in the invention of certain theoretical artifacts or tools—namely intervals, scales, chords, and even discrete pitches. Thus, the scale and other structures are not given in nature, but are the result of human activity in the extra-musical domains of writing, teaching, and reflection. I return to this in some detail later.

In addition to intervals and scales there are more abstract structures that are presumed to influence music, yet are independent of human origin. One example is the "golden section"—when two entities, such as passage lengths or rhythms, are thought to create a ratio such that the smaller is to the larger as the larger is to the sum of the two. In cases where the golden section is invoked as an explanation for musical forms or rhythmic complexities, it is as though the ratio preexisted somehow in nature or mind. Another example is the concept of *Urform,* a simple skeleton underlying the diverse compositions of a particular style type. Schenker's (1954, 1979) proposal regarding tonal music was that all (or at least the best) common practice pieces could be found to be based on an *Urform* that consists of a single, long-term harmonic progression from dominant to tonic and a melodic line that descends to tonic. What composers do is elaborate or flesh out this basic skeleton.

Note that in the case of the golden section and *Urform,* as well as in the case of intervals and scales, no one doubts that music is in a real sense "made" by human beings. Composers put the marks on paper. Yet the structures that I have subsumed under the music-as-nature rubric are peculiarly extra-human, for they entail the presumption that the structures were there before composers came along to make use of them. There is also the presumption that composers, except by force of will, cannot help but use them or that when they do turn their backs on such structures they imperil musical integrity.

Not only structures but also processes might be candidates for some natural, built-in influence on musical outcomes. One example is the idea of an evolutionary or teleological process in music, by which the artform gradually progresses along a predetermined path toward ever higher states of quality. Such a view found favor in the late nineteenth century when, under the influence of simplistic interpretations of Darwin, scholars saw musical forms, instruments, and styles all evolving toward betterment. The work of Sir Hubert Parry (1896) is only one example of the view that medieval and primitive musics are species evolving toward what nineteenth-century Europe already enjoyed.

The above views, particularly those on scales, intervals, and the like, are tied to a broader set of assumptions about mathematical order and its role in music. This theme, a legacy of the Pythagorean worship of numbers, has been applied in full force by nearly every music theorist and acoustician since that time (see, for example, Rameau's theory of 1722, translated in Strunk 1950; and Benade 1960). At root the view holds that music is not merely *organized* but *ordered* precisely. Moreover, such order is based on arithmetic or mathematical relationships embedded in the tonal structure, rhythmic structure, or long-range form of a composition. Two critical assumptions are that (1) such relationships are based on the system of natural numbers, *which themselves preexist and are given in nature,* and (2) that for some reason the human mind, in listening and composition, prefers and selects mathematically ordered relationships.

Music as nature theories, if they were correct, could give a nice account of music's universality across cultures and individuals, since gods, perfect ratios, overtones, and natural numbers could be assumed to do their work similarly in all times and places. The difficulty with accepting such theories is that they cannot simultaneously accommodate the vast differences among types of music, much less music's continual change. The fact that much music, even in the West, shuns the intervals, scales, and other structures presumed to be so natural would seem to cast doubt on such theories.

The music as nature theories contrast sharply with the cognitive approach put forth here, because the latter assigns no central role to nonhuman entities and instead holds the root of music to be human thought.

Music as Sound Stimulus

A final theory of music—music as sound—underlies several of those pre-viously mentioned, particularly music as trait, nature, and communica-tion. On this view music is fundamentally a subcategory of the general class *sound,* and as such shares at least some similarities with other sounds such as speech and noise. Music in some sense consists of vibrations, is perceived through the ears, and so on; composition may be regarded as the act of assembling and organizing sounds, while listening is a matter of perceiving and storing them. The thesis of music as sound has not, oddly enough, led to a comprehensive theory of music that can accom-modate the facts about music discussed earlier—that music changes and is diverse, for example. This is perhaps because, in its baldest form, the theory is rather like searching for the nature and causes of painting and sculpture in the characteristics of pigment and clay. The thesis has yielded, however, a most prodigious tradition of scientific inquiry into music—mostly in the fields of acoustics, psychoacoustics, and information processing—that has generated hundreds of research reports on music perception since the late nineteenth century. The assumptions on which this view necessarily rests are these:

(1) Music is best defined as a type of sound: an external stimulus which activates, excites, imposes upon, or otherwise stimulates the mind.
(2) Music may be broken down into its component sounds—e.g., isolated tones and chords—without loss of essential musical characteristics. That is, isolated tones, chords, or other entities that have been ab-stracted from the more complex realm of music proper nevertheless retain the character of music.
(3) Knowledge about how sound is perceived and remembered (whether ordinary sound or the above component sounds) is relevant to the question of how music is perceived and remembered.

The above assumptions represent the kernel of my dispute with much of the contemporary experimental research on music, as I discuss in a later chapter. Here, I want to consider these only briefly before taking a look at their research implications.

The first assumption appears, at first reading, to be a difficult claim to argue with. We can see quite clearly that when music occurs, strings and air vibrate, sound travels, the ears do their job, and so forth. But on closer inspection there are two difficulties: One is that the definition of music as sound radically underspecifies the object in question; the vast majority of sounds are not music. The other is that music can and frequently does occur in the absence of sound; it may be entirely internal or imaginary, as it probably is during much of composition, the recollection of familiar pieces, and so on. Whether such imaginings are sound-like is at least debatable. For certain no activation of the hearing apparatus is directly involved. On these two counts, then, sound appears to be neither necessary nor sufficient for the occurrence of music. As I hope to show, music's defining characteristic is not that it involves sound—and its perception and storage—but rather that it involves a particular set of thought processes. Moreover, these processes operate in part on the domain of *time*, not sound, and in part in a more abstract, even formal, domain. Musical *sound*, however, arises more as a consequence or by-product of musical thought than as the *stimulus* of it or the raw material on which it works.

The second assumption—that music is composed of or can be broken down into smaller units such as tones and chords—is one that is intuitively suspicious at the same time that it is practically convenient for a variety of purposes. Countless studies of pitch, interval, and chord discrimination and memory depend on this assumption for their purported relevance to music. But the assumption is a suspicious one nevertheless, for we know that the stimuli used in such studies are never, under any circumstances, considered or listened to as music. Their claims on musical relevance must depend on the assumption that the musical whole can be assembled from what, by themselves, are nonmusical parts. More importantly, such studies assume that perception occurring with stimuli of one, two, or three tones or chords is not fundamentally different from that occurring over a complex piece of music.

I have one argument and one observation to make with regard to the above assumptions. The argument, to which I return later, is that the very derivation of tones, intervals, and chords depends on the conscious, usually intellectually motivated *analysis* of compositions, and that it is the cumulative history of analysis that gives rise to such units. Further, my claim is that although analysis is useful and necessary for intellectual purposes, there is no reason to believe that the units of analysis are also the units of perception. Put simply, the fact that we can see tones, intervals, and chords in the composition (on paper) is not reason to presume that those are also the components of our perceptual experience of music.

My observation, which I offer with only half an apology, is that for all practical purposes the decades of research on tones, intervals, and chords have yielded almost no convincing theory about how complex music is constructed, perceived, and remembered. In plain terms, as Burns and Ward (1982) put it in a recent review of research on interval perception, "the perception of isolated melodic musical intervals may have little to do with the perception of melody" (p. 264).

The third assumption in this series—that knowledge about how sound is perceived is relevant to how music is perceived—is, like the others, beguilingly obvious on a certain level. We know from research, for example, that pitches cannot be heard above or below certain frequency limits, we know pain thresholds for decibel levels, and we know a great deal more about the perception of ordinary sound. It makes a certain amount of sense, therefore, to compose music and design concert halls with such knowledge in mind, but the real question is whether such knowledge has only practical implications for the execution of music-making or whether it explains in some fundamental way the nature of music or the source from which it springs. Close consideration of all or nearly all our knowledge about the perception of sound reveals very little that is actually relevant to musical questions. To take an extreme example, knowledge about how the ear works is capable of explaining little more about music than does knowledge about any other organ.

Music research that comes out of the information processing tradition is especially interesting in this regard. The vast majority of studies begin with the assumption that music can be meaningfully broken down into components such as tones, intervals, chords and more general factors such as scales and contour patterns. The experiments show that alterations in the stimuli along one or more of the dimensions mentioned (interval, chord, scale, contour) produce alterations in the responses of listeners. For example, listeners are not likely to perceive a melody as being the same as it was before if its intervals are changed. From such a result this conclusion is drawn: If altering a melody's X factor produces a change in listener response, then listeners must be perceiving and storing melodies in terms of the X factor. This boils down to a wholesale confusion between the features of the stimulus and the elements of perception and cognition. On this view, the elements and processes of cognition will be exactly isomorphic to the factors we are able to find (however unlimited their number) and manipulate in experiments.

The thesis of music as sound contrasts with the present view of music as cognition because the latter view holds that music is actively generated (even in perception) not simply "processed." Although many of the information processing approaches to music hold that internal cognitive processes *influence* perception (hence they hold that perception is not veridical), the cognitive approach offered here claims further that such processes *determine* it.

In the foregoing pages I have proposed that the central task for a theory of music is to come to grips with facts about music's universality, diversity, change, and acquisition. I have suggested that a cognitive definition of the artform best does this, and that such a definition diverges from other conceptions of music as trait, communication, behavior, nature, and sound.

We may now ask about the methods by which musical cognition may be studied. There are two broad approaches: One, the province of music theory and analysis, is aimed at the musical *object* and attempts to uncover through the analysis of compositions the general principles by which compositions are organized. The other, the province of psychology, is aimed at the human *subject* and the processes that are brought to bear in musical activity. Both of these approaches are parallel routes of attack on the problem of musical cognition and both must ultimately come to similar conclusions. For the principles of musical organization that are uncovered through analysis are the principles employed in compositions *composed and heard by humans*; and the psychological processes known to be implemented during composition and listening must, of course, affect the way music ultimately turns out. We shall see that the interplay between these parallel methods is crucial for understanding musical cognition.

CHAPTER 2

The Idea of Music
as Cognition

The somewhat circuitous path of this chapter has the aim of presenting
a framework for thinking about music. I begin by defining several concepts and then cite examples of them in the formal or "classical" Western
tradition. I conclude by discussing the several implications of this framework for current theories of music perception.

PRELIMINARY CONCEPTS

Music is a cultural phenomenon. To say so is to emphasize that it is born
of groups of persons—here called musical communities—who share common understandings about the way music is to be composed, performed,
and heard. Their shared understandings give rise to a musical *style,* and
the processes necessary for understanding it may be distinguished from
broader, more generic processes that allow us to understand, as we do,
more than a single style. The implications for cognition of musical styles
and communities, among other things, are brought out below.

Musical Style and Style-Specific Processes

The term musical style refers both to a body of compositions that share
similar features and to the principles governing how such compositions
are composed. More importantly, common features *exist at all* in a body
of compositions because shared principles are in use by the composers
and listeners who generated the style. Thus, to speak of styles—such as
"classical," jazz, folk, and rock—is to recognize that special features are
characteristic of all the compositions said to be in a particular style. Finer

distinctions among substyles can also be made—for example, baroque, Dixieland, blues, and heavy metal—and these represent even more particular features and principles common to the compositions in question. These principles are of necessity cognitive principles. They are adhered to, if not wholly consciously, by composers who create music and listeners who understand it. The following are examples of style principles from "classical" substyles, which I have stated in the form of rules, as though one were adhering to them in composing and listening:

(1) To divide a long span of music into smaller pieces, come to rest at certain points around the first tone or chord (the tonic) of the scale (a rule from the eighteenth-century common practice period).
(2) In forming a melodic line, balance upward movement with descending movement; if there are skips or leaps, balance them with stepwise motion in the opposite direction (a rule from renaissance counterpoint).
(3) To transform or vary a short melody, play it backwards, note for note (a rule from the twentieth century and some earlier styles).

Theoretically, any style can be described in terms of explicit statements of its principles. But in practice it is difficult to do so because common features and principles can only be gleaned through the rigorous formal analysis of a sizable subgroup of the compositions that constitute a style. Thus, it is primarily the several styles in the "classical" Western tradition that have been so analyzed—much less so the popular styles—because they have been amenably written down in notation and for a variety of other reasons are the traditional grist of analytic scholars. An inescapable conclusion of this analytic tradition, however, is that the classical substyles employ consistent principles in the construction of music and that consistent features keep showing up across many individual compositions. This is evidence that consistent *cognitive* principles, for composing and hearing, are put to use in constructing music that is experienced—to cite the rules above—as divisible, well-balanced, and varied.

There are virtually hundreds of style principles that imply cognitive processes, but note that such processes are specific to particular, individual styles. These style-specific cognitive processes can be distinguished from what I will describe later as *generic cognitive processes,* which are those that cut across a large number, perhaps all, musical styles.

Style Change

The most interesting aspect of musical styles—and the critical one for cognition—is that they change. All musical styles undergo transformation over time, which results in the rise of new styles. This means that the (cognitive) principles put to use by composers and listeners change in a slow but continuous way over the course of several to many years. There can be no doubt about this. To give the obvious example, no modern composer writes in the style of Bach or Mozart; it has been almost a hundred years since a serious composer adhered to the principles of the common practice period. Similarly, listeners gradually but continuously make minor adjustments in what they are willing to accept, so that even new, unfamiliar works are understood. Thus, the principles on which new pieces are based are incorporated into what listeners know and accept about the style at hand.

Examples of style change are perhaps most easily recognized in the field of popular music, where the changes seem particularly rapid. One type of change is the normal, gradual change to which all music is susceptible. Rock music, for example, has changed dramatically from the "rock-'n-roll" form of the 1950s, which was then a working-class form, to the "rock" of the 1970s and '80s, which is now a middle-class phenomenon (Shepard et al. 1977). A second type of change is a style blend, the seemingly instantaneous change that results when two styles of music are combined to create a new one. I am personally familiar with two of these. One is *con junto* music of the American southwest (see recordings by Flaco Jimenez),[1] a blend of German-immigrant and Mexican musics. In these compositions—some of which sound like a polka or waltz sung with Spanish words—melodic, rhythmic, and timbral features of the parent styles have been fused to create a new one. Another example is "dawg" music, a recent bluegrass/jazz fusion that results in a style not easily classed as either true jazz or true bluegrass (see recordings by David Grisman).[2]

Exactly why styles change is not clear. A possible explanation is that style change results from a subtle but definite interaction—even a discourse—that goes on among composers, listeners, and performers, combined with a tendency among music-makers and audiences to seek new

[1]Recording: *Flaco Jimenez y Su Conjunto.* San Antonio, Texas: Disco Grande Records, 1976.
[2]Recording: *David Grisman—Quintet '80.* Burbank, Calif.: Warner Brothers Records, 1980.

and interesting variations on the musical climate at hand. Part of the implicit agreement between music-makers and audiences seems to be the generation of slight variations on the shared rules or principles of a musical style. Something of a "bending of the rules" takes place, and the style gradually though continually changes. Whatever the cause of style change (and its causes are not completely known), the conclusion is inescapable that it does occur. We may go so far as to assert the apparent *necessity* of style change.

Two issues which I shall not discuss at length here are worth brief mention at this point. One is the issue of repeated hearings. Listeners do seem to enjoy repeated hearings of the same compositions—even the same performances of the same compositions—often over a period of years. How the desire for and enjoyment of repeated hearings square with on-going style change, and the necessary, concomitant changes in listeners' cognitive processes, remains to be wholly worked out. A second and related issue is how audiences manage to understand—and enjoy or even prefer—styles of music that are no longer composed in contemporary times. Although the penchant for old music is a distinctly modern phenomenon, it is so widespread as to be of serious consequence for any theory of music. Unlike language, where older grammars and styles of speaking are not generally used once they are replaced, "outmoded" musical styles live amicably with new ones. Compositions from earlier centuries are being replayed and reheard continually in modern life. It's not entirely clear how this can be reconciled with the fact that style—the principles by which people hear and compose music—must change. But the probable explanation may go beyond a simple sociological one, for example that the middle class prefers the security of the familiar or pretends an interest in historical artforms.

A more likely explanation is that, when the medium of discourse among music-makers and listeners is older music, the tendency for style change is exerted in the form of *performance variation*. That is, new interpretations are made up; new relationships are discovered and pointed up in the playing of old artworks; new tempos, new accents, new and subtle changes are imposed on the old works at hand. The performance or rendering of music itself becomes a sort of "style." Continued performance variation in the execution of old works is, then, the analogue of style change. Were this not so, were performance a matter of mere reproduction not in need of continued fluctuation, then we might expect the definitive performances recorded on disc to put an end to the need for further performances, either live or recorded. Actually the opposite seems true. If concert programs and record sales provide any measure, there is no end in sight on the number of alternative performances of a piece that can be tolerated. Even aside from the technical advances in auditory reproduction that make new recordings desirable, performers and listeners seem willing to accept increasingly subtle changes as cause for a new performance of a seemingly familiar work. In short, people insist on changing their music.

Musical Communities

I have said that style change is inherent in musical cognition and that it results from interaction among the composers, performers, and listeners associated with a particular style. I call such a group a *musical community*. The term can be used on the same variety of levels that the term musical style is used: We can speak of the Western art-music community, or the community of baroque, eighteenth-century Germany, for example, and of the many popular musical communities of contemporary culture. All styles have musical communities that create them, however small that community may be (as is the case, for instance, with the community of modern avant-garde music). Styles are carried out and undergo change as a result of the cross-influences among composers, performers, and listeners. It is obvious how composers and performers execute their influence (they create the music), but listeners too have their role. They are not only the consumers of new works or renditions, but they are the carriers of consistency in the style. Gradually, however, the listeners change, as each new experience with music in some way changes the listener and makes tiny steps toward style change.

The emphasis on community interaction is meant to underscore this point: True style is a cultural matter and it is never invented instantaneously in isolation from some audience (however small). No single person sets out alone to create a system of style principles. Rather, such principles evolve gradually from composer/listener interaction, and they are always the result of group-human forces. Style, in the sense I propose it here, is analogous to a language or system of discourse, the shared understandings of a group, and not to, say, a personal, idiosyncratic code.

The distinction is important for it leads directly to this conclusion: Not *all* of the things that composers or performers do involve principles of style. Put another way, composing (when it is legitimate) will always rest on some of the shared principles of the community. It may, however, embody some other features that are irrelevant to principles of style. This point is particularly important for twentieth-century music.

Consider the case of twelve-tone compositional technique, developed by Schoenberg and practiced by Berg, Webern, and others. An over-simplified description of the technique will suffice here: An initial series of tones (called a row) is set out. In the course of composing the piece, the composer always uses the tones in exactly the same order. He may transpose them up or down by the octave, he may use several tones simultaneously, and he will use whatever rhythm, meter, and so on he chooses. But the order of tones is predetermined. Alternatively, the row may be used in the form of some variant of itself, such as an inversion (mirror-image of intervals), retrograde (backwards), or retrograde-inversion (both).

The purpose of the technique is to equalize all twelve tones of the chromatic scale, so that some are not favored over others in a way that produces the effects of traditional harmony and tonal center. The intent, in fact, is to forge new works not based on traditional means.

But a question is raised: What are the style principles of this repertory? In such compositions people probably do not hear tone rows. Although there is no unassailable experimental evidence, few musicians (even aficionados of the style) claim to hear row orders. Anecdotal evidence suggests that row identification, when it occurs, is almost always attributable to a characteristic motive or interval that happens to be embedded in the row. Thus, the hearing of true row orders is rare if not impossible. We must draw the conclusion that the particular configuration of notes is unrelated to the cognitive principles of hearing and composing that people use for this music, even in its own community.

This is not to say that such a compositional technique is unwholesome. (On the contrary I applaud it.) But it is to say that such a technique is not an element of style within the definition of style, meaning cognitive principles, that I propose here. Put otherwise, not all of the things that composers do, or that can be uncovered through analysis, are stylistic principles.

What, then, *is* the style of such music? One answer is that the style is defined not by the complex successions and orderings of pitches, but by other parameters that are likely to give rise to our understanding of the piece—relationships among textures and melodic lines, rhythmic development and variation, large-scale form, and so forth. The style, then, is not necessarily defined in terms of what the composer *ostensibly* did with the pitches (however necessary and desirable that was), but rather in terms of what *else* he did and how it is, thus, that the piece is understood. Such understanding is perhaps likely in terms of texture, rhythm, and parameters other than fixed pitches.

I might add that a similar situation obtains with regard to un-notated musics. I am thinking here of both Western and nonwestern musics, including contemporary popular forms that are for the most part conceived and transmitted from person to person without the aid of notation. For example, most jazz and rock defy precise notation; much folk and primitive music remains wholly un-notated except for specimens of the repertory that scholars have attempted to write down. It is not clear what are the style principles of such music, for there has been only fragmentary analysis of them. It is conceivable, however (in my opinion likely), that their style principles reside in precisely those parameters that are not accurately captured in notation, perhaps intonation, timbre, dynamics, phrasing, and so on. The tendency has been to view such musics as static, repetitious, and unelaborated, principally because of the biased focus on the traditionally notated parameters of melody, harmony, and rhythm. However, the style of un-notated musics may be carried through other parameters.

To summarize, I have thus far set out a notion of style as the shared principles of creating and understanding music that are in use by a particular community. I have stated that style change is a fact of music, and that such change results from the necessary interactions among the performers, composers, and listeners of a particular community. Two aspects of musical communities remain to be described: the act of reflection, by which I mean the post hoc analyses of musical compositions, and the phenomenon of transmission, the means by which style principles are acquired by new members of the group.

Reflection on Music

It is not clear what we are doing when we engage in music-making. It is not at all clear why music affects us. In creating and listening to music, we experience organization, coherence, and deviation, but it is not immediately obvious how such effects are caused, or where in the music they lie. Music is all the more difficult to pin down on this matter because it is a passing, temporal thing that will not hold still while we look at it. We cannot stop it at some point and say, "there, *that* is the pattern . . . the repetition . . . the form," for whatever we point to evaporates and is lost. Music unfolds in temporal experience; it is always continuous and in flux. Still, we have the definite impression that music involves a characteristic experience, principally one in which the flow of temporal events is organized in some way.

Every culture appears to have beliefs about music and beliefs about why and how music's effects are worked (for some examples, see Merriam 1964). I hesitate to claim that such belief about or reflection upon music is universal, but if it is not universal it is at least very widespread. People think about their music. They reflect on it in order to see how it works and to see what it is they are doing when they engage in it.

I can give an example of elementary reflection from American folk music. I have been told that one of the traditional ways that senior fiddlers teach young boys to play is like this: The boy sits next to the fiddler and their legs are tied together (one leg each). As the fiddler plays and stomps the beat, the boy's leg goes up and down too. So it goes for several lessons, and only after much practice at stomping will the boy ever hold the instrument. This is an example of reflection. From the ongoing flow of music, the beat has been abstracted and represented. Thus set apart, it is made concrete (with stomping) and so it is taught.

For our purposes it is irrelevant whether the method is pedagogically sound, or whether, in fact, a steady beat is actually desirable or necessary in the cognitive construction of this music. It is, in short, irrelevant whether a steady beat is truly intrinsic to the style. What is important is that reflection and abstraction have taken place, and here for pedagogical purposes.

Reflection may be considered an after-the-fact heightened awareness of some aspect of music thought to be important for its understanding. We do not know the degree to which conscious reflection is a universal characteristic of the world's musical communities, but reflection is certainly the rule where a community has developed one or both of the following ideas:

(1) *The idea of a composition.* That is, a single, repeatable artwork is conceived that is cut off in time with a beginning and an end. Such a

concept is not the rule in some preliterate societies and probably not in the early music of the West (see Carpenter 1967; Shepard et al. 1977), where music-making is continuous and improvisational, and the concept of an isolable, replicable composition is not in use. But wherever a *repeatable* composition is conceived, there will be reflection upon it as to its salient and necessarily repeated features.

(2) *A written notation of music.* The vast majority of world musics are not recorded in written documents, but where notation is in use, reflection has taken place. Notation is, in fact, an act of reflection, for it arises from a consideration of *which* features are most salient and in need of recording. No form of notation records all aspects of a piece of music. Our current notation of lines and dots records approximations of pitch and duration, but it does not record intonation, loudness, exact phrasing, timbral and tempo changes, and so on. Additions to the notational system have been made over the past few hundred years (new signs and markings, new words written in), and new forms of notation continue to be developed in our own century. Still, notation gives us only an approximate model, not an exact image, of what goes on in a piece of music. Notation, then, is only a record of what has been reflected upon and thought important.

To summarize: Reflection involves some explicit, post hoc consideration of a piece of music. Reflection speaks to the questions: How does this music work? What is its structure? What accounts for its coherence and interest?

Transmission and Pedagogy

In the fiddling example above I anticipated a critical point: that one of the principal aims of reflection is to aid pedagogy and the transmisson of style principles and understandings to new members of a musical community. Certainly not all acts of reflection lead unequivocally to sound pedagogical practices, but some form of reflection on music is always and necessarily employed in pedagogy and style transmission. I do not address here the question of how style is actually acquired by new members, but it is clear that an artform in flux, so to speak—whose styles change and whose every instance of occurrence is fleeting and temporary—would require a reflection-and-transmission process to insure preservation of those most central, stable principles of style. Music, then, is just the sort of artform that would call for conscious reflection and transmission.

In Western musical history, reflection and transmission have evolved into a highly elaborate and formal system. Reflection has taken the form of detailed analyses and theories, and style transmission has taken the form of formal pedagogy, for musicians both within and outside educational institutions. The discipline of music theory best exemplifies this form of reflection, and its aim for the past several hundred years has been unchanging: to formulate and codify the stylistic principles of Western music and, where possible, to generate guiding rules that can be learned by novice musicians. Predictably, music analysis and music pedagogy are inextricably bound in their histories (they remain so today) and many treatises on music, both ancient and modern, have been intended as textbooks for students.

An example from the eighteenth century will demonstrate this point. Composers at that time wrote their music down with roughly the same modern system of notation that we use today. But (as always) many important features of the style were left un-notated, and performers were expected to improvise them. Trills, appoggiaturas, and other ornaments were not written out; cadenzas were not written out, or only the general lines were sketched; chords in need of arpeggiation were not written out; the precise stops to employ on the organ or harpsichord were not indicated. Keyboard players had an especially difficult task. In ensemble pieces, a harpsichordist would be given only the left-hand bass line, and he was not only expected to figure out the harmonic progression as he went along, but to improvise a suitable and interesting arrangement of it as well. In short, many aspects of the piece had yet to be composed or created, even after notation.

We have, then, a classic case of musical style principles that are clearly employed by a musical community but which do not find their way into notation. The style principles in question are, for example, the manner in which trills are executed at the middles or ends of phrases, the special way appoggiaturas are treated when they are dissonant with the bass, the particular harmonic progressions that are employed, the types of melodic lines that will be improvised. All of these are particular style principles by which people understand this music. In the eighteenth century such style principles were everywhere in use, but seldom put down in notation. Somehow they had to be acquired by novice musicians who sought to compose and perform in the style. The situation called for someone to observe and reflect on the current musical practices, and write down the rules of the style for learners. Several musician-scholars undertook this task, and two of the most popular textbooks, still in use today for our rendition of eighteenth-century music, are *Essay on the True Art of Playing Keyboard Instruments,* by C. P. E. Bach (the son) and *Treatise on the Fundamentals of Violin Playing* by Leopold Mozart (the father). These books, and many others like them, are examples of conscious reflection upon the actual musical practice of the day, distilled into stylistic rules or principles for learners (see translations: Bach 1949; Mozart 1948).

There are countless examples of how this same process has occurred repeatedly in Western music. Musical style principles, whether for performing, composing, or listening, are distilled from music by theorists who observe and reflect upon practice and subject it to systematic analysis. The resulting principles find their way into the curricula and texts of formal music pedagogy. The list of such pedagogical/theoretical works is long, covering the fields of harmony (e.g., Forte 1974; Mitchell 1948; Piston 1962), counterpoint (Jeppesen 1939; Salzer and Schachter 1969), composition (Hindemith 1942), and even listening (Bamberger and Brofsky 1975; Cogan and Escot 1976; Crocker and Bassart 1971; Salzer 1952; Wink and Williams 1976).

Generic Musical-Cognitive Processes

Thus far I have proposed the notions of *style* and *musical communities,* and I have alluded to the role of *reflection* in the transmission of style to a community's new members. I have suggested that, in the West, such reflection and transmission have been undertaken largely through formal analysis and pedagogy. Most importantly, I have emphasized that style *change* is continuous and inevitable, and that it implies a concomitant change in the style-specific cognitive processes shared by composers and listeners. This brings us to a further claim: that in addition to changing, style-specific cognitive processes, there must also be some generic cognitive processes that are stable across different styles. I refer to these as *generic* processes because I conceive of them as panstylistic, and I have avoided the stronger term *universal* only because it is difficult to demonstrate true universality. The reader should note, however, that I intend the term *generic cognitive processes* to refer to those cognitions applicable to many if not all styles. It is the specification of these generic processes—

and the monitoring of their development during childhood—that is the principal focus of the remaining chapters.

I can best draw the distinction between style-specific and generic cognitive processes by referring to the rules mentioned earlier. For example, "to come to rest at the tonic" is a particular style principle, but the fact of music being divisible by temporary resting points (that mark pieces or "chunks") is a generic cognitive process. Similarly, balancing skips or leaps with stepwise contrapuntal motion is a stylistic principle, but the formation of a coherent, organized, and memorable melodic line is a generic process. Playing a melody backwards is a matter of style, but the act of doing so for the purpose of transforming or changing musical material is a generic cognitive process.

Put otherwise, the activities of "chunking" music into pieces, forming coherent units or lines, and transforming musical material can give rise to a variety of stylistic manifestations. It is true that the distinction between generic and stylistic processes is often difficult. But the distinction must be made, for a confusion of the two leads to ethnocentric (or style-centric) notions of what musical cognition is about. As I take up shortly, style principles, particularly those associated with the common practice period, have too often been assumed to be human universals.

As background to this point, I give below a brief summary of the different substyles that characterize the Western classical tradition, and I focus on the interplay that has gone on among style, reflection/analysis, and pedagogy. My purpose in doing so is in part to show how very changeable have been the style-specific cognitive processes that a culture apparently employs in music-making, and in part to argue that the results of the style/analysis/pedagogy interplay have had some unfortunate consequences for modern psychological research. The results of reflection and analysis, I argue, have been largely misread, and attention has been devoted almost exclusively to the tonal, common practice style.

Some comments are in order about why I choose the art music or "classical" community as the exemplar of the style/analysis/pedagogy interaction. I choose it because it maintains the most rigorously formulated and intensely administered system of style codification and transmission of any style community in the West. This is so because it is the only community whose music, throughout its history, was consistently put down in writing. The resulting analysis and pedagogy, over centuries, have made it the most influential of Western style systems, and its influence has been felt even in scientific investigations of music, as we shall see. I do not choose Western art music, however, out of a conviction that it is a superior style. Indeed, I would deny the superiority of some types of music over others, and I construe style as a neutral concept; it is, quite simply, the set of principles by which a group understands its music. Certainly *within* style, there are individual artworks that are more or less successful manifestations of that style's principles. But the issue of *style* and *quality* are two different questions, and they ought not be confused. Thus far I have maintained that the several popular forms—folk, jazz, rock, etc.—are separate *styles*; that is, they have their own intrinsic principles by which the organization, coherence, and deviation in the music are understood. My assertion remains a hypothesis, however, for no comprehensive analyses of those forms have been conducted (although now there are some beginnings), and hence we do not know exactly what principles are operating. Were it to be shown that such musics do *not* constitute separate styles—i.e., that their principles are not different from the art-music style—then the stage would be set for evaluative comparisons among the individual artworks of a more general, comprehensive style (perhaps a general tonal style). In such a case popular musics could be considered subtypes or offshoots of the classical style. Such disparate pieces as rock tunes and symphonic works could then be compared along the same lines, with the same criteria, perhaps with the former considered inferior to the latter.

I think the likelihood of establishing such an all-encompassing, general style is minimal, however. We do not now evaluate medieval chants against symphonic works, because we know them to be separate styles. The same is true of popular forms, and, reinforcing their separateness as styles is the fact that they appear to be embedded in distinct communities—various age, ethnic, and social groups (see Shepard et al. 1977). These communities have built their own apparatuses for informal reflection and transmission. For example, aficionados of these styles have emerged as critics and commentators, and there is active communication about the conduct of the style. (See, for example, any issue of *Rolling Stone*,[3] or the more scholarly contributions such as the *Journal of Country Music*,[4] or any number of books on the Beatles, e.g., Mellers 1973.) In

[3]*Rolling Stone*. New York: Straight Arrow Publishers.
[4]*Journal of Country Music*. Nashville: Country Music Foundation.

short, popular forms are probably true styles. It is not clear what their style principles are, particularly since the repertory is largely not written down. More than likely the principles involve musical parameters (such as intonation and timbre) that are not captured in traditional notation and exploited in classical composition.

I turn now to a case study of one community, the classical tradition, and to a description of its styles, reflective analyses, and pedagogy. I then turn to the influence of these matters on modern psychological research.

CASE STUDY: THE FORMAL WESTERN TRADITION

We do not know how music sounded in any age other than our own. We come to educated conclusions about it based on written documents (treatises and notation), on a few facts about what seems true of people in general (their limitations in vocal range, for example), and from the few extant communities that have maintained a style for hundreds of years, such as the Catholic monasteries, which today are the last surviving preserve of Gregorian chant. Electronic recordings will erase the doubts that future historians may have about the music of our present age, but when we now look back on the music of earlier times, we can depend only on written documents. There is perhaps one advantage to this. Reflection—describing and explaining music—always follows rather than precedes practice, and it does so at a considerable distance. Hence our written documents, the treatises and even the earliest examples of notation, usually describe the characteristics of music that people had consistently been employing, often for generations.

Take Gregorian chant. The early Christians were doubtless intoning prayer texts from the days of their earliest worship, but they did not begin to notate it until the ninth century.[5] For hundreds of years chant melodies were improvised, not fixed, and musicians transmitted them orally, retaining what they needed in memory. Of course, notation, when it came, was not invented full-blown. Sometime during the ninth century scholars began to add symbols above the words of a text to remind singers of a rising or falling line. Over generations, the practice changed to placing symbols at higher and lower points on the page, and not until the tenth

[5]Technically the term *plainsong* more properly refers to chants in general, while Gregorian is a specific type, but I use the latter and more familiar term generically here.

century was a single horizontal line occasionally placed among the high and low symbols, or perhaps just imagined (so it appears from the manuscripts) by the scribe. This was later expanded to two lines, and finally four lines were in use by the eleventh to thirteenth centuries. Throughout, there was never a concept of fixed or *absolute* pitches as we know them today (Grout 1973). A *relative* system of whole and half steps, with the attendant system of letter names, did not appear until the tenth century when, and consequently for the first time, singers were miraculously able to "sing by sight alone, without hesitation, music that they have never heard" (St. Odo of Cluny, *Enchiridion musices,* ca. 935).[6] The crystallization of the octave into whole and half steps and the systematization with letter names took a long time to evolve, but once it did, scholars and teachers such as Odo celebrated the achievement in various manuscripts surviving from that period. Odo writes that "with God's help alone I taught certain actual boys and youths . . . something which until now ordinary singers had never been able to do, many continuing to practice and study singing for fifty years without profit." That is, young singers were now able to sing any number of pieces "at first sight" without having heard them sung in advance. So great a feat was this that Guido of Arezzo traveled to Rome to convince a doubting Pope John XIX of its efficacy, and John "did not dismiss the subject or leave the place where he sat until he had [learned] to sing a verse without hearing it beforehand, thus quickly finding true in his own case what he could hardly believe of others." "What need I say more?" Guido concludes (*Epistola de ignoto cantu,* ca. 1030).

Thus, notation and pitch-naming developed only slowly (spurred on by the Church's desire to spread and standardize chant) and scholars were called upon to reflect on the music, distill its seemingly essential qualities, and write those qualities down. The essential quality of chant in those days was pitch fluctuation within a very narrow range. Medieval musicians employed a style that is very different from our own. They made use of only a tiny portion of the available pitch range, wavering around pitches and refusing to regard them as fixed or absolute. They settled or rested—indeed even ended chants—on pitches that would be unexpected to our ears, and of course they used no harmony. They shunned the concept of

---

[6]Translations of all the historical treatises predating 1800 that I mention in this section can be found in Strunk (1950).

fixed time values, and even the idea of a fixed composition, for which was substituted continual improvisation, seems not to have been in use. Certainly they used no major or minor scales, no chords, and no tonic-dominant tonalities. These now-common notions, even the concept of twelve fixed pitches dividing the octave, were yet to be developed.

Sometime before the ninth century, people began to "harmonize" chant melodies with the simultaneous singing of parallel melodies (a practice called organum). At first much of the harmonizing went on as a series of parallel intervals. (An interval is the distance between two simultaneous tones.) Note for note the melodies often matched at a consistent distance, and thus there was no independence of line. We may assume that people harmonized at an interval they found auditorily acceptable; in this case they frequently chose parallel fourths and parallel fifths—that is, a continuous succession of fourths or fifths, something that sounds quite odd to us today.

Gradually the separate lines became more independent—that is, they could move in different as well as parallel directions—and so a number of different intervals would be used. Music-makers did not treat all intervals with equal regard. The octave, fourth, fifth, and unison (same note) were treated as consonant; that is, these intervals appeared frequently, moved in parallel succession, and held prominent places such as the beginnings and endings of phrases. It is worth noting that the medieval consonance-dissonance concept here does not exactly square with our own. The continuous, parallel fourths and fifths of medieval music sound dissonant and harsh to today's ear. (Indeed, later centuries had rules prohibiting parallel fifths.) Thirds and sixths only gradually achieved true consonant status, being considered "imperfect" consonances by the fourteenth century. Hence dissonance is not a universal matter, but rather an element of style. The definition and treatment of dissonance vary from style to style and hence constitute some of the *changing* style principles by which people create their music.

Medieval Theory

Medieval theorists wrote a great deal about their music in both practical and speculative treatises. Chant melodies, as they were notated, came to be categorized by their ending note, range, and characteristic melodic patterns. For unknown reasons, this categorization led to a system of eight scale-like *modes,* which medieval theorists, enamored as they were with the Greeks, erroneously named according to what they knew of the Greek modes or keys (Grout 1973). Not only the pitches but also the rhythms of melodies were subjected to scrutiny, the result being a companion system of rhythmic modes. In short, and like all music theorists since, medieval theorists analyzed, documented, and codified the music of their day.

Their primary purpose in doing so was to define good singing and teach it to beginner musicians. Many treatises were written to influence pedagogy, and they are filled with commentary on the voice and its music that makes today's reader know how similar is medieval to contemporary man. Medieval theorists wrote about the modes and rhythms and intervals and the singing of prayer texts because they wanted to ensure a good crop of church singers. Consequently one finds mention in these old treatises of the predictable problems of music teaching—the problems of attention and memory, particularly that of young boys in church choirs, and the normal difficulties of learning a large body of melodies and texts (see Strunk 1950). In large measure the advances of medieval theory—the development of whole steps and half steps, the use of letter names, the development of mnemonic devices and rules that describe the proper execution of style—were owing to the desire of theorists to transmit the singing style then in use to novice musicians on their way into the style. This same pattern continues through all periods in Western music history—the analysis of style, and theories about how it works, make their way into the writings and teaching methodologies of the day, and hence effect style transmission.

But many theorists were not satisfied with describing the style and instructing novices. They went a step further and sought the ultimate rightness of their musical system—a solid connection between music and nature. God having provided an orderly universe, it was held that music too must have its orderliness, and this order was pursued with passion over the centuries. No other theme in the history of Western music was held for so long, so fervently, and so uncritically as this one. Order, not just in man but in the succession of tones, became the theme of treatises from Boethius' work in the 500s, to the anonymous *Scholia enchiriadis* of 900, to Rameau's 1722 *Traité,* to Schenker's theory at the turn of the twentieth century. Each era looked for an orderly basis for music and each era found it, in God, science, or psyche. In the middle ages, the root of musical order was found in numbers.

Rhythms and melodic intervals were subjected to such analyses as would uncover the perfect ratios and symmetries held accountable for their beauty (a notion that persists in some quarters even today). The octave was especially singled out because a string divided in two created it (hence a two-to-one ratio), but the other intervals were given similar treatment in terms of numerical ratios. Reason, most especially mathematical reason, was thought to be the key to the secret of beauty perceived by mere senses and, through number, music joined the brotherhood of arithmetic, geometry, and astronomy. We take pleasure, Boethius held, when reason shows us the likeness of "what is well and fitly ordered" both in ourselves and in our music (*De institutione musica,* ca. 500). From this, says Boethius, noting his concurrence with Plato, "the soul of the universe is united by musical concord." Thus Boethius provided the cradle for many centuries of music-and-number speculation. His sixth-century treatise was popular through the middle ages and was printed even a thousand years after he wrote it. But if Boethius anticipated the modern arithmetic speculation that was yet to come, other medievalists anticipated the predictable response to it that still rings familiar today. The teacher Guido shrugged off Boethius' treatise as "useful to philosophers, but not for singers" (*Epistola de ignoto cantu*).

The Horizontal Style

But to return to the facts of medieval style. In the years before 1500 people conceived their music in primarily a *horizontal* style. That is, they conceived it as multiple, simultaneous melodies, first two, then three, and later four melodic lines over the course of generations. The emphasis was on a successive, horizontal dimension, particularly on smooth melodic line, and only secondary attention was paid to vertical, simultaneous sonority (most notably at crucial points, such as the ends of phrases). Music from these centuries sounds strange to us, for it was composed and heard with no major-minor tonalities, no chords, and no tonic-dominant cadences; it contains seemingly harsh dissonances, and what consonances appear are the hollow-sounding fifth and octave. All of these persisted in a modal framework (*not* the major-minor scale system) through most of the renaissance.

But slowly, over centuries, people were changing their musical style. By the fourteenth century some of the *vertical* sonorities produced by the horizontal melodic lines resembled chords or inverted chords as we know them today. By the fifteenth century composers began to use *pairs* of vertical sonorities that today resemble our tonic-dominant cadences. By the sixteenth century the melodic lines might clearly form a succession of triads and inverted chords, and the lowest melodic line might act as a fundamental bass, moving by a fourth or fifth. These two new characteristics, triadic succession and fundamental bass movement by fourth or fifth, produced the cadences and tonal centers that are the earmark of the later "common practice" period, with which we are now so familiar.

Throughout most of the renaissance, however, music was still conceived in a horizontal style—in terms of multiple, horizontal melodies drawn from the old church modes. Although vertical, chord-like sonorities appeared, they were *not conceived* as such. Rather, the horizontal constructions gave rise to vertical chords secondarily, almost incidentally. Later this trend would be reversed; that is, vertical chords would be seen to give rise to melody, and not vice versa. But this change was so important, so divergent from what had gone before, that the later treatises give it elaborate and special mention as, for example, Rameau's *Traité* of 1722. Prior to the vertical conceptions, a composer might write out one whole melody, then add one or more melodies to it, and "chords" of whatever stripe might come along as they will. Of course the composer would pay attention to these at cadence points, but elsewhere they were not his primary concern. Not until the 1520s do we find mention of an alternative technique of composing, and it is so important that the writings of Pietro Aron give it special treatment: that of composing all four parts of a composition simultaneously—that is, composing the vertical sonorities as one goes along. (Aron wrote *Toscanello in Musica* in 1523, among other works.) Thus the concept of chords as we know them today grew only slowly, and they were not integral facts of musical style for Western man until the end of the renaissance. Put more simply, chords as they are known in modern tonal theory were not part of the musical cognitions of people in the West for more than a thousand years. It is worth noting that the same is true for the concept of major and minor scales. The first systematic treatment of the major/minor phenomenon did not appear until

1547. At that time, Glarean's treatise *Dodecachordon* proposed some additions to the then eight-mode system, and his additions, the Ionian and Aeolian modes, are equivalent to our current scales.

While renaissance composers slowly moved toward the newer vertical or harmonic style reflective of major-minor tonalities, theorists were busy analyzing the music, distilling practice into rules, and writing pedagogical documents. From the horizontal, melodic dimension emerged the discipline of *counterpoint*; from the vertical dimension emerged the new discipline of *harmony*. These two disciplines remain even today the principal areas of study for all formal students of music. The rules of renaissance counterpoint, as formulated in the 1500s, influenced virtually all students and composers for the next four hundred years. These rules, aimed at how to make good horizontal melody, concerned such things as the maximum number of skips in one direction, the balancing of skips with stepwise motion, the preferred approach and departure from dissonance, and the suitable consonances or resting points. Zarlino's treatise of 1558 (*Istituzioni armoniche*) contains such contrapuntal rules, and Zarlino is also one of the earliest scholars to mention vertical triads. Still, renaissance counterpoint remained intimately tied to the old church modes (not to the major-minor system), and even after two centuries of rule-formation, the last and most authoritative treatise on renaissance counterpoint (Fux 1725) was entirely based on the modal system. This treatise by Fux— appropriately titled *Steps to Parnassus* (translation, 1943)—was based on the counterpoint style of the foremost composer of the late renaissance, Palestrina (1525–1594). Fux's book contained rules and exercises for students, and it was used for generations. Haydn learned counterpoint from this book. A modern rendition of it by Jeppesen (translation, 1939) is still used in universities and conservatories today. Put briefly, some version of Fux's 1725 documentation of the renaissance contrapuntal style has influenced every counterpoint textbook since that time. (See, for example, Salzer and Schachter 1969.)

The Invention of Harmony

Although the counterpoint theorists had made mention of the new, vertical style, a systematic treatment of its primary characteristics, triads, scales, and fundamental harmonic progressions, was yet to be undertaken. The initial steps had been taken by Zarlino in 1558 and followed by the figured bass theorists thereafter. Meanwhile, the style moved increasingly toward the vertical, harmonic, hierarchically organized style of the baroque era, the beginning of the now familiar common practice period. The first theorist to systematically document the new style and put forth a lasting theory about it was Rameau (1683–1764), himself one of the great composers of the day. Rameau surveyed the music of his time and, paying respects to Zarlino, formulated a theory of harmony to explain the organization, movement, and feeling for tonal center in the music about him (*Traité de l'harmonie,* 1722). His theory made concrete and explicit the style characteristics that had been employed in the previous few decades—such things as triadic harmonies based on the major-minor scale system, bass movements reflecting clear dominant-tonic relations, and modulations to new key centers. To explain these and other phenomena Rameau employed the concepts of chord roots, chord inversions, octave equivalence, and other concepts that remained the stuff of harmonic theory for common practice for the next three hundred years. Rameau's theory was virtually unrivaled until Schenker's *Harmony* (1906) at the turn of the twentieth century. Even then its basic concepts were not all overturned, and it is still held by some today.

Rameau's theory is the womb of all the notions that are held, by scholars and laymen alike, about music of the common practice period, the eighteenth and nineteenth centuries. In it we find the central notions of scales, chords, keys, and the rules of chord progression and modulation that are now to be found in everything from popular, self-help books to formal textbooks. Predictably, Rameau's harmonic theory made its way into the regimen of all formal students of music since the eighteenth century. In one form or another, the basics of Rameau's contribution still surface in current textbooks. (See Mitchell 1948; Piston 1962.)

But Rameau, like his medieval and renaissance predecessors, was not content to merely document the musical practice of his time (see Palisca 1961). He wanted further to establish the roots of music in nature, and if not through God, then through science. For otherwise, he asked, "how shall we be able to prove that our music is more perfect than that of the ancients . . . ?" Rameau set about showing that the entire tradition of harmonic practice was derivable from the numerical laws governing interval ratios and from the overtone series (the higher frequencies generated from a fundamental tone). He thus put forth, in the early 1700s, a scientific explanation for music that based the entire artform on a single, pill-sized principle. Music reduced to scales and chords, and these to the single, fundamental tone (and its overtones). He marveled at the simplicity of this reduction: that all harmony, all melody, all the infinite diversity of music—"all this arises from two or three intervals arranged in thirds whose principle is summed up in a single sound." In this, as well as in the more practical aspects of the theory, Rameau's treatise influenced all the harmonic theories and textbooks that followed.

In the two hundred years between 1700 and 1900, the common practice or tonal style prevailed. There were changes, of course. The baroque polyphonic tonality was gradually replaced by classical homophony, and that by the lusher, more chromatic tonality of the nineteenth century. Through the two centuries of tonal style, theorists managed to apply harmonic theory (mostly Rameau's) in their analyses of current styles. The most comprehensive statement of tonal theory was Schenker's *Free Composition* (1935/1979), a diversion from Rameau's that accounted even for some nineteenth-century tonality. It is today regarded by many as the premier tonal theory, though not without controversy (see Narmour, *Beyond Schenkerism* 1977). Schenker's theory has seen pedagogical implementation in two major textbooks (Forte 1974; Salzer 1952).

But by the late nineteenth century style changes started to take shape in Western music that tonal theory could not explain. Composers, as always, insisted on tampering with style, and in the twentieth century those tamperings were many and vast. Styles proliferated. The early departures from traditional tonality were at least modal or pentatonic (e.g., Debussy), but the later ones were atonal and then serial (e.g., twelve-tone music), intentionally devoid of all tonal center and traditional consonance. Even later ones shunned discrete pitches and made use of the entire pitch spectrum (e.g., computer-generated music and avant-garde pieces for instruments), and finally compositions with *non*-pitched sonorities made their way into the style (e.g., strictly percussion pieces such as those by Warren Benson). New methods of sound-generation implemented these styles. Old instruments were played in new ways (on the body of the instrument, for example); and non-instruments were used for music-making—like ordinary objects and computers. New forms of notation and composition are in use, including aleatoric (random) means and provision for extensive performer improvisation.

In short, the changes have been vast, almost revolutionary. In some ways there has been a return to the premises of early Christian chant—

there is no fixed composition built of single tones and solidly notated. One point is clear: The major-minor system of traditional tonality cannot account for contemporary music; indeed, that system of scales, chord progressions, and conventional consonances was only employed for two and a half centuries, and it has been out of use now for nearly a hundred years. Contemporary music theory faces a great challenge, indeed crisis, in explaining, without the notion of tonality, the nature of organization and unity in contemporary musics. Controversies abound and there are a number of competing theories. Thus far a theory of the pitch structures in atonal music has been put forth by Forte (1973), and connections between such structures and the rhythmic events in atonal pieces have been sought (Forte 1980). Work continues, meanwhile, on the tonal music of earlier periods, some of it with implications for music in general, across styles, and hence for modern forms. (I consider theories by Meyer and by Berry to be examples of such.)[7] Still, a full account and explanation of modern music are a long way off. The attack moves slowly, and the pedagogical offshoots of modern theory are even further off in the future.

Summary

(1) In all periods there are characteristic musical styles (e.g., chant, contrapuntal style, harmonic style), and these styles are followed at some distance by reflection—that is, notation and analysis. Such reflection influences style transmission, principally through formal pedagogy.

(2) In the West, style has been defined primarily in terms of pitch and rhythm. These are the two parameters most accurately captured by notation and most thoroughly subjected to analysis. Pitch, which provides both harmony and melody, has been given the most attention, rhythm considerably less. (Only two modern rhythmic theories are widely known, those by Cooper and Meyer 1960; and Yeston 1976.) The other param-

---

[7]As discussed in chapter 1, Meyer's theory (1956, 1967, 1973) is drawn from musical analysis wedded with elements of perception psychology and information theory. The central premise is that all music embodies implications and realizations, that it creates expectations in listeners familiar with the style, and that it varies the resolution of those expectations by calling upon previously established norms both in the individual piece itself, and in the style from which it comes. Berry's thesis (1976) is difficult to summarize succinctly. It concerns temporal movement in music as a function of intensities in the various parameters of harmony, melody, texture, etc.

eters—timbre, dynamics, etc.—have not been given rigorous analysis and are not precisely notated.

(3) Styles change. There are few universals across style. No consonance/dissonance concept has proved universal (see also Maher 1976), nor concept of harmony or tonal organization, particularly the system of major-minor scales and triadic chords. Ultimately, the task of a cognitive theory of music will be to articulate cognitive processes that are pan-stylistic.

(4) Historically, music theory has been followed at close range by speculation about the ultimate source of music and its laws. Once reduction and analysis give rise to style principles, the source of those principles is sought. Typically, the source is thought to imbue music with order (especially mathematical order), whether the source is located in God, in Nature, in science, or in mind.

PSYCHOLOGICAL RESEARCH IN MUSIC

We have seen that reflection, particularly formal analysis, plays a determining role in style transmission and pedagogy. Reflection tells us, ostensibly, how music works, what it is made of. Hence the history of reflection and analysis could not help but influence the conduct of modern psychological research in music. It is worth taking a close look at this because the influence of analysis has been a pervasive and not unmixed blessing. I argue here that much psychological research has mistakenly focused exclusively, and also misinterpreted, merely the *results of reflection*—that is, scales, chords, and discrete pitches—rather than been concerned with music itself. Initially I direct my argument to the case of scales and chords—the main pillars of common practice tonality—but later I extend the argument even to discrete pitches. That is, I propose that isolated pitches, particularly as they appear in pitch perception studies, are themselves only the products of reflection and not the elements or building blocks of music. (That is to say, the *idea* of discrete pitches is an after-the-fact notion about music, not that the individual subject generates pitches from personal reflection.) A word more on my purpose and main points here. My aim is not to give an overview of the normally underestimated but nevertheless vast research literature in the psychology of music. (Contemporary lines of work, such as that of Deutsch, Dowling,

Shepard, Siegal, and others,[8] are traceable at least back to Helmholtz, 1877/1954.) Rather, my aim is to question the pervasive assumption that scales, chords, and especially discrete pitches are the units of musical compositions—hence also of music perception—and, more generally, to persuade the reader that an answer to the question, what *is* a musical composition? has serious consequences for psychological research. I first give attention to scales and chords because they have been so influential in determining initial research questions, forming the actual stimulus materials, and dictating interpretations of results. Hence we begin by taking note of where scales and chords come from in the first place.

Scales and Chords

Scales and chords do not exist in music. There is seldom a time in real music when a rising melodic line determinedly marks out all the diatonic steps within an octave, and there is rarely a time when tones collide at the perfect point to make a triad. Rather, music moves helter-skelter in many directions, and we discern scales and chords in it because we attempt to bring order to the goings-on there. Our music is composed of horizontal, melodic succession and vertical, simultaneous sonorities. Scales and chords (that is, chords based on triads)[9] are an attempt to systematize and explain those successive and simultaneous events.

Let us consider a metaphorical description of how scales and chords could be "discovered" in music.

Imagine a mythical analyst who is faced with a good number of compositions, all of which sound interesting and unified to his ear and which also seem to evidence certain effects—centers of gravity, states of flux, points of resolution, and so on. He seeks to explain these effects and, beginning with the notated score, he makes a number of observations. First, there are thousands of pitches occurring, but he is able to reduce these to a manageable number by labeling them with recurring names at

[8]A review of research by some of the recent contributors to music psychology can be found in the proceedings of the National Symposium on the Applications of Psychology to the Teaching and Learning of Music, Ann Arbor, Michigan, July 30–August 2, 1979. See *Documentary Report of the Ann Arbor Symposium,* Reston, Va.: Music Educators National Conference, 1981.

[9]Here I use the term *chords* in the narrow, technical sense—meaning the triadic chord, not any simultaneous compounding of tones.

their octave equivalents. (It is fortunate that of all the pitches and pitch fluctuations that occur in performance, only the twelve notated types concern him now; otherwise discrete pitch notation would be a preliminary problem.) Next, even among the twelve types of pitches, he observes that some reoccur continuously, others appear rarely, and certain ones never. In pieces that end on D, for example, the likelihood of E-flat, G-sharp, or A-sharp anywhere is small, but that of E, G, or A is very great, even though they are acoustically close in pitch to the rare ones. This is different from what happens with F and F-sharp, however, since in some pieces one occurs, and in some the other, and it is different still from C and C-sharp, since the former occurs often in early pieces (historically), and the other is used in later ones. How can he explain this? Over the years our analyst develops a system of separating the few frequently occurring pitches from all the available ones, reducing all to a single register, and when he lines them up on the staff he calls them a scale. Having taken stock of their effects in creating stability, flux, and movement, he develops an ordering system based on whole and half step distances between the tones in question, and when the system is transposed to keynotes other than D, it works just as well in predicting which tones will and will not appear in compositions and what their effects will be. As for the variable occurrence of F and F-sharp, our analyst calls compositions with the former usage "minor" and the other ones "major." In short, he's invented the scale and its major/minor variants.

Imagine now that our analyst attacks the problem of chords. He would be faced with a seemingly infinite number of vertical collections of pitches—or almost vertical ones. Often the tones do not coincide, but those that seem to go together he considers as a cluster. The clusters appear to succeed one another according to certain patterns and to create certain effects (tonal center, movement, etc.). He reduces these vertical collections by removing their redundant notes at the octave and inverting the notes so that they stack up in thirds. In so doing he invents the notion of octave redundancy (or equivalence) and the ideas of inversion and transposition. He then names these rearranged collections according to the bottom notes and observes their relation to the scale. In short, he develops the idea of triads or chords, and he is on his way to a theory about harmony.

The above description of how a mythical analyst might invent scales and chords is technically in error because it presumes that the invention was the work of an individual. In truth, the invention was the work of many who reflected on music and especially of scholars who studied, wrote, and passed on the enterprise to future generations of scholars. But the above description is not in error in its presumption that scales and chords are invented after the fact, because analytic reductions can elucidate a style only *after* that style has made its way into the public domain. Clearly, the results of analysis are retroactively descriptive of style, *but they are not necessarily the elements of music*. They are, at best, powerful analytic inventions, but they are not the cognitive "building blocks" from which music is created or heard. Let me emphasize that the act of reflection/analysis is capable of telling us a great deal about the cognitive organization of music. Indeed, insofar as a musical composition is a record of some person's musical thoughts, we may expect formal analysis to elucidate the structure of such compositional thought. But the mere *artifacts* or *reductions* that result from analysis, such as scales and triadic chords, are not to be confused with the *elements* of music or of thought per se.

This in no way implies that composers generally fail to make use of their knowledge and training in the domain of scales, chords, keys, forms, and the like when they work at writing music. Indeed, once scales and chords have been discovered and enter the culture's store of knowledge through whatever mechanisms of musical education, they likely play an important role in the total act of composing music. For example, eighteenth-century and later composers would have made considerable use of their knowledge about scales and chords in the course of working out their musical ideas. But this is knowledge *about* rather than *in* the domain of music I defined earlier. I wish to distinguish the employment of such knowledge about music from *composition proper*, by which I mean the aural-cognitive judgments (perhaps intuitive) that composers use in order to form organized, interesting wholes from the infinite sound resources they have available. Similarly listeners, as well as composers, may be affected by whatever knowledge of scales and chords they possess at the moment of their hearing a piece. Still, this is not to say that scales and chords are themselves the central elements of listener cognition. I insist, then, on a distinction between music-as-such—the stuff in the interchange between music-makers and listeners—and the analytic artifacts that follow from reflection on it that are transmitted educationally, however powerful their effect.

Scales and chords, however inevitable from reflection, have been awarded a musical prestige out of proportion with their pedigree. The widespread infatuation with these items is nothing short of a historic phenomenon, and no other concepts have commanded quite so much reverence as these supposed symbols of music's essence. All schoolchildren sing their scales, and all pianists make their fingers practice them; it is no wonder that scales and chords have been the object of so much research attention. In fact the music-psychological enterprise has devoted enormous attention to scales and chords, on the questionable assumption (not uncommon even among musicians) that the artifacts of analysis are also the elements of composition and the units of perception. Simple chords, for example, have dominated the harmony sections of several of the music aptitude and achievement tests. Hence research on harmony has likewise focused on the isolated chord, the simple discrimination of major and minor chords, the judgment of mere *number* of notes in a chord, and the possible association of single chords with colors. (This latter issue has been elucidated recently by Kowalcyk, 1976, who not only found little evidence of color-chord association, but also found that inversions of chords were not associated with the same color as the chord itself!)

Scales too have figured disproportionately in music research, chiefly through their influence on the design and conception of studies. Several investigators have started with the assumption that the scale preexists, that it is given even in advance of composition. Hence scale tones are defined as the elements from which music is created (e.g., Rakowski 1979), and they are assumed to be the fundamental units by which it is heard. The assumption that musical compositions are heard in terms of scale tones has led to a number of studies on the perception of isolated pitches drawn from the major scale (usually C major). Some of these have been useful in confirming that the perception of relations among tones does in fact conform to what scale theory would predict (e.g., Balzano 1977; Krumhansl 1979). For example, two tones a major third apart may be judged more similar than tones a second apart, even though the latter are acoustically closer in pitch. But it is not surprising that modern Westerners would perceive scale tones in such a way. Indeed, it is precisely these tonal relations that the scale is designed to reflect (for our common practice compositions), and Westerners are universally acculturated to this tonal system at a very young age, perhaps as early as 5 and certainly by 6 or 8 (Zenatti 1975; see also 1976).

Scale studies do provide a useful confirmation of Western scale theory, but as mentioned in chapter 1, there are problems with certain conclusions that have been drawn. Specifically, (1) attributing a peculiar specialness or power to this mere analytic device would seem to be misguided, and (2) claiming that the scale is an innate factor in human perception is certainly arguable. For example, one assertion is that the scale itself is responsible for music's having variety and interest, since the scale contains many different sizes of intervals (Dowling 1978). In this assertion the cart erroneously precedes the horse, for on the contrary it is surely *music* which first contains the intervals, and the scale only reflects them. Further, music's variety cannot possibly be due to the various distances between notes. Imagine what a listener must do were this in fact so: Consciously or unconsciously he would have to register each incoming interval with a degree of particularity that would give rise to either interest or boredom (for example one step, then three steps, now four steps, etc.). But what listener is aware of the hundreds of intervals that sweep him even in a short passage? More importantly, most music contains intervals *not* contained in the scale—tenths, fourteenths, thirty-fifths, and so on— and these intervals cannot be said to exist in the scale unless the operation of transposition and the construct of octave redundancy are applied. (Octave redundancy refers to the notion that a tone may be moved up or down by the octave and still be considered equivalent to its original.) These notions, transposition and octave redundancy, are, like scales, the product of analytic reflection, and they too developed only gradually in Western music scholarship. They are not inherent facts of perception. In fact, the perception of octave redundancy (or equivalence) in some musical settings has not been confirmed by research. (See Deutsch 1972; Dowling and Hollombe 1977; Pederson 1975; Thurlow and Erchul 1977.)

A related assertion similarly focuses on the scale's finite number of steps. Some have claimed that, by its very nature, the scale conveniently meets the demands and limits of cognitive processing (Dowling 1978; Rakowski 1979), since it conforms to the "seven-plus-or-minus-two" condition (Miller 1956) that is presumed to be the number of items readily cognized. The more central fact overlooked, however, is that while the scale contains seven steps, music does not. Rather, thousands of pitches can reach the listener in only a very short period of time. The scale, as an analytic reduction of music's pitches, is simply incapable of acting as the principal explanation—or even description—of the complex cognitive processing that must be necessary to handle so vast a number of bits of information. The reason is that it is very unlikely that the principal cognitive process employed in such a situation is the reduction of several thousand tones, ranging in frequency from 20 to 4,000 hertz, to a mere seven steps.

The preoccupation with seven steps inevitably confronts the fact that many nonwestern scales violate the "seven-plus-or-minus-two" principle. Some have attempted to rationalize this by claiming, for example, that the twenty-two pitches of an Indian scale can be effectively reduced to seven if we note that Indian melodies use only seven or so focal pitches, with the others used as neighboring, ornamental ones (Dowling 1978). The difficulty with such an observation is that it necessarily rests on our willingness to accept as legitimate (for the purposes of this argument) the analytic-reductive strategy that I described earlier as the source of scales in the first place. That is, the separation of focal pitches from ornamental ones is precisely what led to our own scale, no less than to the new seven-note Indian scale. What is troublesome about employing a reductive strategy here, in addition to the fact that the act of reduction is never unbiased, is the fact that there are virtually no limits on the way any scale can be "reduced." The Western scale, for example, might reasonably be "reduced" to tones 1, 3, and 5, or perhaps even 1 and 5 (or at least an argument can be made for such reductions), and theoretically there is no reason why virtually any scale could not be "reduced" to any size or made to approximate practically any other scale. Thus reducing a twenty-two-note scale to seven tones is specious.

Although some writers have merely asserted the scale's specialness by citing its interval variety, convenient number of steps, or universal applicability, others have claimed that it is in fact innate to human perception or cognition. One view holds that the physiological mechanism underlying pitch perception is scale-based: "The ear first divides up the incoming sound waves into many narrow frequency bands, using the filtering properties of the basilar membrane. These bands are laid out roughly in accordance with the well-tempered scale" (Searle 1979). Occasionally assumptions of scale innateness lead to the insistence that proper music must be based on the diatonic system if it is to conform to human physiological or cognitive constraints. Such a tonality-centric view of music calls for a wrist-slapping of modern composers because they shun what has stood the "test of time" and instead base their compositions on some other structures (e.g., Shepard, p. 153).[10]

It is difficult for the claim of scale innateness to accommodate the variety of scales extant cross-culturally as well as the fact that, even in the West, the diatonic scale as we know it did not exist before 1600. Although it is possible to argue for a gradual evolution in Western music toward a style that did match up with the presumed physiological or cognitive constraints, it must be said that such a match lasted only a short time, from about 1650 to 1900. More importantly, and with regard to claims about the basilar membrane, it should be pointed out that a basilar membrane laid out in frequency bands (from low to high, say) is likely to be "roughly in accordance" with virtually *any* scale likewise laid out from low to high, not just the Western, well-tempered one. In fact it would be an odd coincidence indeed if the frequency bands did not approximate *some* scale.

But even granting that the ear embodies an approximate conformity to the diatonic scale, it is clear that the basilar membrane (or whatever structure) has exerted no appreciable influence on the way the world's music actually turned out. Virtually all music except Western music between 1650 and 1900 is not based on the well-tempered scale, yet it is or was well-cognized by its audiences. That music in a particular epoch temporarily conformed to what the basilar membrane supposedly dictates does not make the basilar membrane a central force in music. A similar argument may be made in art: That depth perception is part of the human equipment does not invalidate art that makes no use of depth or perspective. In sum, that the basilar membrane embodies the scale is at worst unlikely, and at best largely irrelevant.

In summary, I have suggested that psychological research has been too narrowly concerned with the artifacts of analysis instead of with music. In particular, scales and chords have been awarded a degree of attention out of proportion with their ability to explain the central facts of human music-making—that understanding music is universal, that there are mul-

[10]R. N. Shepard. "Individual Differences in the Perception of Musical Pitch." Paper presented at the National Symposium on the Applications of Psychology to the Teaching and Learning of Music, Ann Arbor, Michigan, July 30–August 2, 1979. *Documentary Report of the Ann Arbor Symposium,* Reston, Va.: Music Educators National Conference, 1981.

tiple styles of music, and that musical styles change. The problematic assumption regarding the centrality of scales and chords is tied to a more fundamental assumption: that the single discrete pitch is the basic unit of processing in music listening and composing. In what follows I explore the question: Can discrete pitches be considered the universal elements of musical cognition, or are they too just the artifacts of reflection?

Discrete Pitches

When we listen to music, a magnificent number of pitches bombards our ears. Without question we not only have the twelve chromatic pitches to contend with, but also, in almost all music, there are fine gradations of pitch, pitch wavering, and tremolo effects that add to the vast number of pitches we hear. We can cite many examples of music that contains more than just the twelve discrete scalar pitches: many nonwestern musics use quarter-tones or smaller divisions; much folk and popular singing in the West uses pitch wavering; modern composers use quarter-tones and even continuous movement along the pitch spectrum, especially in electronic music but also in music for natural instruments. But even discounting music intentionally composed outside the twelve-step system, we needn't look far for music that contains more than just twelve pitches. Almost all music (save solo keyboard) is performed and heard with fine gradations in pitch, since most vocalists and instrumentalists perform with vibrato and "slide" smoothly from pitch to pitch. Our question is not: Does music contain more than twelve pitches? for surely it does. Rather, our question is: Are the twelve isolable pitches the primitive, fundamental units, the "building blocks," of listening and composing?[11] More generally, Where do discrete pitches come from? Do they preexist as the primitive basis for our music-making? My argument is that they do not, and that discrete pitches arise only as a result of reflection *upon* music and notation *of* it. That is, they arise after music, not before it. (I could give a similar argument for numerically calibrated durations not being the fundamental processing unit of rhythm, but I do not pursue that argument here.)

In my view the most plausible explanation for the invention of discrete

---

[11]There is a similar issue in speech perception: namely, that no two tokens of the same utterance type are ever exactly the same, yet diverse tokens may be categorized as belonging to the same phoneme class. Still, there is some question as to the perceptual reality of phonemes, which I take up below.

pitches is the following. In our early history the frequency band did not naturally divide itself up into the twelve chromatic pitches. (This is certainly true given the cross-cultural differences in scales.) Instead, there was singing, and here I am thinking of chant, with fine gradations and fluctuations of pitch, "wavering" along the pitch spectrum, but no discrete, separated tones. As early notation developed, these fluctuations collected about isolated pitches and were notated as such. That is, the fine gradations were reduced, condensed, and collapsed into single tones. Most probably, the development of notation and the consequently necessary act of reflection brought about the isolation of separate pitches.

Over centuries, as the artillery of notation increasingly played a role in composing, music-makers came to rely on the tool of discrete-pitch conception and notation. This was all the more necessary with the rise of complex polyphonic music (two or more singers simultaneously), and with the use of instruments which were more disposed, by their physical limitations, to the production of one tone at a time, whatever those specific tones were (and we do not know what they were). Thus with the invention of notation, discrete pitches became irrevocable features of Western style. Eventually they became the backbone of composition, performance, and analytic activity. This does not imply, however, that they are the fundamental, natural units of cognitive processing, or that the twelve discrete pitches preexist. Rather, like scales and chords, discrete pitches are the artifacts of reflection, and in particular of written notation. Though they came very early in our history, they form part of our knowledge *about* music-making, not our musical knowledge per se. They are part of the rational knowledge employed in the act of composition, but they are not the elements of *composition proper,* by which I mean the aural-cognitive judgments, the heard organizations that result in pieces of music. My claim is that, as a fact of cognitive processing, these heard organizations are not constructed piecemeal by conglomerating isolated tones. Rather, they come about, in both composing and listening, from cognitive processes such as transformation and closure. Such heard organizations may be implemented or described by modern scholars with the tool of discrete pitches. But however necessary and convenient that tool, it is not the set of building blocks, the initial, pre-given units that are added up to make a composition.

I hold, then, that in our early history musical style could not have been conceived in terms of discrete pitches. Instead, isolated pitches resulted from written notation. Thus, they are not the generic or universal cognitive units of composing and listening.

There are a few bits of historical and psychological evidence that bear on this issue. First, in the early days of medieval chant, the pitch range in use was very narrow, only an octave or two compared to the several we use now. I believe it is unlikely that, during these several hundred years, people based an entire style on just the few pitch-steps in this narrow range. More probably they used many fine gradations of pitch over the narrow spectrum available. Second, Western music notation began only in the ninth century. If the style had been conceived at that time in discrete steps, we might expect it to have been notated sooner, since any discrete symbols, letters or numbers, could immediately be used as pitch designators. As it was, the first forms of notation did not even show discrete steps, but only the general rising or falling of melodic line. In short, notation and the idea of discrete steps appear to have developed in synchrony. And third, the invention of discrete steps, when it came, did not immediately give rise to the concept of *fixed* pitches. Indeed, the very concept of a fixed, absolute pitch (e.g., '440' A) was foreign to the medieval period (Grout 1973; Trietler 1974). Once established, the concept of absolute pitch proved malleable over time, for systems of instrument-tuning changed throughout history. They continue to change today as orchestras and other ensembles deviate from the '440' rule. In short, there are changes even now in music's "fixed" pitches. More importantly, the idea of discrete pitches, fixed or not, does not appear to have been an a priori condition for music-making throughout history.

The psychological evidence on this problem is meager, but two issues are relevant:

(1) If discrete pitches are the fundamental processing units, then the perception of isolated tones should precede, and be easier than, the perception and cognition of larger wholes. The evidence suggests this is not the case.

(2) If discrete pitches are the fundamental processing units, then the perception of the frequency spectrum should universally be in terms of discrete categories that mark off the spectrum by steps. Here too the evidence is that this is not universally the case.

With regard to the first issue, the evidence is that the perception and discrimination of single pitches is extremely difficult, more difficult, seemingly, than other musical tasks in which we routinely engage in everyday life. Over the past sixty years enormous amounts of data have been collected with the several standardized pitch or interval perception tests, those by Kwalwasser and Dykema (1930), Lundin (1949), and Seashore (1919, 1930, and 1960), for example. I will not attempt to summarize here the many studies devoted to pitch perception; however, the following results are important: (1) Pitch perception tasks are difficult—e.g., determining which of two tones is higher or lower, telling the number of tones in a chord, or determining whether two intervals are the same or different. (2) Such tasks are more difficult for children than for adults, more difficult for nonmusicians than for musicians. These results, while predictable, tell us that discrete pitch perception is not a primitive, simple, or universal skill. Moreover, our informal observations tell us that almost everyone (including children) can sing or recognize simple melodies, will listen to and recognize even very complex pieces, and, in short, can understand music to some degree when there are whole phrases, whole compositions, and perhaps hundreds of pitches occurring. Still, almost everyone finds single-pitch perception taxing. It appears that the perception of single pitches does not necessarily precede the perception of groupings of multiple pitches. In other words, the discernment of single pitches is not the prerequisite to the perception of musical wholes.

With regard to the second issue, that of categorical perception, the evidence is that musicians acquire categories for pitch that are analogous to the phonemic categories for speech (Siegel and Siegel 1977a, 1977b). However, persons without musical ability do not use categorical perception, particularly when tones are presented in isolation from some musical context, such as a chord (Blechner 1978). Thus, the categorical perception of pitches does not seem to be universal, primitive, or innate.

The issue of whether discrete pitches are the fundamental processing units of musical cognition sees a parallel issue in speech perception—specifically, whether the phoneme is the fundamental unit of larger linguistic entities (syllables, words, and sentences). No one doubts the reality of phonemes, since they clearly are responsible for alphabets and rhyming, for example, but the issue is whether some basis can be found for their *perceptual* reality. In a phoneme- and syllable-identification task, Savin and Bever (1970) have shown that phonemes are perceived only after the whole syllable is perceived, not before. However, McNeil and Lindig (1973) provide evidence that this could have been an artifactual result of the experimental design, and results similar to McNeil and Lindig's were obtained by Healy and Cutting (1976). Nevertheless the question of phoneme processing is still open, and the experimental technique of using phoneme monitoring (the method employed thus far) is still under consideration (Frauenfelder et al. 1980).

Note that the arguments about phonemes in speech and pitches in music are parallel but not exactly congruent, because it cannot be assumed that musical pitches are the precise analog of phonemes. (Or are they more like syllables or words, for example?) Moreover, it is not clear that discrete scalar pitches in the sense I describe them here have *any* direct analog in speech. Nevertheless, the general issue regarding the fundamental processing units is similar in both domains.

In summary, I have held that, however much the twelve scalar pitches are now integral facts of Western style, their genesis lies in reflection and the invention of writing, not in some innate perceptual mechanism; discrete pitches are the artifacts of reflection and cannot be considered the elements of music cognition. Thus measures of music perception whose stimuli consist of isolated tones (or even chords) that bear little resemblance to that which we know as music, are unlikely to yield information about music proper.

The misconception about the role of discrete pitches in music cognition stems from the attempt to chop the artwork into small bits to study it more closely. More generally the fault lies with a questionable conception of what the artwork is. Indeed, some investigators have explicitly disavowed a willingness to entertain such questions as "What is music?" But implicit assumptions about the object under study are always and necessarily made; the failure to consider fully music's nature thus risks the making of erroneous assumptions and in my view is responsible for mistaking analytic artifacts for the building blocks of music. Specifically, the most common implicit conception of a musical composition is that it consists of *preplanned organized sounds* (such as pitches). Two debatable assumptions underlying this conception are the following: (1) that a musical composition is a fixed object residing in the external environment; and (2) that it can withstand repeated reductions on its constituent elements without loss of musical integrity. My counterproposal to this artwork-as-object is a definition of music as cognition. Before elaborating this in the following chapter I next give closer consideration to this "problem of object."

The Problem of Object

The difficulty of defining what music is can be grasped by attempting to generate a definition that reasonably encompasses the objects or occasions known as music. A more concrete representation of this problem is to assign ourselves the task of imagining a concert program consisting of several compositions, performed in a typical concert hall, and asking the question, Where in this setting lies the music and by what criteria can it be identified? The naive, outside observer—the proverbial Martian, say—would have a difficult time identifying the music by the criteria we would normally suggest. Imagine, for example, that the details of the concert program are the following. It includes music from all of Western civilization: chants, improvisatory pieces, a late Beethoven sonata, a symphony, and electronic pieces. Among these pieces, some are notated and some are not; some use instruments but some do not; some use discrete pitches and some do not. The singers use words, but sometimes not. The performers play together or alone, but when together they do not play or sing the same material. What is sung ranges from song to chant to *Sprechstimme* ("speech-song"). What is not notated ranges from the totally free, performer improvised, to the totally fixed—that is, prerecorded on tape. What is nonpitched ranges from discrete rhythmic pulses (in solo percussion pieces) to blurred sonorities in timbre-based pieces for instruments or machine. It is a strained vision but none of it lies outside our Western tradition, where pieces of music are long or short, sung or played, fixed or free, and with and without tones, instruments, or notation. Imagine, too, these details of the concert: There is an audience of listeners that includes naive and sophisticated laymen, plus critics and composers, one of whom is non-hearing. There are environmental noises both inside and outside the concert hall, and the entire thing will be electronically recorded on tape.

Our questions, then, are: Where in this setting is the music? and by what criteria can the artworks on stage be distinguished from the traffic noise, the applause, or the players tuning up? Questions such as these haunt all formal considerations of music, and answering them is more difficult than might be thought. Most of the immediate answers do not hold up because they include things that cannot be considered music, or they leave out things that certainly are music. The least useful definitions of music are those that start from the assumption that the *artwork is an object.* For example music cannot be called a *collection of sounds* because the traffic and environmental noises are sound collections but we do not consider them music. Neither is music simply *organized* sound or *structured* sound because many such sounds aren't music; doorbells, curses, and everyday greetings are organized sound but they surely are not music. Other qualifiers might be added. Music could be organized sound with *non-semantic, artistic intent,* but this begs the question. What is artistic?

We might further constrain the class of musical sounds that could be organized, such as the finite class of discrete pitches, scale members, or frequency ranges that delimit musical material. But in this case mere *scales* might qualify as musical compositions because they are clear cases of organized musical sounds, yet we know they are not music. In no way do they function as compositions, either aesthetically or socially, in the ordinary meaning of that term. Additional qualifiers similarly fail. A definition such as "that put forth by a *bonafide music-composer*" leaves out much of the music throughout history, and music specified by the *location, setting,* or *condition under which it is heard* is untenable because music indeed occurs in autos, churches, concert halls, and virtually everywhere. Most certainly music is not simply *notated,* organized sound, or even preplanned, pre-fixed, or preconceived sound. Improvisatory pieces, for example, would be omitted from such a definition. This last is perhaps the worst hurdle for a conception of music as a specific object. Musical pieces seem not to exist prior to performance; once played, they evaporate, and when repeated, they are nevertheless somewhat different.

The seemingly obvious and often implicitly accepted definitions of music, then, are faulty in one regard or another. Attempts to further modify the definition of music to encompass all cases leads increasingly to a subjective conception, a definition of music in terms of some receiver. It is clear that the electronic tape recording of the program will not do as the "receiver" whose record can symbolize what music is, for the tape recording will meet with as many objections as did objective definitions of the live performance. Rather, the artwork needs to be defined in terms of the activity of some human subject. In this conception, there are thus at least four different objects: the piece as composed, the piece as performed, the piece as heard (there will be many here), and the piece as remembered (still more again). The artwork/object is now an object that is not constant across time. Rather, we have many objects, for there are many performance renditions of a piece, and for any single playing the listeners will never be in agreement on precisely what was heard, the performers are each playing and hearing different material, and our composer who is non-hearing hears nothing at all, though surely he has a conception at least of pieces he composed. The object, if there can be said to be one, is a fluid, changing thing, or else there are multiple objects, each constituted from some human-subjective point of view. At best, the central artwork/object is an idealized, hypothetical piece—the area of overlap among all the individual performances and conceptions of the work. This artwork is not a fixed, external object, but an abstract and fluid one that rests on human cognitive construction in all phases of its existence—composing, performing, and listening.

This conception of music not as a fixed object but as a cognitive construction is consistent with what is probably the common popular or folk view of music. For we all come to the artwork expecting that repeated hearings will be slightly different, believing that the performer's rendition always diverges from the composer's intention, and knowing that, as listeners, we vary enormously in what we hear. My claim is not so much that artworks are cognitive, for surely we intuitively know this, but rather that formal investigations of them have ignored this intuition. The focus has been on the bits and pieces of artworks, a tone here and there, a chord, a scale abstracted from hundreds of passages, rather than on the generic cognitive processes that give rise to whole pieces.

In summary, a conception of the artwork as a clearly specified object external to the human knower is untenable. Further, the artwork must be defined in terms of the human processes that give rise to it, from both the productive and receptive points of view. In the following chapter, I give an elaboration of this cognitive conception of music and then propose a set of generic musical-cognitive processes that are consistent, in my view, with both a constructive definition of the artform and with the multiple, divergent styles or "languages" that we find across history.

CHAPTER 3

Some Processes

DEFINING MUSIC COGNITION

To begin, I construe music as the activity of *thinking* in or with sound and for this reason I favor the term musical "thought" or "cognition" over "music" alone. Musical thought may be defined as human aural-cognitive activity that results in the posing of artworks embodying finite and organized sets of temporal events described in sound. Several aspects of this definition warrant attention.

First, the emphasis is on organization in an ongoing, temporal context, rather than on the perception of the physical entities of sounds (or silences) per se. The temporality of music is its defining feature, and the role of specific pitch, duration, loudness, and timbral characteristics of sound events is of only secondary importance. Sound is the medium through which interesting temporal events are organized, but however necessary sound is as the carrier of music, it is by itself an insufficient definition of the artform. The principal characteristic of music is movement in time—the exploration of simultaneous and successive events that embody points of arrival and stasis, points of departure and continuation, and a train of event-to-event similarities and transformations.

A second aspect of the definition is its particular light on the subject/object relations of the musical enterprise. Indeed any definition faces this task, to portray the disposition of the knowing subject (the processes he brings to bear) and that of the musical object (on which those processes act). The extremes in the subject/object equation bear easy caricature and will be familiar: too narrow a focus on object (sound waves pour into the ear and the musical composition is stamped on the mind); too central a role for the subject (no musical sounds exist until the subject invents or hallucinates them); too facile a description of the happy interaction between the two (the subject and object create each other). The present conception may be called one of subjective construction; that is, it leans to the side of the subject insofar as it locates the organization of musical events in the activity of cognitive processes (that is to say, organization resides in the mind, not in the piece) but it also presumes the existence-as-object of a finite collection of musical sounds in the external environment. On this ground (the dimension of subjective construction) the present definition parts ways with other conceptions of music, particularly those with too narrow a focus on some assumed musical object.

Third, the definition emphasizes aural-cognitive activity—that is, thought having to do with sounds—and it excludes all such thinking that does *not* involve sound. "Sound" here may be construed as including not only actual sounds in the physical environment but also mental images of sounds that occur internally—that is, sounds occurring in the imagination (the terms "inner ear" and "inner voice" may be invoked here) and not merely represented there through some nonaural cue such as verbal pitch names, visualizations of music notation, or images of colors, spaces, or objects. In fact all such nonaural material is excluded from this definition of music, including items that may be *about* but not *in* music, such as the following: entertainments about musical characteristics that reach the level of verbal description ("The music sounds jagged"; "This sounds like such-and-so"); conscious awareness of the compositional or performance techniques of the piece; speculations about historical or biographical matters; verbal labelings of the progress of musical events (say, moving beyond felt changes in harmony to the exercise of labeling them after audition). Moreover, when words occur in the artwork itself, their consideration is excluded from the definition of music if it is their semantic meaning that is the focus of attention. (But words may be defined as music to the degree that it is their temporal and sound qualities that are entertained.)

There are a few other stipulations in the definition. The mention of *human* aural-cognitive activities is meant to exclude environmental and animal sounds such as traffic noises, doorbells, and birdcalls that occasionally make their way into other definitions of the artform. The condition of *organized* temporal events omits from the musical category both randomized and totally serialized sound collections (as in aleatoric and serial musics) that remain unorganized by the listener. (Often, however, music can be meaningfully heard irrespective of the techniques of its generation, a fact that allows a measure of aesthetic legitimacy to compositions that would otherwise be crippled by their music-as-object condition.)

Finally, the definition of music calls for the activity of posing an artwork. There are three such activities: composing, listening, and performing; and although they appear to have little in common as overt activities (in fact they call upon dissimilar motivations and abilities) they are rooted in a common set of basic musical-cognitive processes. Indeed, it is impossible to assume that the life of an artform could proceed without such a common core of processes. The term composing refers to all deliberate acts of combining sounds within a specified time frame for the purposes of creating interesting temporal events. Composing may or may not involve the fixing of an aural organization of events (as through visual notation or electronic recording), but it always involves sound events that are to some degree intentional and planned. In this definition most forms of improvisation are acts of composing; most activities involving chance or random sound collections are not. The term listening refers to an active organizing and construing of the temporal events heard in a composition. The term performing refers to a hybrid activity involving both listening and composing (in the sense of creating a certain interpretation within the bounds of a composition's pre-specified materials).

The activities of composing and listening embody the clearest and most exemplary functioning of what I have called musical thought, and although I argue for a core set of processes that crosses each, I do not imply that listening is the mere reception of whatever is the result of composing. Indeed this would be a faulty portrayal of the artwork—a fixed object with properties injected or composed into it, those same properties being pulled out of it and received in listening. Composing and listening share certain musical-cognitive processes (which I later describe in detail) but they must be conceived as independent functions. Moreover, composing and listening both involve other activities that are unique to each, and many such activities, although they may be necessary or desirable accompaniments to composing and listening, are not necessarily musical in the sense proposed here. In particular, all of the following nonaural activities are excluded from the present definition of musical thought.[1]

---

[1] The exclusion of *nonaural* processes from the definition of musical thought does not necessarily entail the exclusion of other (especially *aural*) processes that might occur in both musical and nonmusical domains. Indeed, some processes that are not limited to music (for example, transformation) may be included in the present definition of musical thought, provided they occur aurally.

(1) In composing, the pseudo-compositional acts of a predetermining sort such as arbitrary or expedient selections of key, instrument, or tone row; any nonaurally motivated acts such as the spelling out of words with pitch names (e.g., B-A-C-H); the use of symbols (e.g., in the baroque period the descending chromatic line for death); the use of explicit representational devices (for painting thunder, cuckoos, or clock-tickings); and even the logical, premeditated, or intellectual working-out of a theme or tone row so that it is convenient for some later purpose (e.g., a canonic theme that works backward as well as forward, or a row that embodies properties that predispose it to certain manipulations later on).

(2) In listening, those instances of attention that are for ordinary intellectual purposes, such as the determining of technical or historical integrity, all reflections rooted in verbal or visual imagery (including extramusical emotional reflections); and monitorings of the piece for isolated, preselected events such as the appearance of a favorite instrument or theme.

(3) In performing, the activities of decoding notation and coordinating muscular activity.

All these activities are specifically excluded from the category of music proposed here because they rest on thought processes, of whatever necessity, integrity, or desirability, that are nonauditory.

Having given examples of what musical thought is not, I turn now to what it is. Musical thought is the activity of thinking temporally with sounds, both simultaneous and successive. An example of the path such thought might follow in the designing or hearing of a piece of music would perhaps be this: Some temporal space and an initial level of activity are defined. (A rhythm or pulse is established, not just for tones, but for the entire pace of harmonic, timbral, and thematic changes.) The acoustic space is defined (most broadly by register and timbre) and separate horizontal lines of activity are set up that may meet, part, or cross. Large areas of time are divided and subdivided; small units are created, then chained together. Memorable collections of sounds, perhaps patterns, undergo change (as when themes are transformed), and relationships of relative similarity and difference evolve. Hierarchies in a structural background arise if some sounds circumscribe, prolong, or elaborate others in such a way as the latter seem more prominent and fundamental. The rhythm of vertical formulations creates areas of instability, movement, and tendencies toward change, as well as stability, repose, and closure.

Rhythmic and dynamic activities also create patterns of movement and closure. Sound parameters interact; rhythmic, timbral, and pitch activities are congruent or dissimilar in level of intensity. Throughout, patterns of change, repetition, and silence imply and forecast events which may or may not actualize.

In short, things happen. Musical events occur. The job of thought is not just to follow but to construct such events.

Thus far I have defined music as a cognitive activity and have proposed a strict definition which excludes all forms of nonaural activity. I have held that composing, performing, and listening are the external manifestations of musical cognition and that at the root of all three activities lies a common set of generic musical-cognitive processes. The task of describing these generic processes is undertaken in the following section. It is worth emphasizing here that such processes always occur through the medium of some musical style or "language," and we have seen that such styles vary in the rules or principles they employ. Throughout Western history style principles have varied with respect to the types of closure, transformation, grouping, etc., that were employed. Style principles are themselves cognitive; that is, they describe how the participants of a particular musical community understand the specific style they share. Our purpose here, of course, is not to catalog specific style principles (there would be hundreds of them), but to propose some general or generic cognitive processes that likely cut across a variety of styles. We must assume that people employ such generic cognitive processes in the course of effecting a particular musical style, because they surely do not alter their minds every time a new style makes its appearance. Indeed, styles change continuously, and at least in modern times people are exposed to a variety of styles at any one time. If there were no generic, pan-stylistic processes, we could only understand one style at a time, perhaps only one in a lifetime.

The several processes I propose here are generic and pan-stylistic. While it cannot be proved that they are universals, they certainly encompass a good many styles, and I cite examples of them from Western art music, jazz, and folk or "primitive" music. Unquestionably they are general enough to account for more than just the single style of the common practice period, which has occupied the bulk of the research attention thus far. On the other hand, they are cognitively more specific than some previous attempts at identifying musical universals. Harwood (1976), for example, claims "pitch perception" as a universal cognitive process in music, but while this is undoubtedly correct, the level of description is roughly analogous to claiming "vision" as a universal cognitive process in art. As such it is far too general to be a useful predictor of how humans actually construct or organize their music in composition and listening. In sum, my aim here is to identify cognitive processes at a level of description that, regardless of the *particulars* of style, is generally indicative of how the music of various communities ultimately came out and is generally descriptive of what it takes for music to be understood. I describe two categories: *temporal processes,* which concern relations among discrete events (succession and simultaneity) and *nontemporal processes,* which concern more general and more formal properties over large sections of a piece of music (closure, transformation, abstraction, and hierarchic levels).

TEMPORAL PROCESSES

Music is organized, in the acts of both composing and listening, along two dimensions, the simultaneous and successive. The Western scholarly tradition has elevated these two dimensions to formal musical disciplines: that of harmony (the simultaneous dimension) and of counterpoint (the successive). But all music, Western or not, embodies these dimensions by virtue of its temporal nature. It is perhaps unfortunate that we are able to speak of the two separately, for they always coexist in experience. Nevertheless, I discuss them separately below and call attention to some of the cognitive issues at stake in each.

Succession

With respect to the successive dimension, the mental operation of chaining, grouping, or horizontally adding events is required. Some initial, short unit is conceived, then successive units are added to it. Two or more units together are reconstituted into a unified whole, a single but longer unit, rather than remaining a series of bits glued end-to-end. The successive dimension unfolds in time, beginning with shorter units that extend to create new, longer units. I describe four sub-processes here:

(1) *Idiomatic construction.* In any piece of music, a basic, coherent unit must be conceived. Units may be melodic fragments or motives, longer

melodies, rhythmic patterns, harmonic or timbral sequences, or any coherent "block" or area of sound that acts as a cohesive unit. Although
they may vary in length, units have the quality of being for the composer
or listener a single tight cell that coheres, remains potent in memory, and
which can be extended or acted upon after its initial statement. Indeed,
composers may often begin work on a piece by first fashioning a cell or
unit on which it will be based. In his jazz text, Collier (1975:132) refers
to this initial step as "starting from nothing"—the specifying of the central, opening unit. Whether such a unit pervades the entire piece, or only
provides a springboard for other, different units, the necessity of specifying *some* coherent unit or units seems to be incontrovertible.

I have termed the construction of such units *idiomatic* construction
because a unit's coherence depends critically on its abiding by the organizational rules of some idiom. For example, the so-called tonal idiom is
universally understood in the West. The difference in musical "sense" or
logic between the opening six tones of our national anthem and those
same six tones mixed up at random is that the former adhere to our tonal
idiom. Different cultures have different musical idioms, of course, and a
single idiom can give rise to different styles. For example, Western folk,
rock, most jazz, and classical music between the seventeenth and twentieth centuries are generally participants in the tonal idiom. But despite
differences across styles and cultures, the important point here is that
some *idiom* is employed for the purpose of constructing an initial, coherent, well-organized musical unit.

The psychological implication of idiomatically constructed units is this:
Sound events that are logically discrete and isolable (e.g., pitches) in fact
are perceived or felt as a continuous gesture. The separate tones of a
melody are perceived in a continuous sweep so that earlier tones are somehow tied to later ones, even after the former have quit sounding. The
result of this—that the effect of now-silent tones is still felt upon the
remaining tones of a unit—is that units project shape, contour, and direction. The "rising line" of an ascending melody is impossible without
the knitting together of earlier and later tones, though the former have
ceased by the time later ones sound. The idiomatic construction of units
is a matter of cohesion during or within succession.

(2) *Motivic chaining.* Motivic chaining is the cumulative or additive
process by which any two or more units (or motives) are combined successively into a longer one. This process is obviously necessary for music

to continue beyond the single, graspable unit, for in all music events are chained or connected or follow one another. But note that we may speak of the process as "retroauditive"; that is, there is a building up of the whole successively, as an extension or unfolding, of which one becomes aware only in hindsight. That is to say, there is not a whole segmented into parts glued end-to-end, for there can be no temporal whole *prior* to the chaining of parts. Rather, the whole is known only in the experience of temporal succession.

(3) *Patterning.* When motives or units are chained repetitively, patterns result. In the successive dimension, the primary types of patterns are repetition and alternation, which, in tonal music, may be combined with modulation to produce sequences. Nevertheless, repetition and alternation appear to be evident in all music, especially monophonic folk music (Nettl 1956a). Repetition and alternation are also conspicuous in jazz, and at least one jazz text (Collier 1975) makes explicit suggestions for their use.

The important cognitive issue, however, is specifying *what* for the human subject constitutes a perceived repetition or alternation. Developmentally, does the child perceive repetition *as* a repetition, or as something different (perhaps because a repetition is never exact and is always transferred or delayed in time)? Most importantly, patterns give rise to two forms of expectation: continuation (of the pattern or sequence at hand) and cessation (since ultimately all patterns cease). For example, in tonal music the traditional harmonic/melodic sequence combines modulation with melodic patterning to produce a strong sense of expectation and arrival at a tonal center. Nevertheless, the general process of chaining one or more units repetitively so that perceived patterns result, appears to be a near-universal process in understanding music.

(4) *Phrasing.* This process concerns larger-scale attempts to group musical events into clusters, "chunks," or phrases, which may or may not be equal in length. Of primary concern here is the nature of the boundaries that obtain between phrase "chunks." In Western music the boundaries between phrase groupings are signaled by repetitions of previous material, any change in theme, rhythm, texture, or dynamic level, melodic or harmonic changes or resolutions, or by absolute length (since at some point an event sequence must have a phrase boundary). In actual practice phrase boundaries are signaled by a combination of factors, though not in all cases are the boundaries unequivocally clear; two phrases may share

an overlapping section, or a boundary may be ambiguous. Suffice it to say that some larger scale divisions in the temporal progress of a composition are made. With regard to nonwestern and especially primitive musics, it is not clear whether the cues to phrase boundaries are identical to those mentioned above, but there is at least rudimentary evidence of phrase grouping in all sung forms. That is, repetitions or points of change in text, pauses for breath, or any change in timbre, register, or vocal performer could signal a new phrase. The important point is that, whatever the particular phrase boundary cues in use, it seems likely that all musical spans of substantial length must be subdivided into chunks or phrases that facilitate the processing of the whole, longer span.

Simultaneity

The simultaneous dimension in music calls for the operation of combining and synthesizing musical events, vertically adding or superimposing one event on another. The critical issue here is whether and how two events may be superimposed and retain their identities intact, or whether and under what conditions they form a new whole which is perceived as an integrated event. The standard three-note chord is a case in point. Only in the most abstract sense can it be considered three events or tones superimposed, for in the course of a composition chords are likely to be perceived as true integrations of tones.[2] Indeed, so unified and well-blended an entity is the chord that even determining the number of tones comprising a chord is a difficult and specialized skill thought to be reflective of musical talent or ability. Wing (1948, 1961) included such a task of determining chord components in his musical ability test battery, and the task has been associated with auditory acuity even among musicians (Shuter-Dyson, and Gabriel 1981).

But there are other examples of cognizing simultaneous events. One may be called *timbre synthesis*—simply, the combining of two or more timbres (e.g., instrumental tone colors) with the result that such syntheses may range from tight, unified blends to separable, distinct juxtapositions.

---

[2]The simultaneous compounding and integration of tones occurs in all chords, whether we define them narrowly as triads (e.g., C-E-G) or broadly as any cluster of tones (e.g., E-G-C-F). That tones blend and integrate in the formation of chords or vertical clusters, however, in no way bears on whether those clusters are themselves isolated units with respect to their surround, when they occur in a composition.

In a study of timbre synthesis in three- and four-year-old children, Serafine (1981) found that young children have extremely accurate perception and memory for simple timbres *as single entities,* but they are unable to imagine or predict simultaneous combinations of them *even* when the combinations involve very distinct, separable timbres (e.g., a bell and drum). This suggests that simple perception and memory are not sufficient for timbre synthesis; rather, a more advanced cognitive operation for combining or synthesizing appears to be necessary.

Yet another example of the construction of simultaneous events is that of *motivic synthesis,* the compounding of any two or more motives or units, such as multiple melodies or rhythmic patterns. Consider a measure of any musical composition whatsoever that entails at least two simultaneous instances of melodic or rhythmic activity. The two parts, melodic fragments, say, are superimposed so that they both sound together. The question at hand is how, whether, and under what circumstances two fragments are combined or added to achieve a particular result: either a unity in which the parts retain their individual identity, or in which they are subordinated to produce a new whole. In either case, the elementary process at hand is the act of combining melodic or rhythmic events in a simultaneous context.[3]

On a larger level, over the course of the composition, a process I have termed *textual abstraction* involves the organization of simultaneous areas or streams of activity. That is, the collage of simultaneous sounds that has been identified as the composition must be subdivided (vertically) and organized so that a definable *texture* emerges. Described most generally, textural organization involves the putting together of what-goes-with-what and the separation of the "whats" into various components that contrast and interact. Examples of organized textures would be contrasting figure-versus-ground, or melody-against-accompaniment textures or, say, polyphonic textures (such as counterpoint or fugue) in which two or more simultaneous parts are of equal prominence.

In the case of melody/accompaniment textures, those parts of the texture that are construed as accompaniment are cast against a melody that stands in relief, is put into the foreground, so to speak; in the case of the fugue, the separate parts are streamed into horizontal threads that may

---

[3]It should be pointed out that among the rules governing such a process, some may be particular to music and others not.

meet, part, and cross. Note that in this activity the subject must actively construct such textures—melodies against background, melodies against each other—for there is no inherent reason why textures must be organized as such, particularly when produced in the same register and timbre. To take the example of a fugue again, the separate parts are cast into a linear format, stratified in a parallel manner, and understood as a linear, stratified pattern, not as, say, what would be logically just as possible, a sequence of overlapping zig-zags. Organizing the texture is one aspect of how the mind constitutes and makes sense of the composition on a larger, more global level.

It is important to note that the most general types of texture, monophonic, homophonic, and polyphonic, occur across cultures and in different types of music. Russo (1968) gives examples of counterpoint, figure/ground textures, and even voice-crossing in jazz, and Nettl (1956b, 1973) gives many folk music examples of both the mono- and polyphonic textures. In one case, Nettl (1973:115) gives an example of an Italian folksong in which two voices alternate in playing the dominant role in a melodic part. This seems to be evidence for a conscious awareness of the prominence of melody, such that it is shared among voices.

The more general problem, however, is that we are not certain how various textures, especially complex ones involving two or more parts, are actually heard. Are all the parts of equal importance and thus independent? Or is one part subsidiary to or dependent on another? To what degree does a melody stand out against its background? Of primary importance is the question of how textural organization develops from early childhood. Assuming that a child subject may be made familiar with two or more parts as individual entities, how and under what conditions will he construct a compositional texture when the parts are together and interacting?

In sum, whatever the nature of the texture (homo- or polyphonic, etc.) and whatever the cues to textural organization (timbral and registral separation, for example), one aspect of cognitively organizing a composition is construing the texture or areas of activity that occur in the piece.

NONTEMPORAL PROCESSES

The processes here are nontemporal in the sense that they do not result from immediate, note-to-note, phrase-to-phrase reality; rather, they are more formal, logical, abstract operations performed on musical material.

Of course, the processes here are temporal in the sense that all music is temporal—that is, it unfolds in time; however these processes are to be distinguished from the temporal processes in the previous category, which are tied to surface level, event-to-event groupings. The present category of nontemporal operations has four processes: (a) closure; (b) transformation; (c) abstraction; and (d) hierarchic levels.

Closure

Music embodies periods of both movement and stasis (or closure). The term movement describes time spans which generate expectations of continuation and advancement toward some point of rest and arrival. Closure refers to points of stasis and stability which imply cessation. It is movement which propels us forward in time and closure which brings us to rest, to the end of a section or piece.

In Western music it has been principally melody and harmony which effect movement and closure, while rhythm and density of rhythmic/tempic activity may also play a role. Unstable, unresolved melodic intervals which generate movement away from themselves are, for example (in the common practice tradition), the intervals of a fourth or seventh; the more stable, closed intervals are the third and octave. Harmonically, the least stable chordal areas are the dominant and the vii chord, the most stable the tonic.

These assertions about common practice tonality are simple enough—that certain tonal combinations generate movement, others closure. But the important point is that every style alternates movement and stasis, though the principles or cues for closure vary from style to style. Nearly all Peyote songs, for example, end with four long, even notes on the tonic; many Plains Indians' songs end with a descending third or fourth followed by several repetitions of the final tone (Nettl 1956a). Such closure techniques contrast with the typical tonic chord of Western tonality, or the other devices for closure in contemporary Western music, but closure is both ubiquitous and necessary in all musical styles. Surprisingly little research has been devoted to the cognitive aspects of closure in music.

Transformation

In much the same way as abstraction (described below), transformation in its broadest form is responsible for many unity-generating effects in music, for it results in the awareness of similarity in the face of ostensible differences. Two musical events or structures may be perceived as related, hence in some sense cohesive, if some similarity obtains between them, even as there is discontinuity in other features. I speak of transformation as the more general source or cause for similarity/difference relationships, for the nature and degree of similarity and difference between two musical events can be logically described by the steps that would be entailed to transform one event into the other. That is, similarity/difference relationships are themselves relative, psychological judgments; and transformation is the more general process or operation that effects or results in similarity and difference. We may imagine that individuals vary with respect to the quality and number of transformations of musical events or structures they are able to perform (whether in listening or composing), and that they also vary in how such transformations affect their similarity/difference judgments. Mention of the more general operation—transformation—is preferable to the mere figurative judgment of similarity-difference, for the similarity judgments of two people may be equivalent (as measured), but the system of transformations used to effect that similarity may not. I propose, then, that while the process at hand involves the detection of similarity across divergent musical events (and thus generates unity), the process is best thought of as rooted in the operation of transformation—the step(s) that would need to be accomplished in order to transform the first musical event into the second.

It should be pointed out that logically, not aurally, any musical event may be transformed into any other, so long as an infinite number of steps or transforming operations is allowed. In the extreme, musical events that are related by only vast and numerous logical transformations would not necessarily generate similarity relations or, hence, unity. Our concern, then, is with those transforming operations that do result in aurally perceived similarity or at least aurally experienced unity and cohesiveness. The transformations, even the similarity, may or may not be accessible to a conscious awareness, but the logical transformations in question must result in the experience of aural cohesion. We presume, then, to describe heard similarity and thus heard unity as the relationships of transformation that obtain between two musical events or structures.

I distinguish three types of transformation operations. The first is *relative repetition,* including (a) identity or exact repetition (with only temporal displacement) and (b) repetition with figurative changes such as transposition of key or register, changes of mode, tempo, accompaniment, or dynamics. In tonal music repetition with figurative changes is commonplace, but it also occurs in other styles. Collier (1975) gives jazz examples of both literal and tonal transpositions, the former being simply a change of key and the latter involving, in addition, certain adjustments in the scale degrees used so that the tonic/dominant (or some other) relationship is preserved. Nettl (1956a:198, 1973:85) gives examples of Cheremis songs employing transposition to a lower pitch as well as *tonal* transposition, which indicates that some special scale relations may be preserved.

Beyond such techniques of relative repetition, a second level of transformation is *ornamentation*. This process involves the alteration of a musical event through the addition, overlay, or superimposition of other events, usually with a result that is substantially more changed than with relative repetition. An example would be the classical ornamentation that occurs in early theme and variation forms, the addition of turns, trills, and repeated notes to melodies undergoing variation, but any form of melodic alteration through the addition of musical material would be a form of ornamentation. Examples abound in the jazz idiom, and several are given by Collier (1975:89–90), who considers this one of the primary techniques employed by the jazz artist when he "plays around the melody" (p. 82). A striking example from American folk music can be found in the transcriptions of fiddle tunes (e.g., "Buffalo Gals") as elaborately ornamented by traditional players (see Guntharp 1980). The results of ornamentation preserve the original event intact, as the scaffold for whatever has been added. The transformation here is alteration through addition, but without substantial tampering with the original event itself.

While both relative repetition and ornamentation maintain the presence of the original event, yet a third level of transforming, which I will call *substantive transformation,* may not. In this case the transformed event is left recognizably related to its original form, but in ways that are more abstract. For example, only the contour may be preserved, and transformations may have been applied to the rhythms or tonal sequences. Jazz instances of this, for example, are given by Collier (1975:163). Or the contour and tonal pattern may be preserved and substantive changes may take place in the rhythm, through the addition of rests, syncopation, or augmentation and diminution (lengthening and shortening of durational values). An example of an African song with the same tonal pattern repeated over different rhythms is given by Nettl (1956a:200). Examples from the tonal art music tradition can be found in any theme and variations form, as well as many other pieces. Further, substantive transformations may be applied to tonal sequences, such as inversion (turning intervals and contour upside down), retrograde (the sequence in reverse or backward), or even retrograde inversion (both operations). Such transformations occur in Western art music in both tonal and atonal music. Examples in the jazz idiom are given by Collier (1975) and Russo (1968), the latter of whom gives an example of such transformations applied to the tune "Bill's Blues" (p. 685).

The above examples do not exhaust the methods of substantive transformation that may be applied to one or more parameters of a musical event (contour, rhythm, dynamics, tonal sequence, etc.). There may be expansion, contraction, or omission (elision) of material, or any number of abstract operations that may be applied to an event. Indeed, not all forms of transformation have been as precisely formalized as strict inversion, retrograde, and so on, and a complete catalog of all techniques of transformation would come close to a catalog of all compositional technique itself. The critical point here is that transformation as a cognitive process, in both composing and listening, does occur, and it is one of the processes that contributes to our understanding of music and the changes that take place from one event to the next. One of the continuing problems is the identification of which transformations are, in fact, perceived as such by listeners, and which may be considered only formal, logical transformations that are perceived by listeners as new, unrelated material. This question is still open to experimental scrutiny. The evidence thus far is that adults can perceive inversions of brief melodies, but with some difficulty (Dowling 1971); transformations involving retrograde and retrograde inversion are even more difficult, perhaps impossible in certain contexts (Dowling 1972).

Abstraction

Abstraction is the process by which some aspect of a musical event is removed or considered apart from its original context and is relocated elsewhere in the composition. Some relationship or connection between the original appearance and later appearance is thus implied. For example, *motivic abstraction* occurs when a subunit or fragment of a theme is removed and reused in a new theme. *Property abstraction* occurs when some general property—only the rhythmic pattern, tonal pattern, or harmonic progression, for example—is abstracted from one section and reappears in another.

Such abstractions are ubiquitous in Western art music (any work of Beethoven provides a ready example), but they also appear in other styles. Collier (1975:164) gives examples of rhythmic abstraction and reuse in the jazz idiom, and Nettl (1956a:197) shows a clear example of identical rhythms over different melodies in a Comanche Indian Peyote Song. Moreover, Pflederer (1966) has provided evidence for children's understanding of this process, in the case where the same rhythm occurs under tonal deformation.

Abstraction is typically thought to be a generator of unity and wholeness in compositions, because it represents the parsimonious use and reuse of the same or similar material over long spans of time. Abstraction is in some cases a prerequisite to the process described above (transformation) because even before a tonal sequence can be transformed, say, by an alteration in its rhythm, there must be a process that allows for that particular tonal sequence to be abstracted from its original context and compared to or connected with its later, transformed version. Thus, the process of abstraction/relocation involves the removal and reuse of some part of a whole, or just some property of the whole, and the drawing of connections and relationships between the old and new versions. In so being abstraction is thought to be one of the unifying processes in musical compositions.

But there is a problem with abstraction. We do not know the degree to which abstracted and relocated fragments or properties are indeed perceived as related to their original version, or whether they are perceived as new music. While evidence for the understanding of abstraction has been demonstrated under laboratory conditions, usually in short musical fragments that can be immediately compared, we do not know how this process operates over the longer time spans of whole compositions. The problem is made more difficult by the fact that certain abstractions, especially rhythmic property abstractions, can be found across entirely different pieces of music. Yet it is unlikely that listeners draw important connections and relationships between the two pieces. The reader can prove this for himself by considering whether the nursery songs "Twinkle, Twinkle Little Star" and "Baa, Baa Black Sheep" are in fact the same tune. Most people probably do not draw intimate connections between these two songs, but on closer inspection they have identical melodies, with only different texts and minute alterations in rhythm. (Incidentally, both of these are also identical in tone sequence to the children's alphabet song, "A, B, C.") A more sophisticated example is provided by Yeston's (1975) analysis of the Mozart C-major piano sonata (K. 545) and the popular song, "Hey there, you with the stars in your eyes," both of which share the same abstracted tonal sequence, with differences in rhythm.

In sum, the precise unity-generating characteristics of abstraction are still open to question. Nevertheless, it appears to be a prevalent process in many musics, and some rudimentary evidence for its aural understanding has been found.

Hierarchic Levels

This process can best be illustrated by an example. Imagine a person listening to a piece of music. He is bombarded with a vast number of sounds and, over the course of the composition, must impose upon them an overriding structure that allows him to organize or make sense of the multiple sounds. One way of doing this is to construe the sounds (or tones) along a continuum of more important/less important. That is, certain tones can be identified as the important, primary, or focal tones, and these, in succession, provide the overriding structure of the piece. Other tones of less importance, "weight," or primacy circumscribe and elaborate the basic structure. We may imagine, then, that a musical composition embodies an underlying structure composed of its most important or focal tones, and other, less important tones have the role of circumscribing and elaborating these focal ones. Note that the designation of more and less important is not descriptive of the overall *aesthetic function* of certain sounds or tones. Certainly non-focal, elaborating tones are aesthetically obligatory, for who would listen to just bare structure? But the point is that some tones have greater importance or primacy in terms of organizational structure, and together these constitute what may be called the *structure* of the piece. A musical composition, then, embodies some basic, underlying structure composed of its primary, focal events. Such a structure transcends the bit-to-bit, one-tone-after-another nature of the piece on a purely physical or acoustic basis. The cognitive process of hierarchic structuring involves the imposing of a more simplified, reduced structure, on the vast array of sounds in the piece.

Perhaps more than the other processes mentioned thus far, hierarchic structuring has been investigated through the formal, theoretical analysis of Western compositions. The process of identifying the underlying structure, the succession of focal tones or events, proceeds roughly as follows: Beginning with the notated piece, tones that are least important in terms of structural function are removed. What is left is a skeleton of the piece consisting of the most primary events. But the process may be continued even on this skeleton structure: The least important tones may be omitted, and an even further reduced structure of focal tones is left. It is in this sense that the process of structuring is *hierarchic*; that is, several *levels* of structure may be in evidence, each level embodying increasing primacy or weight among focal tones. In terms of the cognitive process employed by a listener, this means that the structuring is not simply a matter of applying a single, dichotomous criterion of more or less importance. Rather, the structuring proceeds in a relative way, with tones construed along a continuum of more-or-less focal, relative to each other.

What is the evidence that such focal tones exist in music and provide an underlying structure? The formal analysis of Western tonal music, particularly from the eighteenth and nineteenth centuries, provides the most abundant examples. The work of Heinrich Schenker (1935/1979) is perhaps the most comprehensive theory of structural and elaborative functions in tonal music, but structural analyses are employed by many theorists of tonal music (see, for example, Forte 1955). Berry (1980) has discussed at length the assumptions that are employed in the identification of structural levels: the notions of tonal primacy or weight, the rhythmic displacement of focal tones over long spans of time, and the principles of counterpoint that govern movement from one focal tone to another. But there are other examples outside the tonal, art music tradition. Strunk (1979) has provided evidence of structural levels in early jazz pieces by Cole Porter and Benny Goodman. Nettl (1956b:200) discusses an example of a Rumanian folksong in which elaborative tones cluster around a focal tone of B-flat. Elsewhere Nettl (1973:144) discusses the tendency of many folk melodies to cluster around a nucleus of one or two tones.

An example of hierarchic structural levels in the Western art music tradition is given in example 3.1, where the opening bars of the Prelude from J. S. Bach's *English Suite* No. 2 are shown.[4] The bars labeled "fore-

---

[4]Thanks to Deborah Stein for providing these reductions. For simplicity the reductions shown here utilize conventional notation rather than the alternative system developed by Schenker.

Example 3.1

3. Model

Foreground reduction

ground reduction" represent the focal, structural tones of the piece. The reader can verify, for example, that of the seven tones in bar 1, the four eighth-notes in the reduction represent the main melodic line in that measure. Similarly, the remaining bars have been reduced to the relatively few focal tones shown in the reduction.

In Schenkerian terms, the above represents a first-level or foreground reduction because some of the tones are in fact ornaments, embellishments, or passing tones for *even more focal* tones in the reduction. That is to say, the reduction itself can be further reduced so that only its more focal tones are represented. Such a representation may be termed a "middleground reduction," in the Schenkerian terminology, and an even further or deeper level of reduction is at the "background." Thus structural levels are hierarchic in the sense that a deeper level of reduction (e.g., background) is contained within the level above it (middleground), which in turn is contained in the level above it (foreground). Example 3.2 shows the middleground level for the Bach phrase. It shows that the overall movement of the original phrase is generally that of two open fifths on the tonic, followed by movement to the dominant and return to the tonic.

The Bach example represents, in addition to hierarchic levels, Schenker's notion of compound melody. That is to say, the original, single-line melody (i.e., one note at a time) is thought to *structurally* embody two simultaneous melodies: an upper melody represented by the notes with upward stems, and a lower melody represented by notes with downward stems. Thus, the single A in bar 1 is assumed to provide a tonic base through bars 1 and 2, until it descends to the leading tone, then the dominant, and is understood to return to the tonic at the end of the

Example 3.2

Middleground reduction

phrase. (Actually, in the original piece the A occurs there an octave be-low.) Whether one accepts the theoretical assertion that Bach's original single-line melody is in fact conceived as two simultaneous melodies (im-plicitly by either composer or listener), the example stands as a formal representation of how a piece *may* be hierarchically structured. Suffice it to say that, while there is debate about the precise nature of such struc-tures in music (theorists differ in their renditions of structures, for ex-ample) it seems clear that listeners employ some principles of organization in which a vast array of sound is construed in terms of central, focal tones or events. There is tentative evidence for listeners' identification of struc-tural, as opposed to nonstructural, tonal sequences in musical pieces of this kind.[5]

In the previous paragraphs I have described a set of temporal and non-temporal processes that are generic and pan-stylistic. I have alluded to questions about the nature and development of these processes, especially as they emerge over the life span from childhood to adulthood. Although there are practical reasons for an interest in such questions—for example, knowledge of childhood cognition is sure to improve education—there are also theoretical questions about music that I believe are addressed by developmental research. Before turning to the developmental experiments reported in the next chapter, I briefly discuss the theoretical rationale for such research.

AIMS OF A DEVELOPMENTAL APPROACH

Change as it occurs over time in animals and humans is the topic of developmental psychology. It is useful to think of *changes in the state* of an organism, such as its physical, emotional, and cognitive state changes.

---

[5]M. L. Serafine. "The Cognitive Development of Structural Levels in Music." Paper pre-sented at the Society for Music Theory, Los Angeles, November 1981.

The developmental psychologist is concerned with (1) the causes of change (all of the factors that may account for it); (2) how change is best characterized (gradual, sudden, uniform, in stages, etc.); (3) the degree of stability in a state once it has been reached (for example, whether remnants of earlier states are either incorporated into or supplanted by later ones, whether regression to earlier states is possible, etc.); and (4) more generally, the degree to which change can be said to occur at all. That is, there may be sufficient continuity between early and later states that what appears to be change turns out to be superficial or irrelevant. A useful analogy for the problem of development is the relationship between an acorn and a tree. Here the forebear is very unlike the final form, yet slow change in the former gives rise to the latter. Metaphorically speaking, the developmental psychologist is interested in characterizing the relative contributions of environmental soil and water (else no acorn becomes a tree) and of tree-ness embodied innately in the seed (all things planted do not become trees). He is also interested in the degree to which truly fundamental differences between early and later forms need to be included in the account of where trees come from (for example, do acorns "operate" in ways that trees do not?), and whether atypical state changes such as regression could apply to the species at hand.

Vastly more difficult than the acorn-to-tree problem, however, is the case of animals, particularly humans, and especially where culture and cognitive matters are involved. Cognitive developmentalists have addressed the problem on a large scale only in this century, and their main focus has been on areas such as number, space, time, general reasoning, and language. There are no readily accepted answers to the questions posed above, and we have had to settle for (1) delineating the approximate ages at which particular cognitive developments occur; and (2) making direct comparisons between children and adults (or between younger and older children) in an attempt to ascertain whether true or only superficial changes have taken place. This latter question is often expressed as the issue of *qualitative* as opposed to *quantitative* changes and differences. The notion of qualitative difference implies that children's minds—consequently their ways of viewing the world and their understanding of concepts like number and time—are fundamentally different from adults' in the way they work. The notion of quantitative differences, on the other hand, implies that child and adult minds are essentially alike except that the latter has accumulated a larger number of experiences.

The questions surrounding Piaget's famous conservation experiments are a case in point. In one of several variations on this task, the child is shown two identical glasses containing the same amount of either "continuous" or "discontinuous" substance (water or kernels of dried corn). After the child agrees that both glasses contain the same amount, the contents of one are poured into a differently shaped container—for example a tall, thin cylinder—and the child is asked whether the remaining glass contains the same amount as the cylinder, or whether one has more. Young children, around 4 or 5, typically assert that the cylinder has more because it is "higher" (or, as one child explained to me, because kernels of corn grow larger when put into a tall container, although they subsequently return to normal size when put into a glass). Older children, usually by the age of 6 or 7, understand that quantity remains the same or is conserved despite changes in shape.

The classic question here is whether the understanding of conservation results from a true qualitative change in how the child's mind works, or whether it results from the accumulation of a requisite number of experiences. This issue turns on whether conservation ability can be taught at early ages, for if training is *not* effective, then the young child's mind might be thought to be qualitatively different in how it operates, and if training *is* effective, then what the young child lacks is apparently only experience. A vast number of studies have addressed this issue, but because types of training and definitions of conservation vary from study to study, there is no interpretation of results that meets with everyone's satisfaction. Perhaps the wisest conclusion is that training is generally *not* effective for very young nonconservers, although it may be effective for older children who are nearer the age when they would acquire conservation on their own. Training, then, helps these children achieve the concept somewhat sooner. Interpreters of developmental results tend to variously emphasize either the early futility or the later success of training efforts depending on their point of view. Recently attention has shifted away from conservation itself to the question of whether young children possess more primitive concepts which may underlie conservation.

What is important to us here is that the aim of raising such questions is epistemological. The aim is to determine where knowledge or understanding comes from, and whether its source is principally inside the organism or in the external environment. Knowledge that arises externally may do so in two ways: (1) by virtue of the perception of features of stimuli, or (2) as a result of learning (that is, special experiences germane to the knowledge at hand, particularly those followed by reward or reinforcement). In the case of conservation, for instance, the child may be thought to have accumulated many experiences of *seeing* substances poured from various containers and eventually noticing that amount remains the same irrespective of shape. (Of course, the beauty of Piaget's conservation task is that young children do see what adults see, but they understand it differently.) Alternatively, the child may be thought to come to an understanding of conservation by way of finding it rewarding in some way to make use of the concept; it may be advantageous for a particular purpose, he may be praised, etc. Thus, the aim of making child/ adult comparisons and assessing the effects of training is this: To the degree that a type of knowledge is substantially different in children and adults *and* is resistant to training, then to that degree knowledge is rooted in the subject's internal cognitive operations and not in the external world, through the perception of stimulus features or through learning. Knowledge of this type is the most likely candidate for a human universal.

Although it may seem obvious and even empty to claim that children and adults have dissimilar responses to tasks, in fact there are many areas in which the young child's abilities (even the infant's) meet or exceed that of the adult. Color perception is one example and certain kinds of auditory discriminations for speech sounds are another. In these cases the young child's perceptual apparatus is fully functioning and he meets with success on perceptual tasks. It is on this ground that the question of music becomes critical. For to the degree that music is a matter of *perceiving the features of external stimuli,* then children should have perceptions of music that are similar to those of adults. And according to traditional music-as-sound theories, this is precisely what one would expect. For there is no reason, on this view, to suspect that the child's perception, say, of doorbells, music, or any other sound would be different from that of the adult (provided the child paid attention to it, of course). On the other hand, to the degree that music is a matter of internal cognitive operations, then we would expect wide differences between children and adults and even between younger and older children.

Prior to conducting the research reported in the following chapters, even I, who on the theoretical grounds described previously held to a subjective/internal or cognitive view of music, considered it likely that children would at least have the same perception of *temporal events* in

music as did adults. For even children should understand that two melodic fragments strung together create a longer melody consisting of the
two fragments in question. And among the formal processes I considered
it possible that both children and adults would similarly understand closure—that is, discriminate between a melody that comes to an end and
one that does not. We shall see, however, that the results did not support
these presumptions. Rather, there appeared to be wide differences between children and adults and among children of different ages on all the
generic processes described earlier. Moreover, children with musical
training did not consistently perform better than those without training.

To restate the musical question at hand, the issue is whether music
involves something more like color perception (i.e., stimulus feature perception) or more like conservation (i.e., subjective cognitive activity). The
more general question, as I have put it previously, concerns where music
resides. Eclectics will surely argue that music involves both stimulus perception and internal cognition on the grounds that what a listener does is
first detect the stimulus features (pitch, duration, etc.) and *then* mentally
operate on them so as to understand the presence of melody, rhythm, and
so forth. I argue against this view because there is little reason to presume
a two-step process in which the initial perception is of sufficient consequence beyond the fact that nearly all human activities involve feature
perception. For we do not consider color or shape perception to be a
central process in chess, for example, or number or symbol detection to
be a central process in mathematics. Indeed, we would think it odd if the
cognitive psychologists who studied chess, mathematics, or other cognitive activities investigated only the perception of stimulus features that
seemed to accompany the activity in question. Ordinary perception is a
necessary companion to the understanding of music, but the study of it
is no window on how musical understanding occurs. (We return to this
point in the final chapter.)

In summary, developmental research in music—particularly on age-
related differences and the efficacy of training—attempts in the broadest
sense to determine whether music is a matter of perception or cognition,
or put otherwise, whether music resides external to or within the knower.
Unfortunately, the bugaboo that plagues all developmental research is
fully present here also: the difficulty of determining what children actually
understand or can do. Certainly it is possible to design musical tasks that
can be undertaken by children as well as by adults. But the question is

whether the differences obtained result only from children's more limited vocabulary, concentration, social easiness, or other nonmusical abilities, or whether they result from real differences between children and adults in the understanding of temporality, closure, and other musical processes. Differences in irrelevant nonmusical abilities can mask an underlying similarity in understanding, and there is no antidote to this except to design tasks accessible to children and to employ as many types of tasks as possible. The humble issue of task construction, then, is a critical one for a theory of music.

The following chapters report studies that compared adult knowledge of generic-musical processes to that of children at ages 5, 6, 8, 10, and 11 years.

CHAPTER 4

The Development
of Temporal
Processes in the Child

GENERAL INTRODUCTION TO THE STUDIES

The aim of the studies reported in this and the following chapter was to map the developmental pattern—from early childhood to preadolescence and adulthood—that pertains to the processes of succession, simultaneity, closure, transformation, abstraction, and hierarchic levels. For this purpose sixteen tasks were designed and administered to approximately 15 subjects each at ages 5, 6, 8, 10, 11, and adulthood. The major criteria in the design of the tasks were, first, that they have musical integrity and make use of short compositions, phrases, and fragments that could legitimately be called music, and second, that they be accessible to 5-year-olds yet require no major change in form for older children and adults. Accordingly, the tasks and the music employed were identical for every subject, but instructions and pre-task training were more elaborate for younger children. In addition to the musical tasks, two measures of developmental level were employed: Piaget's conservation tasks for number and quantity and the scoring of a human figure drawing made by each child.

The following general description of procedure, materials, and other matters applies to all of the studies reported in chapters 4 and 5.

Procedure

Each subject completed several tasks in two informal, individual interviews. The experimenter and subject sat at a table with the necessary equipment and materials in plain view: one to three portable cassette tape players with small, external speakers and a variety of dolls, blocks, and other props. The experimenter followed a pre-specified interview procedure and recorded the subject's responses on an answer sheet. Subjects did not receive feedback on the correctness of their responses. Children's tasks were conducted at school, in a separate room that provided acceptable but never ideal quiet. (We marveled at the apparently high level of noise, never achieved here, that it takes to jar a child's concentration.) Adults were tested in a quiet university laboratory.

Slightly different versions of instructions were used with younger and older subjects, although the musical material and general task were always the same. Younger subjects (ages 5 and 6) received more explanations, more repetition, and often fictionalized instructions that involved dolls or other story characters. Older subjects (ages 10 and 11 and adults) listened and answered without recourse to responding for or through a fictionalized character. The term "song" was sometimes used with younger subjects while "piece of music" was always used with older ones. Subjects in the middle group of 8-year-olds were divided into two groups: half received the younger version and half received the older version of instructions. Among 8-year-olds, no performance differences were found that could be attributed to this difference in instructions, except in the Rhythmic Abstraction task where the younger version may have enhanced performance.

In the descriptions that follow it will be noted that many tasks entailed the "playing" of music by dolls, various story characters, a magic "echo box," and so forth. It should be pointed out that in most of these cases the sound did not, of course, emanate directly from the object in question. (The exceptions were tasks that used the wood cubes, as described later.) Rather, the sound emanated from a common audio speaker (or speakers) and the experimenter *pointed to* the object that was supposed to be "playing" the music in question. In tasks that involved, for example, three characters "playing" music in turn, the experimenter's pointing to the appropriate character created the illusion that the character was playing, although all sounds emanated from a single source. We found that subjects had no difficulty accepting this illusion. (Older subjects who would of course be aware of it received slightly different instructions and explanations.) This procedure alleviated the problem of subjects having to reorient themselves throughout the task to multiple and spatially separated sound sources.

In addition to the musical tasks, each subject was given a pitch discrimination task (described below). All children were given the Goodenough-Harris Draw-a-Person test, scored and normed according to criteria given by Harris (1963). This task requires the child to "draw a picture of a person" using plain paper and a single, ordinary pencil. The drawing is scored for the degree of detail present in facial and bodily features, clothing, and so on. Raw scores may be considered an index of intellectual maturity and normed scores have been shown to approximate scores on standard intelligence tests (Harris 1963).

All 5-, 6-, and 8-year-olds were given standard tasks for conservation of number (using two rows of plastic chips, one of which is spread out in a longer line) and conservation of weight (using two balls of clay, one of which is flattened into a pancake). Each conservation task was scored as follows: one point was given for a correct conservation judgment ("They both have the same number"); one additional point was given for a correct explanation involving identity ("It's the same clay"), reversibility ("You can put the chips back as they were"), or compensation ("The pancake looks bigger but it's also flatter"); no points were given for nonconservation judgments ("This one has more"). A more elaborate description of the conservation tasks is given in a later section.

The entire group of tasks took two hours to administer. Each child completed only half the tasks, and doing so consumed two thirty-minute sessions separated by several days. The order in which the tasks were given was designed to take maximum advantage of the child's initial attention and concentration. Thus, each session began with one of the "block tasks," which required sustained auditory concentration, and each session ended with what we considered less taxing tasks. The order of tasks was as follows. Subjects in Group 1 received, in the first testing session, the motivic abstraction task first, followed by the motivic chaining and idiomatic construction tasks, which were alternated in random order, and then the conservation and drawing tasks. In the second session they received the rhythmic abstraction task, followed by the phrasing and patterning tasks alternated in random order, and then the pitch perception task. Subjects in Group 2 received, in the first session, the hierarchic levels task, followed by the textual abstraction and closure tasks alternated in random order, and then the conservation and drawing tasks. In the second session they received four transformation tasks, followed by the timbre and motivic synthesis tasks alternated in random order, and then the pitch perception task. Adults completed all the tasks, in the order described above, in one two-hour session divided by a break.

Materials

Musical material for the tasks was composed by a music theorist/composer who received instructions about the purposes and musical specifications for each task. All music was played on piano and prerecorded on tape. In every case where a repetition of musical material was needed, the material in question was reperformed, not simply duplicated electronically. There were, therefore, the same slight, natural variations from one performance to the next that would be expected under normal conditions.

Other materials consisted of a variety of dolls and other toy figures such as birds, animals, and elves which were used with younger children. Different dolls or figures were used on each task to prevent confusion or carry-over that might occur.

The sound playback equipment consisted of a Sharp (GF-8585) cassette recorder with small external speakers (Realistic Minimus 7), which was used whenever a single source was required. Four tasks required three different sound sources connected to a set of "musical blocks," described below. In these cases three Sharp (RD-492) cassette recorders were used with three of the same external speakers.

Subjects

A total of 168 subjects provided the main data for the study: 32 5-year-olds (mean age 5;6); 30 6-year-olds (mean age 6;7); 31 8-year-olds (mean age 8;7); 30 10-year-olds (mean age 10;6); 30 11-year-olds (mean age 11;7); and 15 adults (university students and staff). The children attended a middle-class, suburban public school in which regular and traditional music instruction was provided by a music specialist. All of the children in kindergarten and grades one, three, five, and six were invited to participate in the study (there were two classrooms at each grade level), and those whose parents granted permission were used as subjects.

Half the children in each age group completed the six tasks associated with succession and abstraction (Group 1). The other half of the children completed the nine tasks associated with simultaneity, closure, transformation, and hierarchic levels (Group 2). Thus, each task was administered to approximately 15 children at each age level. The 15 adults completed all tasks. There were approximately equal numbers of male and female subjects at each age level, except that females were over-represented (about twice as many) in the 8-year-old and adult groups. Within each age group half the boys and half the girls were assigned to each of the two halves of the task series, except that there was a disproportionate number of 11-year-old boys in tasks for simultaneity, closure, transformation, and hierarchic levels, and of 11-year-old girls in tasks for succession and abstraction. However, there were no significant gender differences in task performance.

In addition to the above subjects, 34 children ranging in age from 4 to 11, who had received intensive violin training under the Suzuki method, completed the three tasks associated with closure, transformation, and hierarchic levels. Data from these subjects are discussed separately from the data of subjects in the main part of the study.

Subjects' Musical Training

Table 4.1 shows that there was a moderate amount of formal musical training even among subjects in the main part of the study. Most of the older children had received some training while most of the younger children had not. Training is defined as individual lessons on instrument or voice, either privately or as part of the school program. (Numbers in parentheses indicate percentage of that age group.)

Table 4.1. Subjects' Musical Training

Age	5	6	8	10	11	Adult
Training						
Less than 3 months	31(97%)	23(77%)	20(65%)	5(16%)	3(10%)	1(7%)
3 months to less than 1½ years	1(3%)	7(23%)	9(29%)	14(47%)	13(43%)	3(20%)
1½ to less than 4 years	0	0	2(6%)	11(37%)	12(40%)	3(20%)
4 or more years	0	0	0	0	2(7%)	8(53%)
N:	32	30	31	30	30	15

Subjects' Pitch Discrimination Abilities

All subjects were given a pitch discrimination task in which they were asked to determine whether two prerecorded piano tones were the same or different. (Younger subjects were asked to determine whether a fictitious "echo box" made exactly the same sound.) Older subjects completed up to ten items in which interval sizes ranged from unison to minor third. Thus, a minor second was the smallest "different" item tested. Most younger subjects had difficulty attending to the series of ten items, but completed a minimum of the first six items, which consisted of two unisons, two minor seconds (ascending and descending), an ascending major second, and a descending minor third.

Table 4.2 gives, for each age group, the mean and standard deviation (out of a total possible score of 6) and the percentage of subjects achieving a pass criterion of five items correct. Figure 4.1 gives a graphic representation of the percentage of subjects at each age level who achieved the pass criterion. Several points are noteworthy here. First, it is not until age 8 that half the subjects are successful on the pitch discrimination task. Second, a result that we have called "the sixth grade slump" is apparent on this task as well as on several others: 11-year-olds do considerably worse than children a year younger, although there is no immediately obvious reason for this, since training, intelligence, and gender differences do not account for it. Compared to 10-year-olds, the 11-year-olds did not have fewer years of musical training or lower levels of intelligence as estimated by the Draw-a-Person test. Also the subgroup in which 11-year-old boys predominated (mean score = 4.5 out of 6) did not perform differently from the subgroup in which 11-year-old girls predominated (mean = 4.8). We will see a similar decrement in performance among 11-year-olds (whether they are boys or girls) on some of the other tasks as well.

Table 4.2. Pitch Discrimination Task

Age Group	Mean	s.d.	Percent Pass
5-year-olds	3.3	1.8	19%
6-year-olds	3.6	2.3	40%
8-year-olds	4.5	1.8	50%
10-year-olds	5.3	1.6	80%
11-year-olds	4.7	1.3	53%
Adults	5.7	.6	93%

Figure 4.1. Pitch Perception Task: Percent Pass

Third, a modest correlation (r = .31, p < .001) was found between pitch discrimination scores and degree of musical training, even with age partialed out. We will see, however, that both pitch discrimination and musical training are unrelated to success on certain of the other musical tasks.

Gender Differences

The possibility of gender differences was investigated among children in each age group for each task on which a meaningful (usually interval-level) total score could be computed. Gender differences in this sample and on these tasks were virtually nonexistent.

There were no significant differences between boys and girls in any age group on the pitch discrimination task described above. Across the whole sample, the mean for boys and girls was 4.2 and 4.3 respectively.

Similarly there were no significant differences between boys and girls in any age group on the following measures: (1) total scores on the pat-terning task, although there was a nonsignificant trend for younger boys (ages 5, 6, and 8) to outperform girls of the same age (p < .09); (2) total scores on the motivic chaining task; (3) responding "idiomatically" on the idiomatic construction task; (4) total scores on the closure task; (5) total scores on the motivic synthesis task; (6) success on the timbre synthesis task; (7) total scores on the transformation task (Block Task); (8) total scores on the rhythmic abstraction task; and (9) total scores on the hierarchic levels task.

Subjects' Intellectual Maturity

The Draw-a-Person test yields a normal score that, like standard intelligence tests, has a theoretical mean of 100 and a standard deviation of 15. The mean of the present sample of subjects was 103.6, with a standard deviation of 15.1. There were no significant differences among the age groups; the 5-, 6-, 8-, 10-, and 11-year-olds had means of 99, 103, 102, 107, and 108, respectively. (The means of *raw* scores showed a steady increase across the groups, 17, 22, 30, 42, and 46 respectively, where the theoretical range is 0 to 70.)

There was a small but significant difference between the means of normal scores across the two subsamples, each of which completed half the task battery. The mean for Group 1 was 106 and that of Group 2 was 101; $t(151) = 2.08$, $p < .05$.

Younger Subjects' Cognitive Stage

As an approximate indication of cognitive stage, conservation tasks for number and weight were given to children at ages 5, 6, and 8. These tasks were administered in the standard way: for number, the child was presented with two parallel rows of plastic chips (one red, one white) arranged in one-to-one correspondence. After the child asserted that there was an equal number of red and white chips, the experimenter spread the chips of one row into a longer line and asked the child whether there were now as many in one row as in the other, or whether "one has more." Use of the term "less" was avoided, since it is unfamiliar to most young children. Responses were scored "pass" (one point) or "fail" (zero) on each of two dimensions: (1) judgment (one point for the correct response that both rows contain the same number) and (2) one point for a correct explanation containing one or more of the following concepts: (a) identity ("Because they're the same chips as before"); (b) reversibility ("Because you could put them back the way they were"); (c) compensation ("Because it's longer but there's more space in between").

The conservation of the weight task was analogous to that of number. The child held two balls of clay and, after he asserted their equal weight, one ball was flattened into a "pancake" and the child was asked whether each was still as heavy as the other or whether "one is heavier."

Since each task yielded a score from o to 2, the combined scores for both tasks ranged from o to 4. Of 93 subjects at ages 5, 6, and 8, only two earned a combined score of 1, indicating that it was very rare for a child to give one correct judgment and be unable to explain it properly.

In this sample, 38 percent of the 5-year-olds, 73 percent of the 6-year-olds, and 90 percent of the 8-year-olds were classified as conservers, where the criterion was correct judgment on both number and weight *or* correct judgment and explanation on at least one of the tasks. Mean combined scores (range o to 4) were 1.2, 2.0, and 2.8 for 5-, 6-, and 8-year-olds respectively.

Across the two subgroups of subjects, each of which completed half the task battery, there were no significant differences in mean combined score at any age level. The means for Groups 1 and 2 respectively were 1.8 and 2.1.

Subjects with Intensive Musical Training

In addition to the main body of data from the subjects described previously, data on three of the musical tasks—closure, transformation, and hierarchic levels—were obtained from 34 intensively trained children ranging in age from 4 to 11 years. These children were undergoing violin instruction under the method developed by the Japanese violinist Shin'ichi Suzuki (b. 1898), and all studied with the same teacher who, for the purposes of this project, also acted as the experimenter who administered the musical tasks to them.

The Suzuki method of musical training has the following characteristics (see also Mills and Murphy 1973):

1. *Very early, intensive training.* Ideally children as young as 3 or even 2 years of age can begin the method using specially made, small-size instruments. Training begins with frequent listening to recorded melodies that the child will learn to play. Short but daily practice sessions on the violin and weekly individual and group lessons are the norm.

2. *Musical memory training.* In contrast to traditional teaching methods that emphasize the reading of notation, the Suzuki method relies entirely

on memorization for the first several years of training and introduces notation only after considerable playing ability has been acquired. The present sample of subjects had completely memorized and could play at will any of the pieces on which they had been instructed.

3. *Sensorimotor activity*. In conjunction with the emphasis on memory rather than notation, the method emphasizes repeated, rote muscular activity that calls up well-coordinated motor action in even the youngest children. Drills, exercises, and violin-playing "games" develop posture, agility, playing speed, precision, and the capacity to play almost unnervingly in tune.

4. *Fixed sequence of musical pieces*. One of the hallmarks of Suzuki training is that students generally perform their repertoire at proper, steady tempo, in tune, and from memory. In large part this is accomplished by a prespecified sequence of musical pieces ordered from simple to complex (beginning with folk songs and baroque and classical pieces) and the injunction that no student progresses to the next piece in the series unless the previous one has been wholly mastered.

5. *Parent Involvement*. One or both parents (usually the mother) are encouraged to participate in the child's instruction by observing the lessons, supervising daily practice sessions, and even playing and practicing along with the child. In some cases the parent may actually receive instruction along with the child in order to make possible their joint playing and practicing. In contrast to the sometimes cloistered, sacred relationship between teacher and student and the isolated practice sessions characteristic of traditional intruction, Suzuki training is more likely to be an informal family affair. This is not to say that its emphasis is on fun. Rather, hard work and seriousness of purpose are encouraged if not demanded; but there is also an emphasis on the socially motivating factors of peer and family relationships.

The theoretical or philosophical foundation of the Suzuki method appears to be a behavioristic sort of learning theory that gives a central role to imitation and social reward. Indeed Suzuki has called upon a parallel between language and music, and since in his view language is learned by imitating one's parents, so also music is most profitably learned in this way. There is no question that the method "works" insofar as it is successful in getting large numbers of children to perform a sequence of adult compositions at proper tempo, with precision, and in tune. What observers of the method have complained about, however, is that the method short-changes the expressive, artistic, or interpretive skills in music-making, and at worst may encourage a mindlessly robotic style of playing in its students. Moreover, recent research that denies imitation a central role in language acquisition would seem to undermine the theoretical foundations of the method.

For the purposes of the present study the Suzuki-trained subjects were categorized by their teacher according to the following three levels of accomplishment: (1) Beginning: have mastered basic rhythms, posture, and bowing skill; can perform the folk song "Twinkle, Twinkle Little Star" plus four rhythmic variations on that theme; (2) Intermediate: can perform the above plus 10 to 15 folk songs from memory with confidence and precision; (3) Advanced: can perform all of the above plus 10 to 30 baroque and classical gavottes, minuets, and other pieces, in addition to one or more concerto movements.

Table 4.3 shows how subjects at each age level were categorized by skill. Mean ages for the groups are 4;5, 5;10, 6;6, 7;5, 8;5, 10;7 and 11;11 respectively. There were 19 girls and 15 boys in the sample, unevenly distributed across the age groups. Letters in the cells show the number of boys and girls in each category (B = boy; G = girl).

It is clear that with perhaps four exceptions (a 6- and a 7-year-old only at beginning level and a 10- and an 11-year-old only at intermediate level), the children in this sample outstrip in performance ability their counterparts in the larger sample. The 4- and 5-year-old Suzuki-trained subjects

Table 4.3. Subjects with Suzuki Training

Age Group	4	5	6	7	8	10	11	Percent of Sample
Skill Level								
Beginning: Can play theme and 4 variations	B GGG	BB GG	B	B				29.4%
Intermediate: Can play additional 10 to 15 folk songs	G	G	BBB G	B G		B	B	29.4%
Advanced: Can play additional 10 to 30 gavottes, minuets, and concerto movements	G		B	B G	GGG	GGGG	BB G	41.2%
% of Total Sample	17.6	14.7	17.6	14.7	8.8	14.7	11.8	

who can already play a theme and variations have a head start over the vast majority of their peers who have had no instruction whatsoever. Similarly the 6- and 7-year-olds who already perform at the intermediate level and the 8- to 11-year-olds who perform part of the standard, adult musical literature are far advanced beyond their contemporaries. This is to say nothing of the precocious in the sample, the 4-, 6-, and 7-year-olds who are already performing the adult literature. I have heard these children perform their repertoire in concert and am confident that the skill descriptions accurately match the levels of achievement.

Subjects in the intensively trained sample were given the Draw-a-Person test and those at age 8 and below were given conservation tasks for number and weight. Scores on these measures were compared to the scores of *half* the children in the main sample (Group 2), that is, only those children who were also given the musical tasks for closure, transformation, and hierarchic levels, and against which the intensively trained subjects would be compared. To determine whether there were differences between the main sample and intensively trained sample in conservation scores or in Draw-a-Person scores, two two-way analyses of variance were performed with age group (4, 5, 6, 7, etc.) and subject group (main sample vs. intensively trained) as the independent variables. There were no significant main effects or interactions for subject group, despite the fact that the mean normal score for the Draw-a-Person test among intensively trained subjects was 94.7, slightly lower than the mean of 101.1 for the comparison subjects in the main sample. Thus, the two groups do not differ significantly on the measures employed for nonmusical cognitive stage and for intellectual maturity.

A Note on the Limits of the Study

The research reported here was an initial attempt to pick the lock of music cognition across a major portion of the life span. I adhered to two goals that are responsible for both the strengths and limits of the research: (1) to investigate as broad a spectrum of musical-cognitive processes as possible (in all, twelve processes across sixteen different tasks); and (2) to test as broad an age span as would be feasible (ages 5 to 11 plus adults), meanwhile exposing all subjects to identical musical stimuli. Insofar as all research is constrained by the limits of time, energy, and the endurance of subjects, these goals gave rise to some problems that will have to be pursued in future research. For example, there are fewer items (usually four to six) on any one task and fewer subjects per task per age group (about fifteen) than will allow for optimum hypothesis testing. Also, certain cross-task comparisons cannot be made because different subjects took different tasks. But on the belief that a fuzzy view of the whole elephant is preferable to a clear view of the trunk, I have allowed the data to suggest both well-supported and more speculative conclusions.

In that regard, a word on some of the general statistical decisions may be in order. First, I have sometimes employed the more liberal post hoc tests in analyses of variance, and in some analyses, especially those involving nonparametric procedures, have set the alpha level at .07. These decisions were made on the grounds that the error of not detecting an effect was more serious than suggesting an effect that may not be validated later. Also, I have occasionally used the Pearson correlation coefficient in situations where data on one of the variables was not strictly on an interval scale. In such cases the purpose was always to permit the use of partial correlation techniques to control for the effects of age, which otherwise would give rise to spuriously high correlations among the various musical and nonmusical tasks.

The following sections treat the topics of succession and simultaneity, and chapter 5 covers closure, transformation, abstraction, and hierarchic levels.

TEMPORALITY: UNDERSTANDING THE SUCCESSIVE DIMENSION

Music's most central characteristic is that it unfolds in time. Our experience of it is continuous, and at no time can we stop it to observe more closely what we are experiencing. Under ideal conditions, adults may be expected to employ a kind of continuous tracking of the successive, "one-event-after-another" dimension of music, meanwhile also noting the simultaneous, "one-event-with-another" dimension. The child's abilities in these domains are not so clear, however. I report here four experiments that compared child and adult understandings of this successive dimension in music.

Experiment: Phrasing

In the first experiment, subjects were asked simply to divide a longer span of music into two constituent parts (or phrases), while the music was in progress. The questions of interest are whether children of various ages would give evidence of systematically and intentionally attending to the successive dimension (for example, whether they will divide the same piece in the same place on repeated trials), and if so, whether they will divide the piece according to the same musical cues that are used by adults.

Subjects were told that they would hear a piece of music that could be divided into two parts, each part represented by a cornhusk doll (for younger subjects) or an ordinary wood block (for older subjects). The two objects were separated by about six inches. Younger subjects were told that "*this* doll plays the beginning of the song and *that* doll plays the end of the song. There is one song, but this one starts the song and that one ends the song." Older subjects were told to "pretend that this block stands for the first part and that block stands for the second part." The subject's task was to start with his finger pointing at the first object when the music began and then, at the point when he thought the second part began, to point to the second object.

The experimenter demonstrated the procedure twice using the piece of music shown in example 4.1, after which the child performed the task using the same piece. The conventional or "correct" point of division is between bars 2 and 3.

All the subjects immediately performed the practice trial correctly, except for one 5-year-old who required an additional demonstration by the experimenter and then performed the practice trial correctly. In fact, what was intriguing about the practice performances was the precision and confidence with which even the youngest children performed the task.

Example 4.1

They simply pointed to the second object, often moving the hand in rhythm so as to be precisely in time for beat one of bar 3.

Thus it is not surprising that excellent performances were obtained with the piece of music shown in example 4.2, which subjects divided with no further help from the experimenter. Again the conventional or "correct" division point is at the end of bar 2. Figure 4.2 shows the

Example 4.2

percentage of subjects in each age group who performed correctly with this piece on each of three trials. It is clear that even the youngest children

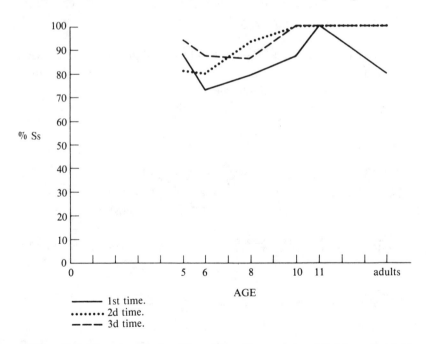

Figure 4.2. Phrasing Task—Piece One: Percentage of Subjects Performing Correctly

favored the conventional division point, and they seemed to know exactly what they were doing (a 5-year-old: "Whew! I got to the other lady just in time"). Although twenty percent of adults erred on trial 1 (an error rate that approaches or exceeds that of all the children), the adults who erred consisted entirely of subjects who gave no answer. At bar 2, they were undoubtedly holding out for a better divider than the dominant chord, and since none was forthcoming they ultimately gave no answer at all. Among children who erred, however, nearly twice as many intentionally divided the piece at places *other than* the end of bar 2 as gave no answer; most often they "divided" at the very end in bar 4. Thus adults did not really perform more poorly than children on this task. All subjects at age 10 and above performed correctly on trials 2 and 3.

Children can, then, track the successive dimension and divide a piece when a clear dividing point—one that is both harmonically and rhythmically stressed—is present. Quite different results were obtained when the dividing point, in what turns out to be an asymmetric two-part piece, is more subtle—in this case a very modest rhythmic stress and a change in texture, as shown in example 4.3. The "correct" division is at the end of bar 2.

As figure 4.3 shows, only among the oldest children and adults was a substantial success rate achieved, and only after an initial hearing. Younger children did not divide the phrase conventionally, even with repeated hearings, although this was not due to misconceiving their task.

Example 4.3

Their spontaneous comments show that they sought a dividing point, but just didn't hear one; that is, younger subjects did not accept the change in texture and rhythmic figuration as the mark of a phrase divider. Five- and 6-year-olds said:

"The second doll never plays—or only a teeny bit."

"There's no stop in between."

"I can't hear it. Can you?"

"I don't think this is working out like I thought it would."

By contrast, one 11-year-old not only heard the division but knew exactly what was odd about the dimensions of the phrase: "The first part's too short."

Again in trial 1 here, there is a difference between the types of errors made by adults and by young children. Adults, if they did not choose the division between bars 2 and 3, were most likely to give no answer at all since they heard no better division after that point. Young children, how-

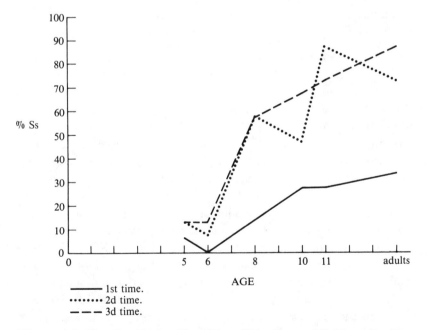

Figure 4.3. Phrasing Task—Piece Two: Percentage of Subjects Performing Correctly

ever, convinced that they must make a division somewhere and hearing no appropriate point, simply move the finger to the second object when the music runs out in bar 7. About half the 5- and 6-year-olds made their "division" in bar 7 (the end of the piece), even on the second and third trials.

Thus, young children appear to be capable of what I will call *scanning* or *monitoring* the progress of a longer phrase and of seeking appropriate division points for it. If a division point is obvious enough—for example, a built-in rhythmic pause at a cadence—they will divide the phrase at such a point. But subtler divisions—such as changes in texture and rhythmic figuration alone—are accepted as divisions only by older children and adults.

A question that arises about young children's scanning or monitoring of an ongoing phrase is the degree to which it is general and global or focused on the particularities of local, low-level events. The following experiment was designed to address this.

Experiment: Patterning

Like the phrasing task, the patterning task assesses the subject's grasp of an ongoing musical phrase, but it also demands attention to a short, three-to-five-note fragment that is contained within the phrase and alternates continuously throughout it. The subject is first trained to associate each of two fragments, A and B, with each of two dolls (see example 4.4). Following several pre-test items in which the subject's asociation of A and B with their respective dolls is verified, the subject is told to listen as the dolls take turns playing some music. When the music stops, the subject's task is to tell "whose turn comes next." Example 4.4 shows two sets of A and B fragments (represented by two different pairs of dolls), each of which appeared under three conditions: (1) a phrase involving static alternation (items 1 and 6); (2) a phrase involving descending tonal movement with alternation (items 2 and 5); and (3) a phrase involving harmonic sequence with alternation (items 3 and 4). The purpose of these conditions was to determine whether tonal or harmonic movement would enhance or inhibit attention to the alternating fragments. In addition, a final item (no. 7) consisted of continuous repetition of the second "A" fragment over a harmonic sequence. The subject was simply asked to tell "what happened here" in this case.

Figure 4.4 shows the percentage of correct responses at each age level on each of the first six items. The different types of items—static alternation, descending tonal movement, and harmonic sequence—clearly do not vary in difficulty. Table 4.4 shows the mean, standard deviation, and percentage of subjects passing at each age level, where the pass criterion is five out of six items correct for the first six items on the task. Note that there is a slight but nevertheless unexpected decrement in performance at age 11. (I return to this point later.)

It is clear that children at age 8 and below had difficulty following a pattern of alternating fragments and indicating which would come next in the series. By contrast, nearly all adults and older children had no difficulty with the task. These results are underscored by item 7 (see example 4.4), in which the same fragment was repeated five times in a harmonic sequence. When asked for a description of this phrase, young children gave no evidence of recognizing that the fragment recurred. (One

Example 4.4

Example 4.4 (continued)

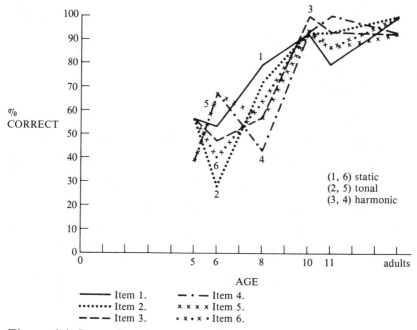

(1, 6) static
(2, 5) tonal
(3, 4) harmonic

————— Item 1.   — · — Item 4.
········· Item 2.   × × × × Item 5.
— — — Item 3.   · × · × · Item 6.

Figure 4.4. Patterning: Percentage of Correct Responses

Table 4.4. Patterning Task

Age Group	Mean	s.d.	Percent Pass
5-year-olds	3.0	1.55	19%
6-year-olds	3.0	.85	0
8-year-olds	3.7	1.63	29%
10-year-olds	5.7	.44	100%
11-year-olds	5.4	.74	87%
Adults	5.8	.41	100%

6-year-old: "It's a whole new song.") It should be pointed out that the task required the spontaneous production of an answer to the question "What happened here?" and such responses are much more difficult for young children than for older subjects. Also, the criterion for success was stringent: the subject had to make explicit reference to repetition ("It's that one over and over") in order to be scored correct. Yet it is somewhat surprising that among 5- and 6-year-olds not one child independently made reference to the repetition. In answer to the question "What happened here?" some responded:

"I don't know."

"There's a low note in it."

"Both dolls mixed up together."

"They made a mistake, forgot the notes."

"It's the same as before—no difference."

It is possible that young children's difficulty with this last item is in fact only a result of performance demands inherent in the task. The subject must reflect on the music, isolate repetition as the dominant feature, and generate the language necessary to describe it. The absence of such skills does not necessarily imply that children do not perceive and understand repetition, which in any case may be partially obscured here by the underlying harmonic changes. Yet there is also the possibility that young children's difficulty with this item reflects a broader difficulty with the idea of musical repetition, or succession, or the necessity of focusing on the shorter fragments or components contained within a longer phrase. We return to these hypotheses shortly. Adults, in contrast, had no difficulty with this item (about three-fourths explicitly described the repeated fragment), while older children were sporadic: 50 percent of the 10-year-olds and 20 percent of the 11-year-olds described the repetition.

With regard to performance across all items on the patterning task, at least four hypotheses emerge, and they are admittedly difficult to consider independently. One hypothesis is that nonmusical task demands, such as attention and vocabulary, mask the competence of younger children. Another is that young children may generally lack the experience with the ideas of alternation and repetition, and so this more general inexperience makes itself known in music also. A third hypothesis is that young children are unable to consider simultaneously both the parts and the whole of a musical phrase; that is, they do not attend to the individual components, the shorter fragments that constitute a longer phrase. A fourth hypothesis is that the very idea of succession in music eludes these younger children; that is, it is the connecting or chaining together of fragments to make a longer phrase that is difficult for the child.

Although the following task was not designed to test these hypotheses separately, it does do the following. First, it requires a different set of task demands and, among other things, requires an after-the-fact memory judgment, instead of an in-progress response to the musical phrase. Second, it does not make use of the concepts of alternation and repetition; rather, it uses two fragments that succeed each other only once. Finally, the task requires the subject to mentally chain two fragments together and also attend to the components of a longer phrase.

Experiment: Motivic Chaining

A critical understanding in the above task, which is directly measured here, is the understanding that a motive A, when combined with motive B, will yield phrase AB. In this task, the subject is presented with motive A, then motive B, and is asked to determine whether, if combined, they would yield a particular subsequent phrase. The subsequent phrase is either "correct" (AB) or "incorrect (AX or ZB) by virtue of a change in the first or second motive. The task involves both memory and prediction skills since the stimuli A, B, and AB (or AX or ZB) are heard in succession, each separated by an interval of approximately one second, and then the subject must answer after all three stimuli have been heard.

Younger subjects were told a story involving three fictitious characters (in this case, elves) represented by small plastic figures of which two (A and B) are identical, while the third has clothing of a different color and is placed about twelve inches from the others. In the story, character A and character B each "play some music," and the job of the third character is "to play the music of this one and then that one all together." In order to facilitate the illusion that the characters played music, the experimenter pointed to them in succession, although all stimuli emanated from the same two (stereo) audio speakers. The subject's task was to determine whether the third character "did it right" and played exactly what the first two had played. Older subjects were given less elaborate story-telling about the characters and were simply told "Sometimes it's easier to hear music when we can look at something that might be playing it. For example, here are three elves . . ." Otherwise, the versions for younger and older subjects were identical.

Example 4.5 shows the musical stimuli used in the task. Subjects were given a demonstration and pretraining involving the fragments marked A and B, which subsequently occurred in a "correct" combination (AB) and an "incorrect" one (AX). Subjects did receive help and feedback from the experimenter on these initial items, and the pretraining was repeated if a subject did not understand or answer correctly. At least six additional items were then given, representing an AB, AX, ZB, AB, ZB, and AB combination, respectively, as shown in example 4.5. Older subjects were given additional items if they were willing to attend to them (not shown), but because it was found that young children would not attend to more than the first six items, only those six were used in the comparisons across age groups. Items 3 and 4 are in an atonal idiom (note that they are in no way random), and each fragment is coherent melodically; the remaining items are in the conventional tonal idiom.

Example 4.5

Figure 4.5 shows the percentage of correct responses at each age level on each of the six items on the task. Inspection of the figure reveals that (1) young children were more likely to answer correctly on items where the subsequent phrase was AB ("correct" or "same" on items 1, 4, and 6) than on items where the subsequent phrase was AX or ZB ("incorrect" or "different" on items 2, 3, and 5); that is, young children may have been subject to a response bias in which they more frequently claimed that the third character "did it right" than wrong; (2) performance on the atonal items was not worse than that on tonal items; and (3) performance did not substantially improve over the six items.

Table 4.5 shows the mean (of six items total), standard deviation, and percentage of subjects passing at each age level, where the pass criterion is five of six items correct. Although adults and older children performed quite well, the majority of 5- and 6-year-olds did not pass this task, and as a group they did not perform significantly better than chance. Among 8-year-olds, only 50 percent passed. The correlates of success among these young children were both training and developmental level. That is,

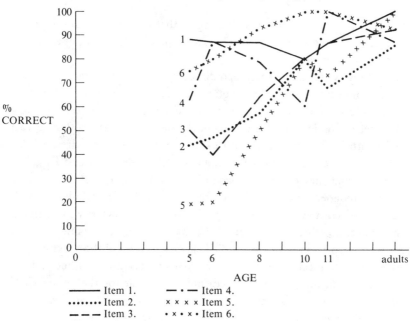

Figure 4.5. Motivic Chaining: Percentage of Correct Responses

Table 4.5. Motivic Chaining Task

Age Group	Mean	s.d.	Percent Pass
5-year-olds	3.3	1.5	19%
6-year-olds	3.6	.9	20%
8-year-olds	4.3	1.1	50%
10-year-olds	4.8	1.2	67%
11-year-olds	5.1	1.0	73%
Adults	5.6	.5	100%

among 5-, 6-, and 8-year-olds, amount of training (in years) was significantly correlated with task score ($r = .36$, $p < .01$), even when age was controlled through partial correlation (since older subjects have more training than younger ones). Similarly, task score was significantly correlated with a combined score for conservation of number and weight ($r = .42$, $p < .005$) and raw score on the Draw-a-Person test ($r = .33$, $p < .02$), with age controlled in each case through partial correlation. By contrast, the partial correlation between motivic chaining scores and scores on the pitch discrimination task were only marginally significant

(r = .23, p < .07). These results suggest that training and developmental level may have more to do with success on this task than does simple discrimination ability.

In summary, young children had difficulty with the successive chaining or addition of two independent motives, at least in a task such as this one. Older children and adults, by contrast, achieved a high rate of success. These results underscore the results of the patterning task in that at least two hypotheses remain tenable at this time. First, young children may be unable to attend to the smaller components of a phrase (A and B) at the same time that they grasp a phrase in its entirety (AB); that is, the parts lose their independent identity and are submerged in the whole. Second, young children may have difficulty with the mental activity of chaining components together successively, such that the necessary connection and flow from A to B is not made. Additional clarification of these hypotheses awaits further research, but it is clear that on account of either or both of the above factors, musical succession is difficult for the young child and cannot be considered an easy or automatic perceptual process.

An additional issue raised by the motivic chaining task is the degree to which the differences between child and adult performances could be due to differences in the perception of the individual fragments themselves, A and B, rather than in how they are chained together. That is, it would seem that conceiving of fragment A or B as a single, coherent unit would offer a special advantage to the subject because a coherent unit is easier to remember and should be easier to identify (when paired with another unit) than are units conceived by the subject as arbitrary collections of tones. In the case of fragments A and B, what makes them coherent units is the fact that they conform to the conventional Western rule system known as the tonal idiom; that is, they are drawn from the diatonic, major/minor scale and they conform to Western rules of counterpoint.

A possible explanation for the results of the motivic chaining task, then, is that subjects who are familiar with the Western tonal idiom might more readily conceive of fragments A and B as coherent and memorable than do subjects who are not familiar with the idiom. Adults and older children would obviously have more familiarity with the idiom than do younger children simply because they have had more experience listening to, and perhaps performing, Western music. Age differences in success on the motivic chaining task, then, might not be the result of internal or structural differences in the processing capacities of older and younger subjects, but rather might be attributable to the more extensive exposure to or even training in the tonal idiom that characterizes the lives of older children and adults. This question reflects the qualitative/quantitative issue referred to in the previous chapter.

The following task was an attempt to assess subjects' knowledge of tonal, idiomatic construction as a means of endowing melodic fragments with coherence. One question, among others, is whether such knowledge is related to the ability to perform the successive chaining of motives as measured in the task just described.

Experiment: Idiomatic Construction

The purpose of the present experiment was to determine the degree to which subjects of various ages are sensitive to the coherence embodied in melodies that are based on the conventional musical idiom. As is discussed more fully below, the task in question simply contrasted subjects' discrimination abilities when the stimuli were coherent melodies and when they were sequences of randomly selected tones. The present experiment does not, of course, provide either a direct or a sufficient test of structural versus environmental (or qualitative versus quantitative) interpretations of the differences across age found in the earlier succession tasks. However, it does address the critical sub-question of whether familiarity with the Western idiom (and such familiarity is entirely an environmental effect) plays an important role in the cognitive-musical processes under consideration here. For example, a strong relationship between familiarity with the musical idiom and success on tasks such as motivic chaining might support the view that the idiom is critically necessary to musical understanding, at least among Westerners. The idiom lends coherence, meaning, and memorability to musical stimuli, hence familiarity with it may account for much of the variance in performance on other musical-cognitive tasks. In such a case, variations in performance on the motivic chaining task, for example, would be largely the result of environmental influences such as exposure to and training in the idiom.

An alternative result—that there is no relationship between idiom familiarity and the motivic chaining task—is more difficult to interpret but more provocative. Ruling out the possibility that the lack of relationship is due to the particular tasks or sample (and this possibility cannot ever be entirely ruled out), then the following interpretation must be entertained: that at least some aspects of musical thought (such as succession, for example) occur without reference to a particular idiom and develop in the child independently of it. Thus a process such as motivic chaining may be a developmental acquisition for which familiarity with even so powerful an idiom as Western tonality is neither necessary nor sufficient. In such a case we may hypothesize that the growth of sensitivity to a musical idiom is concurrent with the development of musical understanding more generally (the processes I have labeled "generic"), but it is not itself the *cause* of that development, or even necessary to it.

The following paragraphs describe the procedures and results of a task designed to measure familiarity with idiomatic constructions. We shall see that the latter of the above two interpretations must be entertained, since success on this task was unrelated to success on the motivic chaining task.

For measuring idiom familiarity a melody discrimination task was used in which three types of items were presented, each item consisting of a pair of melodies which subjects were asked to judge as same or different: (1) simple melodies containing nine tones ("intact" melodies); (2) the same nine tones of which some are left intact and some are randomly displaced ("partly random" melodies); and (3) the same nine tones in random succession ("random" melodies). Of only minor interest is the child's melodic discrimination ability per se. The more important question is the degree to which intact melodies are easier to discriminate than partly random melodies, which in turn are easier to discriminate than random ones. The assumption made here is that if the subject is sensitive to cohesion based on the musical idiom, then he should find melodic discrimination easier when presented with intact melodies than with random ones. Thus, it is not discrimination ability itself that is the measure of familiarity with idiomatic construction, but rather the tendency for discrimination to be easier on intact than on partly random and random melodies, in that order.

The subject was faced with two small, high-quality audio speakers the faces of which measure about 5 × 8 inches. Young children were introduced to these "boxes that play music" with the explanation that "*this* one plays some music" (speaker on the left) and then "*that* one—the echo box—tries to play exactly the same thing" (speaker on the right). The child's task was to tell whether "the echo box" played exactly the same thing. In fact, both melodies of the pair to be discriminated emanated from both of the audio speakers simultaneously and were generated from the same tape source. To give the illusion that "this box and then the echo box" performed independently, the experimenter simply pointed alternately to each of the speakers in turn, which were placed facing each other about twelve inches apart. As in the other experiments in which this pointing technique was used, subjects had no difficulty accepting the illusion that one or another of the boxes was "playing." Older subjects simply received the instruction that they would hear two pieces of music and that the experimenter would "point here (Speaker A) and there (Speaker B) as you hear them."

Example 4.6 shows the twelve items used in this task. Items 3, 5, 8, and 9 are intact melodies; items 1, 2, 11, and 12 are partly random; items 4, 6, 7, and 10 are random. Comparison melodies or "echoes" are shown only for those items in which the comparison is *different* ("wrong echo") from the first or standard melody.

To generate the "different" comparisons, the following algorithm was applied to each of the necessary items: the comparison contains the same nine tones as the standard except that the fourth and fifth tones were interchanged and the second and eighth tones were interchanged. Further, each of the four intact melodies was used to generate a partly random and a random melody as follows: Partly random melodies were generated by drawing two tones at random from the intact melody and then interchanging those two tones; then the procedure was repeated a second time. The random melodies were generated by drawing the nine tones at random and stringing them in succession. It will be seen in example 4.6 that items (5, 1, 4), (3, 2, 6), (9, 12, 10), and (8, 11, 7) are companion items containing the same nine tones in intact, partly random, and random order. Thus, the few subjects who completed only the first six items nevertheless answered every possible combination of melody type and comparison.

One question that may be entertained with respect to random stimuli is the degree to which repetition of the stimulus will eventually cause coherence to be imposed even on a "random" melody. To briefly address this question each subject heard, at the completion of the task, several repetitions of the random melody indicated as the standard in item 6, followed by a "different" and "same" test item utilizing that stimulus. The subject's instructions were to listen very carefully to this melody, to "try to remember it," "pretend you will have to sing it," and so on. Each subject then heard two repetitions followed by a brief repetition of the instructions to refocus his attention and two more repetitions. The test items followed immediately.

Results. It should be noted that 15 subjects, most of them 5- and 6-year-olds, failed to complete all twelve of the items because they could not muster the sustained concentration necessary for this long and purely auditory task. Except where otherwise noted, I have elected to omit these subjects from the analysis rather than to report on fewer items. Thus, at

Example 4.6

age levels 5, 6, 8, 10, and 11 years, there are only 11, 8, 14, 14, and 13 subjects respectively instead of the expected 15 at each age level. To some degree, then, these subjects represent those most willing to undertake the demands of the task, and thus the results are probably biased in favor of superior performances. Nevertheless, as figure 4.6 shows, the youngest children did not perform substantially better than chance when they are scored purely on the grounds of discriminating all three types of melodies. Not until age 8 does the group mean for number of correct items near ten (out of twelve possible items). (The standard deviations are 1.1, 2.1, 1.5, 1.3, 1.0, and 2.0, respectively, for each of the age groups.) Put otherwise, 5- and 6-year-olds answered correctly 58 percent and 63 percent of the time respectively. Eight-, 10-, and 11-year-olds answered correctly about 80 percent to 84 percent of the time, and adults achieved a correct response rate of 86 percent.

Young children's poor discrimination ability on this task is not the result of their having answered "same" and "different" at random. Rather, young children gave a very high proportion of "same" answers no matter what the comparison stimulus was. As figure 4.7 shows, this resulted in their

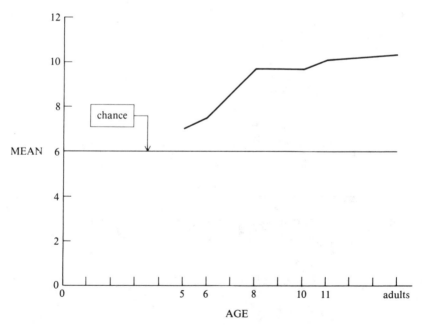

Figure 4.6. Idiomatic Construction: Mean Correct of Twelve Items

scoring correctly on nearly all of the six items in which the comparison melody was the same and scoring incorrectly on many of the six items in which the comparison melody was different. Whether this was the result of a response bias or whether the modified melodies really did sound the same to these subjects is undetermined by these data.

The more important question, however, is whether intact or cohesive melodies were in fact easier to discriminate than partly random or totally random ones, whatever the discrimination abilities of the subject. Figure 4.8 shows that this was generally although not significantly the case at each age level. That is, the null hypothesis that the means for intact, partly random, and random melodies are equal can be rejected for subjects at age 10, $F(2, 26) = 15.59$, $p = .000$, for subjects at age 11, $F(2, 24) = 3.88$, $p < .04$, and for adults, $F(2, 28) = 7.07$, $p < .004$. This contrasts with the results of younger subjects. At age 5 the differences among means for intact, partly random, and random melodies show only a nonsignificant trend, $F(2, 20) = 2.75$, $p < .09$, and among 6- and

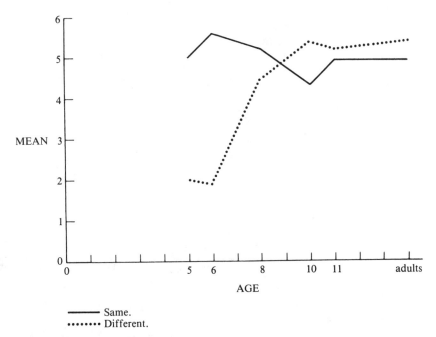

Figure 4.7. Idiomatic Construction: Means for "Same" and "Different" Items

8-year-olds the differences were not significant, $F(2, 14) = 1.00$ and $F(2, 26) = 1.08$ respectively.

Thus, the tendency for intact melodies to be more discriminable than random ones is true for subjects at age 10 and above, but not for subjects at age 8 and below. To the degree that the increased discriminability of intact melodies reflects familiarity with the idiomatic rules on which such melodies are based, the data suggest that older subjects have acquired greater sensitivity to and understanding of these rules than have younger subjects.

This conclusion is further supported by an analysis in which each subject was categorized according to whether: (1) he responded "idiomatically" (that is, performance on intact melodies was *better than* that on random melodies), or (2) he responded "non-idiomatically" (performance on intact melodies was *worse than* that on random ones), or (3) he responded "equivocally" (performance was the same on intact and random

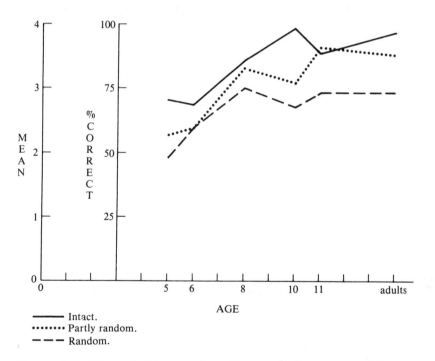

———— Intact.
••••••• Partly random.
– – – Random.

Figure 4.8. Idiomatic Construction: Means and Percentage of Correct Responses for Different Melody Types

melodies). All 90 subjects were categorized in this way, including the 15 who completed only the first six of the twelve items on the task. Only 5 subjects (5.5 percent of the whole sample) responded "non-idiomatically," and these were spread evenly across younger and older age groups.

The more general results were as follows. Among younger subjects (ages 5, 6, and 8), only one-third responded idiomatically, while 62 percent responded equivocally. Among older subjects (ages 10, 11, and adults) these proportions were reversed: only a third responded equivocally and 60 percent responded idiomatically. Thus older subjects were about twice as likely as younger ones to achieve higher discrimination scores on intact melodies than on random ones. Nearly two-thirds of the younger children did no better at discriminating intact, idiomatic melodies than they did random sequences of tones. A turning point in the development of responding idiomatically seems to be at age 8. Here about half the children responded idiomatically and half responded equivocally.

A closer consideration of what sorts of skills the discrimination of intact and random melodies represents will illuminate these results. We may imagine that the child makes at least the following two achievements on the route to being able to discriminate the stimuli at hand. One is to attend closely to and discriminate a stimulus, whatever its nature, purely on the grounds of the absolute physical differences between its elements and the comparison elements, without relying on the extra information that may be embodied in the tonal or idiomatic relationships *among* the elements present. We will assume that this rather "pure" discrimination ability is measurable by the random melodies. The other achievement is to boost pure discrimination by using the extra information contained in stimuli that are organized and rule-governed. The special relationship among elements in an idiomatically constructed melody is an example of such extra information. We may assume that knowledge of such rules and organizational patterns is called upon in the discrimination of intact melodies, which is what makes them easier to discriminate.

Given this distinction, a closer look at figure 4.8 reveals the following: (1) the "pure" discrimination of random melodies is poor in the youngest children (ages 5 and 6), but improves dramatically by age 8, at which point it has reached the adult level; (2) in contrast, the discrimination of intact, idiomatic stimuli follows a slower growth pattern that peaks later, at age 10. Let us consider each of these results in greater detail below.

With regard to random melodies, 5- and 6-year-olds answer approximately at chance (48 percent and 59 percent correct responses respectively). The mean of 1.91 for 5-year-olds is significantly lower than that of any other age group except 6-year-olds, who had a mean of 2.38, $F(5, 69) = 3.17$, $p < .02$, Duncan post hoc test $p < .05$. Moreover, the repetition training at the end of the task did not improve discrimination of a random melody for these youngest subjects. About 75 percent of the 5- and 6-year-olds who had failed random item 6 the first time it was presented (there were 23 such subjects) continued to fail the item even after repetition training on that melody. This contrasts markedly with the results for subjects at age 8 and above: over 90 percent of those who had failed random item 6 the first time it was presented (there were 11 such subjects, spread evenly over the older groups) did pass the item after repetition.

Thus, although 5- and 6-year-olds did poorly on the discrimination of random items, there is a dramatic improvement in this ability by age 8, at which point the correct response rate reaches 75 percent and levels off at what is approximately the adult success rate. The 10- and 11-year-olds and adults have success rates of 68 percent, 73 percent, and 73 percent respectively. Of course, there are no significant differences in the mean scores for random discrimination among any of the age groups at age 8 and above.

The situation is vastly different in the case of intact, idiomatic discrimination. Here there is a more gradual increase in success rate, with 5- and 6-year-olds achieving a correct response rate of about 70 percent, 8-year-olds about 85 percent, and 10- and 11-year-olds and adults scoring close to 100 percent. (There is a slight decline among 11-year-olds, whose success rate dips to 90 percent.) In contrast to the results for random melodies, where 8-year-olds performed as well as adults (mean of 3.00 for 8-year-olds vs. 2.93 for adults), 8-year-olds' mean score for intact melodies (3.43) is now *significantly lower* than the mean for 10-year-olds (3.93), $F(5, 70) = 8.29$, $p < .01$, Duncan post hoc test $p < .05$, and falls just short of significance by comparison to adults (3.87).

To recapitulate these results: 8-year-olds did not find intact melodies significantly easier to discriminate than random ones. Also, although 8-year-olds performed at the adult level on discrimination of random melodies, they did significantly *worse* than older subjects on intact melodies. These results suggest that the "pure" discrimination ability represented in the random items precedes and is not a sufficient condition for sensitivity to idiomatic, rule-governed melodic constructions.

We now turn to the question of whether sensitivity to the rules embodied in idiomatically constructed melodies is related to the ability to add two melodies together successively, as required in the motivic chaining task. The issue here, broadly speaking, is whether the environmental/cultural effect of sensitivity to idiomatic rules enhances the cognitive process I have identified as motivic chaining, or whether, on the contrary, the latter process follows a developmental course that is independent of sensitivity to idiomatic constructions. As shown in table 4.6, there is no relationship between success on the motivic chaining task (where the pass criterion is five of six items correct) and responding idiomatically on the present task.[1] Indeed, across the whole sample, subjects are nearly equally distributed across cells for passing and failing motivic chaining and responding idiomatically and equivocally. (As pointed out earlier, only a negligible percentage of subjects responded non-idiomatically, and even these few are equally divided in their success on motivic chaining).

When the frequencies are displayed separately for younger and older age groups, it is clear that, although more than twice as many older as younger subjects pass motivic chaining and *nearly* twice as many respond idiomatically, there is no relationship between the two abilities within either age group. ($\chi^2 < .01$ for younger subjects and $\chi^2 = 1.8$ for older

Table 4.6. Idiomatic Construction and Motivic Chaining

		Idiomatic Construction		
		Idiomatic	*Equivocal*	*Non-Idiomatic*
Motivic Chaining	All Ss (N = 90)			
	Pass	24	22	3
	Fail	18	21	2
	Younger Ss (ages 5, 6, 8)			
	Pass	5	8	0
	Fail	10	20	2
	Older Ss (ages 10, 11, adults)			
	Pass	19	14	3
	Fail	8	1	0

[1]These results are not substantially altered by lowering the pass criterion for motivic chaining to four out of six items correct.

subjects, ignoring frequencies for the non-idiomatic subjects in both cases.) Thus, sensitivity to the culture's idiomatic rules confers no special advantage in the motivic chaining task, and responding equivocally to those rules presents no particular handicap.

Finally, and perhaps as an additional indication of the independence of these two tasks, the idiomatic construction task shows a different pattern of correlations with other variables. It will be recalled that the motivic chaining task was correlated with both degree of musical training (in years) and the presence of conservation ability in younger subjects and that it was marginally correlated with pitch discrimination. By contrast, success on the idiomatic construction task is unrelated to musical training or conservation, and although it is seemingly related to pitch discrimination across the whole sample, this relationship is eradicated when age or grade is controlled through partial correlation.

Summary

The successive dimension calls upon our ability to perceive that music goes forward in time, with one fragment or unit succeeding another such that longer fragments and then longer phrases are created. Even the young child possesses the skill necessary for scanning the broad outlines of a phrase and dividing it according to conventional cues such as cadence points. However, the simultaneous perception of lower-level units, such as the repeated or alternating motives of a short pattern, remains weak until about age 10 in the present data. Similarly, the capacity to string motives together successively is not generally acquired until age 10 or later. In addition, this development appears to be independent of the growing familiarity with the rule-governed, idiomatic ways in which units are embodied with coherence.

TEMPORALITY: UNDERSTANDING SIMULTANEITY

Many pieces of music involve but a single series of events. A melody played on a solo instrument and a series of sound masses in electronic music are examples because only a single sequence of aural events is under consideration by the listener. However most music, at least in the West, consists of multiple and simultaneous sequences of events, as in polyphonic music (two or more melodies simultaneously), melody-plus-accompaniment pieces, and the more common complexities in contemporary music where masses of sound superimposed on one another are intended to be grasped as distinct but co-occurring. In such cases, the listener is called upon to track two or more simultaneous sequences of events as they move in parallel through time.

The three experiments reported here compare the child's and the adult's grasp of the simultaneous dimension in music. The subjects were children at ages 5, 6, 8, 10, and 11 years (a different sample from those in the succession experiments) and the same 15 adults as used in all the experiments.

Experiment: Textural Abstraction

From the ongoing stream of events that constitute a piece of music, listeners must abstract the multiple and simultaneous sequences at hand and track them separately. Doing this gives rise to the awareness of *texture*, which refers to the general character of a piece of music as it is constituted by its multiple and simultaneous sequence of events or, more simply, its *parts*. For example, homophonic textures comprise two parts—a melody and an accompaniment—and such a texture is ideally understood not as a single sound mass but as two simultaneous parts. Similarly, a polyphonic texture comprises two or more melodies. The purpose of the present task was to determine whether and when children acquire an awareness of the several simultaneous parts that constitute a piece of music.

In the present task the subject was first familiarized with each of three individual parts. Subsequently, any combination of these parts, when played simultaneously, constituted a texture in which the separate parts could be individually tracked. (Simultaneous parts are labeled 1, 2, and 3 in example 4.7.) The subject's task was to listen to combinations of two or three parts and simply indicate how many parts he heard. In the version of this task for younger children, the child was first presented with three dolls, each of which could "play some music." After the child had heard each doll in turn (the experimenter pointed as each "played," but all sounds emanated from the same loudspeaker), the child was told that he would hear some music in which one, two, or three dolls were playing, and he was to indicate "who's playing now" or, if that was impossible, "how many are playing now." The question of interest is not whether the child indicates the correct *ones*, but rather the correct *number*.[2] (Although subjects were introduced to each doll and its melody, they were not specifically pretrained to make accurate associations between them.) In the version of the task for older subjects the procedure was identical except that more sophisticated instructions introduced the dolls.

Example 4.7 shows the two pieces of music used as stimuli, where the three parts associated with respective dolls are so numbered. Piece A and Piece B consume 20 and 25 seconds respectively, so there was ample time for the subject to formulate a judgment.

The two pieces represent different types of musical textures. Piece A is an example of homophony, that is, melody-plus-accompaniment (in this case chords).[3] Piece B is an example of polyphony, where three equal and independent single-line melodies constitute the texture. It is clear that insofar as the polyphonic parts embody considerable rhythmic activity and changes in tonal movement, the resulting texture is busier than homophony, where one part (the chordal accompaniment) is tonally thicker and rhythmically more uniform and slower moving than its companions. This is generally the case when polyphonic and homophonic pieces are compared. That is, composers have typically distinguished the separate parts of polyphonic textures by differentiating them rhythmically. If the parts did not vary considerably in rhythmic pattern, of course, they would be hard to tell apart. The necessity of several distinguishable rhythmic patterns gives rise, when the several patterns are combined, to a busy, complex rhythmic flow. In the case of homophony, on the other hand, rhythmic differentiation among the parts is not so necessary because the difference between accompaniment (e.g., chords or some thicker, uniform harmonic pattern) and the one or two single line melodies above make for a built-in differentiation between the parts. We shall see that polyphony and homophony give rise to some differences in texture perception at different age levels.

[2]Only adults were consistently accurate in identifying the correct *parts* as well as the correct *number* of parts. Even after a single hearing, about 75 percent of adult responses indicated the correct parts on items 1 and 3, the only items that required a choice among the three parts. Children who accurately identified the number of parts showed only a modest tendency to correctly name the bass part (part 3) on items 1 and 3 which, of course, was the easiest part to identify.

[3]Strictly speaking the two upper parts of Piece A may be considered a two-part polyphony, but the convenient distinction I have made here is to refer to any texture with chordal accompaniment as homophonic.

Example 4.7

Four items were scored on this task, two from each piece administered immediately after the subject was familiarized with the three relevant parts. The child's task was to answer "who's playing now?" and answers were scored for whether they indicated the correct number of parts. The four items and their correct answers were as follows:

Piece A:
    1. two parts (1 and 3)
    2. three parts (1, 2, and 3)

Piece B:
    1. two parts (2 and 3)
    2. three parts (1, 2, 3)

A different trio of dolls was used for each piece so that there would be no carry-over from Piece A to Piece B. In the remainder of this section the term "parts" will be used interchangeably with "voices," which is the conventional terminology for textures, even when parts are not sung but performed instrumentally. Parts 1, 2, and 3, then, are referred to as soprano, alto, and bass respectively.

Results. The task yielded two principal results: (1) An early sign of the growing awareness of simultaneous parts is a sensitivity to rhythmic complexity in making texture judgments. That is, the greater rhythmic complexity inherent in polyphony (as opposed to homophony) is at first misread by children as a greater number of *parts*. This misreading completely disappears by adulthood. (2) Despite such early signs, the number of simultaneous parts reliably discerned does not exceed *one* until late childhood. Young children generally underspecify the number of voices they are presented with, often claiming to hear a single voice when presented with two or even three. These results are discussed in detail following a brief description of more general findings.

Age trend and relationship to other variables. Figure 4.9 shows the percentage of subjects at each age level who identified the correct number of voices on each of the four items. There was a clear age trend (increasing success with age), no "sixth-grade slump," and there was greater success on 2-voiced items, at earlier ages, than there was on 3-voiced items.

If the criterion for possessing textural abstraction is set at three out of four items correct, then almost none of the 5-year-olds can be said to possess the ability (only one child did), about a third of the 6-, 8-, and 10-year-olds did, and half of the 11-year-olds and 80 percent of the adults did. The mean number of items correct (of four) increased at each age level, as shown in the following list where respective means are given with their standard deviations in parenthesis: 1.3 (.9); 1.6 (1.3); 1.8 (1.2); 2.1 (.7); 2.6 (1.1); 3.5 (.8).

Among 5-, 6-, and 8-year-olds textural abstraction was correlated with conservation of number ($r = .29$, $p < .03$) and only very marginally correlated with conservation of weight ($r = .21$, $p < .09$), when age is controlled through partial correlation. The pattern of correlations between textural abstraction and other variables was, however, different from that noted for tasks previously described. The correlation with the pitch discrimination task (for all subjects) was significant if low ($r = .20$, $p < .05$, with age controlled), perhaps suggesting that both abilities make use of an analytic strategy that is not necessarily called upon in the sort of chaining-and-memory operations used in the succession experiments. Also, tex-

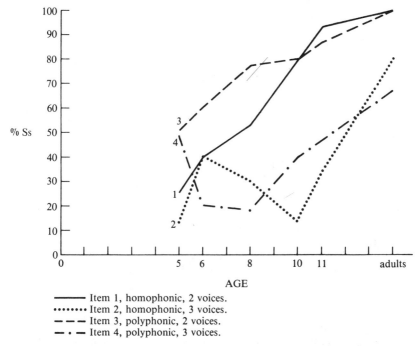

Figure 4.9. Textural Abstraction: Percentage of Subjects Identifying Correct Number of Voices

tural abstraction was not correlated with musical training or with either raw or normed scores on the Draw-a-Person Task, with age controlled.

Sensitivity to rhythmic complexity. As pointed out above, the possession of textural abstraction did not appear in even half the subjects at a particular age level until late childhood, at age 11. Younger subjects performed poorly on the task, although their responses were by no means random. Rather, their responses showed that polyphonic items were consistently thought to comprise more parts than were homophonic items, a result that suggests an early attempt to identify the parts of a texture by reading the rhythmic complexity inherent in a piece of music. Figure 4.10 shows the mean of the *total number of voices indicated* for homophonic and polyphonic items at each age level, whether the number indicated was correct or not. Because there was one 2-voiced and one 3-voiced item for each type of texture, the correct total is 5 and the possible range is a total of 2 to 6 for the homophonic and for the polyphonic items.

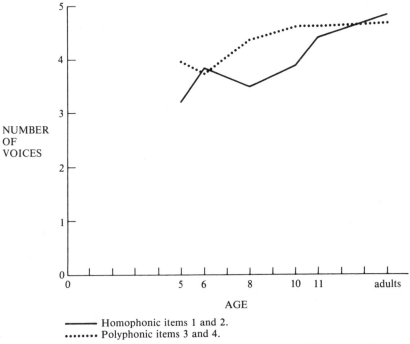

NUMBER
OF
VOICES

AGE

———— Homophonic items 1 and 2.
••••••• Polyphonic items 3 and 4.

Figure 4.10. Textural Abstraction: Mean Number of Voices Indicated for Homophonic and Polyphonic Items

It is clear that polyphonic items were thought to contain more voices than homophonic items at nearly every age level until age 11, when the correct identification of texture parts begins to emerge. The exception is the 6-year-old group, for whom there was virtually no difference in the number of voices indicated for homophonic and polyphonic items (means of 3.8 and 3.7 respectively). However 5-year-olds did indicate significantly more voices for polyphonic items (mean = 3.9) than for homophonic ones (3.2). Even when the responses of these 5- and 6-year-olds were combined, the mean number of voices indicated for polyphonic items was greater than that for homophonic items, t(30) = 1.65, p < .055, one-tailed test. The tendency was even more pronounced among 8- and 10-year-olds, t(31) = 4.21, p < .001. However, there were no significant differences on these items among 11-year-olds and adults.

This sensitivity to rhythmic complexity is, of course, a misreading of the texture insofar as the rhythmic activity inherent in the stimulus is irrelevant to the actual number of parts or voices that it contains. That this sensitivity seems to increase rather than decrease up to age 11 (the point of correctly reading the part-structure) suggests that it may be a necessary or desirable developmental step on the way to understanding the parts of textures. At the least it shows an early attempt to make texture judgments that, while ultimately wrong, are reasonable and nonrandom. At age 11 and in adulthood, with the ability to differentiate and enumerate the parts, reliance upon and misreading of rhythmic complexity disappear, and equal numbers of voices are indicated for both polyphonic and homophonic textures.

The misreading of rhythmic complexity has an interesting consequence among the youngest children—namely, that 5-year-olds can perform more correctly on polyphonic than on homophonic items. This is true of no other age group, as shown in figure 4.11. In this case the mean scores for *correctly* identifying the number of voices have a theoretical range of 0 to

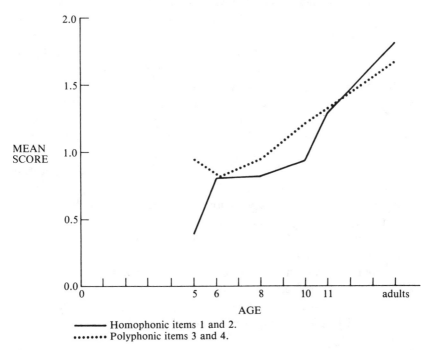

Homophonic items 1 and 2.
Polyphonic items 3 and 4.

Figure 4.11. Textural Abstraction: Mean Score for Homophonic and Polyphonic Items

2, since there are two items of each texture type scored 0 or 1. It is clear that the vast majority of subjects, however good or poor their performance, perform equivalently on polyphonic and homophonic items. Five-year-olds, however, achieve a mean on polyphonic items (.94 correct) that is more than twice that of homophonic items (.38 correct), a difference that is significant, $t(15) = 2.33$, $p < .034$. This is not because polyphony is an inherently "easier" or clearer texture to the 5-year-old ear. Rather, it is because the young child's sensitivity to rhythmic complexity in part overcomes—in the case of polyphony—the almost universal tendency among 5-year-olds to err on the side of *underestimating* the number of voices heard. It is this tendency to hear fewer voices at the younger ages—only in part ameliorated by polyphonic complexity—to which we now turn.

Number of voices heard. There was a general tendency for subjects to underestimate the number of voices that they were presented with, although this tendency diminished with age. Across the four items (two 2-voiced and two 3-voiced items), subjects were presented with a total of ten voices or parts. Yet the total number of voices indicated by subjects was lower than that, as shown by the following respective means for 5-, 6-, 8-, 10-, and 11-year-olds and adults: 7.1, 7.5, 7.8, 8.5, 9.0, and 9.5. Only 2 subjects (2 percent) overestimated and indicated a total of eleven voices heard, while 25 subjects (27 percent of the sample) claimed to have heard a total of *seven or fewer*. All but one of these hard-core underestimators were members of one of the younger age groups (5, 6, or 8 years). Indeed, among children in these younger age groups, a substantial number (38 percent) claimed to have heard only a single voice on at least one of the items where *three* voices had been presented. It is worth noting that underestimators were apparently uninfluenced by any desire or expectation to call upon, at some point, the full battery of dolls. Even when pressed by the experimenter, "How come you always point to just one doll?" one erring 5-year-old explained, "Because I hear so good."

Figure 4.12 shows the mean of the total number of voices indicated for 2- and 3-voiced items at each age level, whether the number was correct or not. Because there were two 2-voiced and two 3-voiced items, the correct total is 4 and 6 respectively with a possible range of 2 to 6 for each.

Even at the younger age levels subjects indicated significantly more voices heard when they were presented with three voices as opposed to

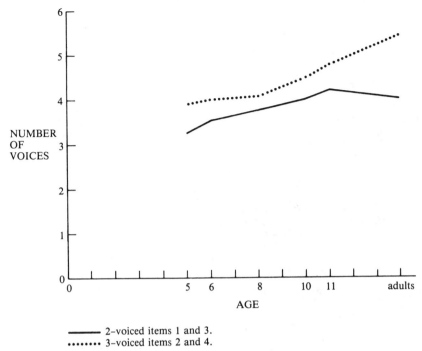

───── 2–voiced items 1 and 3.
•••••••• 3–voiced items 2 and 4.

Figure 4.12. Textural Abstraction: Mean Number of Voices Indicated for Two-Voiced and Three-Voiced Items

two voices. (For 5-, 6-, and 8-year-olds combined, $t(47) = 2.58$, $p < .01$.) But it is also clear that among these younger subjects the difference between number of voices heard on 2- and 3-voiced items was relatively small, whereas among older subjects the difference increased with age until adulthood when it was realistically close to the number of voices actually presented. We may conclude that younger children (ages 5, 6, and 8) are sensitive to the difference between 2- and 3-voiced textures insofar as they indicate significantly more voices in the case of the latter. But the absolute amount of the difference they perceive is not substantial and does not approach what was actually presented. Rather, the tendency to underestimate is pronounced. Beginning at age 10, however, the perceived difference between 2- and 3-voiced textures begins to grow until it approximates reality in adulthood.

These results can be represented in a way that elucidates the developmental trend. Figure 4.13 shows the mean scores for correctly identifying

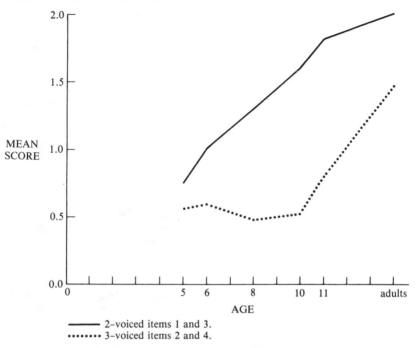

Figure 4.13. Textural Abstraction: Mean Score for Two-Voiced and Three-Voiced Items

the number of voices in 2-voiced and 3-voiced items, where each response is scored o or 1. Thus, the possible range for each subject is o to 2 because there are two items of each type. It is clear that the tendency to perform more correctly on 2-voiced than on 3-voiced items increases with age. Indeed, 5- and 6-year-olds did not perform significantly better on either type, but 8-, 10-, and 11-year-olds did better on 2-voiced items. (For all three groups combined, $t(46) = 8.19$, $p < .001$.) This difference in success rate narrows among adults but is still significant, $t(14) = 2.48$, $p < .03$.

It is also clear that success on the 2-voiced items was considerable by ages 10 and 11. By that age, means for 2-voiced items reach 1.6 and 1.8 (out of possible 2), and 60 percent to 85 percent of the subjects answer *both* of the 2-voiced items correctly. (100 percent of adults do so.) Prior to age 10, the number of subjects who meet this criterion increased steadily from 12 percent of the 5-year-olds to 33 percent of the 6-year-olds and 50 percent of the 8-year-olds. By contrast, performance on the 3-voiced items followed a much slower age trend. It remained poor among children at all age levels (means between .47 and .80) and only a negligible number of subjects was successful on both items, until age 11 when only 25 percent were so. Among adults, two-thirds met this criterion.

The present experiment shows that enumerating multiple and simultaneous sequences of events is a relatively late acquisition. The ability does not appear much before age 10 and even then is restricted to only two simultaneous parts. Enumerating three sequences was out of the reach of most children in this sample. It may be assumed that the youngest children (ages 5 and 6) reliably perceived only a single part under the present conditions, although they did show signs of a rhythmic sensitivity that forecasts the multiple-part processing that they will eventually employ. One question that arises in this regard is whether younger subjects could show increased ability at processing simultaneous parts if stimuli that are shorter, more varied rhythmically, and restricted to two parts were used in a standard discrimination task, which young children often find easier to manage. The following experiment considered this question.

Experiment: Motivic Synthesis

The present task is somewhat analogous to the motivic chaining task described earlier, except that here simultaneous rather than successive combinations of motives (short melodic fragments) were under test. The subject was first familiarized with two motives, A and B. Then, over several items, he was asked to determine whether, if A and B were combined simultaneously, they would yield a particular combination. The combinations presented were either the same (A with B) or different by virtue of a different motive replacing one of the original motives (thus A with X or Z with B). There was considerable memory demand since the subject was required to remember A and B while answering several items.

Two versions of the task were employed, one for younger and one for older subjects. In the younger version subjects were told a story about two girls and their teacher, represented by paper stand-up dolls, each of whom could "play some music." To create the illusion of "who was playing" the experimenter pointed to the appropriate doll, although all sounds emanated from the same two (stereo) audio speakers. In the story, the teacher directs each girl to "play her music" and each girl is associated with one of the motives, A or B. During pretraining for familiarization, the subject heard the motive three times, since the teacher first "shows her how to play it" and then she must "practice it" twice. Following this the subject heard the motive a fourth time and was asked "Did she do it right?" The subject was then familiarized with the second motive in the same way. A memory test followed in which the subject was presented first with motive B, then with motive A, and was asked in each case to determine "who's playing now." Correct answers were taken as evidence that the subject was adequately familiar with the respective motives. If there was an error, the familiarization sequence was repeated. All subjects correctly identified the motives at least by the second familiarization sequence. The task proper began with the "teacher's" request that "the girls must now play their music together at the same time." The subject's task was to determine whether, in each case, "both girls played it right." After several items, new A and B motives were introduced, this time in a similar story about two boys and their teacher.[4]

The version of the task employed with older subjects was similar to the above except that no dolls or stories were used, and the subject was simply asked to listen to some music and answer questions about it. ("Now I want you to tell me what those two tunes would sound like together at the same time. Would they sound like this?") The version for younger subjects was given to 5- and 6-year-olds plus half of the 8-year-olds ($n = 8$). The older version was given to the remaining 8-year-olds ($n = 9$) and all of the 10- and 11-year-olds and adults. There was no significant difference between the mean of those 8-year-olds who took the younger version (5.4 items correct out of 7) and those 8-year-olds who took the older version (5.2 correct), $t(15) = .26$.

Example 4.8 shows five of the seven items on the task. Items 4 and 7

---

[4]Pilot testing had shown that young children found it difficult to attend to the several repetitions and testings during the familiarization sequence. They were asked to listen to and/or answer questions about eight performances of the motives (three hearings plus one test per motive), even in advance of the task proper, which began with four additional items on those motives. Because young subjects' willingness to attend posed some difficulty, we decided to shorten the sequence involving the second pair of motives ("Boys A and B") so that the familiarization sequence consisted of only *two* instead of three hearings of each motive prior to the pre-task testing, and the number of items on the task itself was reduced to three instead of four. Although a reduction in the number of pre-task hearings of the motives may have resulted in poorer memory on the later items, we believe this may have been compensated by the subjects' greater understanding of the task procedures at this point. In any case, all subjects correctly answered the pre-task memory test.

(not shown) are identical to items 1 and 5 respectively. Items 1 through 4 (same, different, different, same) tested the first set of motives, A and B as presented in the first story, which are shown in item 1. Items 5 through 7 (same, different, same) tested the second set of motives, A and B as presented in the second story, which are shown in item 5. In order to facilitate memory for the motives over the course of relevant items, subjects received feedback on whether their answers were right or wrong

Example 4.8

and also re-heard separately the motives under test at two points in the task—after item 2 and after item 6.

Results. Figure 4.14 shows the percentage of correct responses at each age level on each item on the task. The two most important and apparent results are: (1) that there is wide variation in performance across the several items; as in previous tasks, young children appear to be subject to an answer bias such that they more readily answered "same/right" than "different/wrong." Hence they were likely to pass items 1, 4, 5, and 7 and to fail items 2, 3, and 6. Across all items, children at ages 5, 6, and 8 answered "same/right" 80 percent, 70 percent, and 66 percent of the time respectively. By contrast, subjects at ages 10 and 11 years and adults answered "same/right" 51 percent to 57 percent of the time. Since four of the seven items are "same" items, the correct response rate for "same/right" answers would be 57 percent. (2) The "sixth-grade slump" at age 11 is dramatically in evidence on four of the seven items. We return to this point shortly.

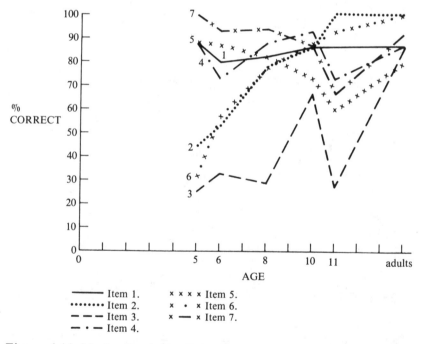

Figure 4.14. Motive Synthesis: Percentage of Correct Responses

Table 4.7 shows for each age group the mean, standard deviation, and percentage of subjects who pass the task, where the criterion is six out of seven items correct. (Recall that a "same/right" answer bias would net a score of at least 4.) As a group, 11-year-olds achieved a mean that is no higher than that of 8-year-olds, and no more of them met the pass criterion than did subjects at age 6. Yet their standard deviation was slightly lower than that for both 6- and 8-year-olds, indicating that the low mean for the group was not due to a few low scorers. Indeed, among the 73 percent of the 11-year-olds who did *not* meet the pass criterion, all of them achieved scores of either 4 or 5 correct out of 7.

It is important to note that the "sixth-grade slump" in this case was not the result of a tendency among 11-year-olds to answer "same/right," as did younger subjects. Indeed, 11-year-olds answered "same/right" a respectable 52 percent of the time, which is comparable to the adults' rate of 51 percent and lower than the 6- and 8-year-olds' rate of 70 percent and 66 percent. Thus, in contrast to younger groups, 11-year-olds were not subject to an answer bias but were simply wrong more often on *both* types of items.

We return in a later section to the performance decrement at this age, but for now it is worth noting that the decrement was observed in two entirely different samples of 11-year-olds—those in the present sample and those who completed the tasks on the successive dimension reported earlier. Thus, the decrement does not appear to be isolated to a single group of subjects, although all the 11-year-olds were drawn from the same school population. Neither can the decrement be due to gender differences, although there was a disproportionate number of boys in the present group (all simultaneity tasks) and a disproportionate number of girls in the other group of 11-year-olds. On the present task, boys (n = 10) achieved a mean of 5.1 items correct and girls (n = 5) achieved a mean of 5.0.

Table 4.7. Motivic Synthesis Task

Age Group	Mean	s.d.	Percent Pass
5-year-olds	4.63	.89	19%
6-year-olds	4.79	1.42	29%
8-year-olds	5.29	1.16	53%
10-year-olds	5.80	1.08	73%
11-year-olds	5.07	1.03	27%
Adults	6.33	.90	73%

Relationship to other variables. The motivic synthesis task showed a pattern of correlation with other variables that is more similar to that for textual abstraction (the other simultaneity task) than to the analogous succession task described earlier, motivic chaining. That is, scores on the motivic synthesis task were correlated with scores on the pitch discrimination task ($r = .20$, $p < .05$) and among 5-, 6-, and 8-year-olds was correlated with conservation of number ($r = .25$, $p < .05$) and weight ($r = .36$, $p < .01$), with age controlled in all cases through partial correlation. The correlation with pitch discrimination may indicate that motivic synthesis, like textural abstraction, requires an especially analytic form of aural perception. The motivic synthesis task was not correlated with scores on the Draw-a-Person task (either raw or normed) or with years of musical training, with age controlled.

Gender differences (among children only) were tested in an analysis of variance in motivic synthesis total scores by age group and gender. The factor of gender was not significant, $F(1, 67) = .13$, and there was no significant grade-by-gender interaction, $F(4, 67) = 2.16$.

Conclusion. The principal conclusion is that the present task gave rise to somewhat better performances on the part of the subjects, where the understanding of two simultaneous melodic motives was required. Whereas the previous task on textural abstraction showed that the processing of simultaneities did not seem to develop much before age 10, the present task showed that at least half the 8-year-olds could perform quite well with shorter motives and an alternative task. The majority of younger children, however, continued to demonstrate a weak understanding of the relation between two simultaneous motives. In addition, there was a severe decrement in performance among 11-year-olds.

The most important question at hand is whether the processing of simultaneous events—in this case melodic events—was truly problematic for young children or whether, on the contrary, it was not simultaneity as such but rather task demands and weak memory for the melodies that led to poor performance. To address this question a task similar to the present one was used in the following experiment, except that isolated timbral sounds, instead of melodies or motives, were used as stimuli. Such a task may be assumed to involve the simplest of all possible simultaneous combinations and might be expected to result in improved performance on the part of younger children.

Experiment: Timbre Synthesis

In its nontechnical sense the term *timbre* refers to the distinctive color of a sound. A trumpet and a violin sound different because their respective timbres are different, even though they may be producing tones at the same pitch and level of loudness. Similarly, two familiar voices are distinguishable, even when identical in pitch and loudness, by virtue of their special timbre. The present task concerns the child's perception of simultaneous combinations of timbres, a commonplace activity, of course, whenever a piece of music involves two or more instruments.

The previous tasks on simultaneity concerned multiple melodies, which may have been difficult to distinguish because they were identical in timbre (piano) and similar in loudness, register (pitch range), and rhythmic character. Thus, insofar as the present task involves, instead, different timbres unconfounded by similar melodic and rhythmic characteristics, it may be considered the simplest and clearest case of simultaneous musical material. The task is analogous to the motivic synthesis task previously described in that the subject is presented with two sounds (A, then B) and is asked to determine whether, if combined simultaneously, they would yield a particular combination. The combinations tested are either same (A with B) or different (A with X or Z with B). The sounds in each case are different timbres produced by ordinary classroom instruments with which most children are familiar (maracas, bells, tomtom, etc.)

The version of the task for younger subjects (administered to 5-, 6-, and half of the 8-year-olds) had three parts: pretraining, the task proper, and a post-task confirmation of discriminability of component sounds. In the pretraining, the experimenter and subject were seated on opposite sides of a table, and each had before him an identical array of instruments: maracas, castanets, bells, jingles, tomtom, wood block, and finger cymbals. The experimenter introduced a "game" in which she played the part of "the teacher" and the subject was to imitate her instrumental performances, that is, to "play a sound that sounds just like this." The experimenter simply played a single sound (e.g., shook the maracas) and allowed the child to imitate. The same was repeated until the child was familiar with all the instruments. The experimenter then played two instruments *in succession* (e.g., maracas, then jingles, one in each hand), and the child's task was to play *both simultaneously*. The general instructions were: "Here's one sound——. And here's another sound——. Now you play both together at the same time." After each of several imitative performances the experimenter asked, "Did you play it right?" and confirmed "Yes, you played it right."

At this point the experimenter concealed her instruments from the child's view with a small screen ("This will make it harder, so listen carefully"), and the game continued with the child always performing *simultaneously* what the experimenter had presented *successively*: wood block with tomtom (or maracas or jingles); tomtom with bells (or maracas); maracas with bells (or castanets). If the child failed to perform any combination correctly, the experimenter reverted to single sounds (still concealed by the screen) and then returned to combinations. All children correctly performed these simultaneous combinations even when the experimenter's instruments were not visible. The correctness of each performance was questioned and confirmed, as before.

The task proper followed immediately. The child's set of instruments was removed, and the experimenter told a story about a teacher and a girl or boy (same sex as subject), represented by dolls, who were playing the identical game that the experimenter and subject had just engaged in. The teacher-doll played "first one sound and then another sound" and the child-doll tried to play "both sounds together at the same time." The subject's task was to tell whether the girl (or boy) in the story "did it right."

All sounds were performed live by the experimenter with instruments concealed by the screen. Items consisted of the seven pairs of sounds listed above for the subject's imitation of the experimenter. Both same (A with B) and different (A with X; Z with B) items were given, and in the different items only one of the sounds was different (i.e., tomtom replaced castanets or wood block; castanets replaced tomtom).

However, not all seven items were exhaustively administered. Rather, the experimenter administered only as many same and different items (a minimum total of four) as were necessary to determine whether the child possessed the ability to identify simultaneous combinations and could be categorized as having passed the task. Children who incorrectly answered more than two successive items were immediately given an optional post-task sequence to confirm their ability to discriminate the component sounds. That is, among children who failed items on the task, the possibility had to be ruled out that failure was due to a perceptual or memory problem for the individual components (A and B) rather than to a difficulty more closely allied with the understanding of simultaneity. Thus, children who failed task items were given a diversion in the story line in which the teacher-doll asks the child-doll to imitatively perform only *one* sound (one instrument) at a time. The subject's task, as before, was to tell whether the child-doll "did it right." Correct responses indicated that the subject had adequate perception and memory for individual sounds, A and B.

But it was also necessary to determine whether children who failed the task had had adequate perception and memory for simultaneous combinations (AB, AX, or ZB) or whether their failure was due to an inability to discriminate these combinations. Thus, the diverted story line continued with the teacher-doll asking the child-doll to "play these two sounds together exactly like this." Again the subject determined whether the child-doll "did it right."

If the subject correctly answered these post-task confirmations, then the original task—where two successive sounds were compared against a simultaneous combination—was resumed. The experimenter proceeded in this way, alternating between the task itself and confirmations of the discriminability of component sounds, until three scores were arrived at (the latter two were contingent upon a "fail" as the first score): (1) Pass or fail timbre synthesis: Does A + B = AB? AX? ZB? (2) Pass or fail discrimination of single sounds: Does A = A? A = X? (3) Pass or fail discrimination of combined sounds: Does AB = AB? AB = AX?

An alternative version of the task for older subjects (administered to half the 8-year-olds and all the 10-year-olds, 11-year-olds, and adults) similarly consisted of pretraining, the task proper, and a post-task confirmation sequence, but without the dolls and story. In the pretraining, the subject played each instrument and listened to its sound. In the task proper the subject was simply asked, "If I take this sound——, and this sound——, will they sound like this—— together?" In the confirmation sequence the subject was asked, "Is this sound—— (A or B or AB, etc.) the same as this sound——?"

Eight-year-olds were equally divided between versions of the task for younger and older subjects. Slightly more of them in the *older* version passed the task (89 percent) than did those in the younger version (63 percent), but the difference was not significant ($p > .20$, Fischer's exact probability test).

Results. The results are clearly shown in figure 4.15. All subjects at age 10 and above were successful on the task and could readily determine what two timbre sounds would sound like together, at least when the sounds are as disparate as those used here. Among 8-year-olds the rate of success was fairly high (77 percent) but among 5- and 6-year-olds success was limited to about half the subjects (44 percent and 60 percent respectively).

There were no gender differences in performance. Among 5-, 6-, and 8-year-olds, 57 percent of the boys passed and 66 percent of the girls passed, $\chi^2(1) = .09$.

Among children who failed the task, failure could not be due to problems in simple perception and memory. Indeed, 17 of the 19 children who failed the task were successful at discriminating both single and combined sounds in the post-task confirmation sequence. These children repeatedly discriminated same and different examples of what the dolls "played" in both the single (A = A? etc.) and combined (AB = AB?) cases. Yet even with the identical story, characters, and task question, they were unable to determine what two sounds given successively *would* sound like if played together. Their failure seems to have been tied to the process of imagining the simultaneity and not to a difficulty in task demands or simple perception and memory.

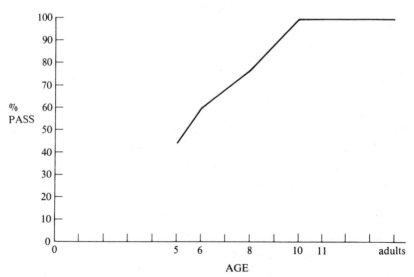

Figure 4.15. Timbre Synthesis: Percent Pass

These results are underscored by a separately published study (Serafine 1981) that investigated the identical phenomenon among an even younger sample of 38 preschoolers, ages 3, 4, and 5 (mean age 4;3). As expected, the rate of success on the task for these children (29 percent) was lower than that for the 5- and 6-year-olds in the present sample (44 percent and 60 percent respectively). Further, while the failure of nearly all the 5- and 6-year-olds in the present sample could *not* be attributed to poor discrimination of single and combined sounds, this was not the case for the younger sample of preschoolers. Rather, among the 27 of them who failed, half (14) did so at least in part because of an inability to answer correctly on those items that required comparison of single or combined sounds. Whether this inability stemmed from inadequate discrimination of the stimuli or simply from misunderstanding or inattention to the task is unknown. The other half of the sample (13) had adequate perception and memory for component sounds but still failed the simultaneity task.

Thus, the discrimination of simple and combined sounds appears to be a necessary but not sufficient condition for the process of mentally combining sounds simultaneously. In the present sample the process was fully accessible to most children at age 8 and above, but was inaccessible to roughly half the children at ages 5 and 6.

Summary

Multiple and simultaneous sequences of events are particularly common in Western music, where the prototypical cases are polyphonic and melody-with-accompaniment textures. In a task that required subjects to abstract from the ongoing stream of events the multiple and simultaneous parts of textures, adults performed very well and were able to identify up to three specific parts. The oldest children, at age 11, although they were not able to identify the specific parts, were nevertheless able to indicate the correct *number* of parts in the texture. Below this age, children performed poorly on the task and often erroneously underestimated the number of parts presented. Young children made a special error—misreading the rhythmic activity of polyphonic textures as a greater number of parts—which is evidence for their emerging sensitivity to the simultaneous dimension in music.

Still, young children were not successful on the motivic synthesis task, which required attention to only two simultaneous melodies. In a follow-up task that used perhaps the simplest and clearest case of simultaneity—a pair of disparate timbres—children below the age of 8 continued to have difficulty with the very idea of simultaneity. Most importantly, simple perception and memory for the individual sounds does not appear to be a sufficient condition for the process of imagining and predicting what a simultaneous combination will sound like.

CHAPTER 5

The Development of Nontemporal Processes in the Child

The temporal processes described in the previous chapter concern relationships among events, specifically the relationships of before, after, and at the same time. It might be expected that these temporal processes are more obvious and easier to grasp than are the nontemporal processes described here—namely, closure, transformation, abstraction, and hierarchic levels—because the latter seem to involve abstract, formal features more characteristic of whole pieces of music than of the relationship between two concrete events. Nevertheless, we shall see that children did better than might be expected on tasks that measure these nontemporal processes.

TONAL CLOSURE: UNDERSTANDING ENDEDNESS

In an earlier chapter I described closure as a generic cognitive process in which pieces, phrases, or fragments were brought to varying degrees of endedness. The particular brands of closure that may be employed are, however, a matter of culture and style, and in the present case we are interested only in that form of closure that is (like idiomatic construction) associated with the Western tonal idiom. That is, in the experiment on closure reported here, closure is defined as a return to tonic: a tonic/ leading tone/tonic sequence in the case of a melodic line or a dominant-tonic harmonic progression in the case of more complex textures. We may expect that, again like idiomatic construction, the understanding of tonal closure would be more sensitive to the influences of exposure and training in the tonal idiom than would some of the other cognitive processes that are not assumed to be tied directly to a stylistic idiom.

Experiment: Closure

The closure task consisted of four items. For each item subjects heard two fragments alternately repeated three times, and the subject's task was to tell which fragment was "finished." Subjects could change their answers in light of repeated hearings. The task was given to approximately 15 children each at age levels 5, 6, 8, 10, and 11 years (the same sample used in the simultaneity experiments but different from those used in the succession experiments) and 15 adults (the same as those used previously). Younger children (the 5- and 6-year-olds plus half the 8-year-olds) were given a version of the task in which they heard a story about two dolls, each of which could "play a song." One of the dolls finished her song, the other did not, and the child's task was to tell which one finished. Older subjects (half the 8-year-olds, plus the 10- and 11-year-olds and adults) were simply told that they would hear one finished and one unfinished piece of music, and they were to identify the finished one. As in the other tasks, subjects heard the stimuli played over loudspeakers. In the version for younger subjects the experimenter pointed to the doll that was "playing."

Eight-year-olds were equally divided between the younger and older versions. Although we expected that the younger version might provide an advantage, there was no significant difference between the mean total score (for four items) of those who received the younger version (2.00) and those who received the older version (2.56), t(14) = .78. Standard deviations in both subgroups were identical (1.4).

The four items (open cadences are unfinished, closed are finished) are shown in example 5.1. As will become clear, the initial strategy of presenting subjects first with a simple, one-line melody (item 1) so that they could grasp the idea before going on to the more complex harmonic items (items 2, 3, and 4) turned out to be wholly misguided. In fact, subjects did better on the musically sophisticated, harmonically complex, and often rhythmically busy items (2, 3, 4) than they did on the single-line melody (item 1). Although it is possible that this was an order effect (task performance may be poor at the start and improve with practice), this hypothesis is at least partly mitigated by the fact that the last three items do not show a general improvement over the course of the task. An alternative hypothesis is that closure in simple, melodic contexts is more difficult than closure in more complex, harmonic contexts because fewer cues and less information are provided in the simpler stimuli.

To adult ears, there can be little question about which of any pair of phrases should sound finished. In item 1 the open phrase ends unconventionally on the supertonic (scale degree 2), while the closed phrase ends conventionally on the tonic preceded by the leading tone. In the remaining items the closed phrases end with unavoidable finality on the tonic preceded by dominant harmony, while the open phrases in all cases do end on a conventional rhythmic unit (that is, some chord of sufficient duration approached in a musically natural way), but the final harmony is not the tonic or tonic-substitute. In item 2 the open phrase ends on a II chord, in item 3 on a diminished seventh chord built on the leading

Example 5.1

Example 5.1 (continued)

tone (extremely unfinished), and in item 4, which contains a pair of two-part contrapuntal phrases, the open one ends with dominant harmony generating an unresolved leading tone in the soprano voice.

In spite of the obviousness with which the phrases in question are open or closed, only adults consistently identified the closed phrases as finished. Young children, responding close to chance, did not answer consistently one way or the other. When age groups are collapsed the mean number of correct responses (on four items) is 2.5 for younger children (ages 5, 6, and 8), 3.2 for older children (ages 10 and 11), and 3.9 for adults. The mean for younger children is significantly lower than those for the other two groups, $F(2, 84) = 12.3$, $p < .05$, Scheffé test. Figure 5.1 shows the percentage of correct responses given by each age group on each item.

Two results are apparent in this graph. First, item 1, closure in a single line melody, appears to be the most difficult of the four items. I return to this point shortly. Second, 5-year-olds appear to perform more correctly on items 2 and 4 than on items 1 and 3. A subsequent analysis revealed that this was probably due to a response bias among 5-year-olds such that they identified as finished whichever doll "played" first. In the present task, closed phrases were heard as the first of the pair on items 2 and 4, and as the second of the pair on items 1 and 3. Across all items, 5-year-olds identified as finished whichever was the first stimulus 66 percent of the time, which is significantly greater than the 50 percent expected by chance ($p < .008$, Binomial Test). Also, although an individual

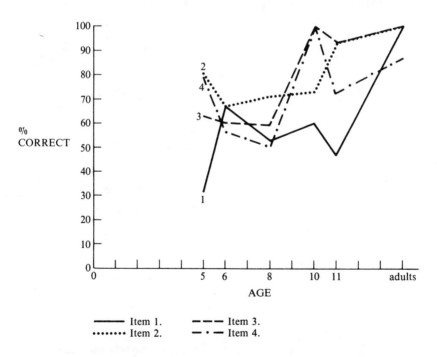

Figure 5.1. Closure: Percentage of Correct Responses

subject can be expected to make a total of two choices for the first stimulus (whether answering by chance or correctly), 70 percent of the 5-year-olds made *more* than two (out of four) choices for the first stimulus, and only about 13 percent gave *fewer* than two choices for the first stimulus. This difference is significant (p < .01). No other age group was subject to this bias; among 6-, 8-, 10-, and 11-year-olds and adults, subjects chose the first stimulus about 50 percent of the time as expected (range: 47 percent to 56 percent).

Returning to the question of closure in single-line melodies and harmonic contexts, figure 5.2 shows the overall percentage of correct responses at each age level separately for item 1 (melodic) and items 2, 3, and 4 combined (the harmonic items). Results for 5-year-olds are undoubtedly due to their response bias and are not valid. Results for younger children (ages 6 and 8) show performance at about chance on both the melodic item and the three harmonic items. Among older children (ages 10 and 11), however, closure responses on the harmonic items are correct nearly 100 percent of the time, while responses to the melodic item remain

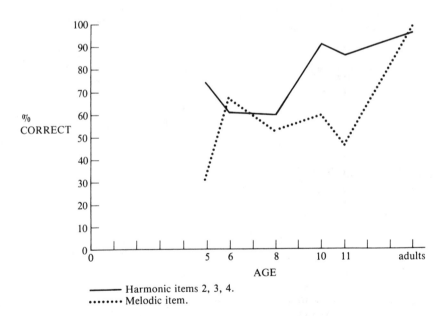

— Harmonic items 2, 3, 4.
•••••• Melodic item.

Figure 5.2. Closure: Percentage of Correct Responses on Three Harmonic Items and One Melodic Item

at chance. Adults are correct virtually 100 percent of the time on both types of items. As has been the case in other tasks, the "sixth-grade slump" appears here to some extent. There is a slight drop from 10-year-olds' 91 percent correct responses to 11-year-olds' 86 percent correct on harmonic items (see figure 5.1 where two of three such items show decline) and a more substantial drop from 10-year-olds' 60 percent correct responses to 11-year-olds' 47 percent correct on the melodic item.

A general age trend can be articulated by defining the understanding of closure as three out of four items correct on the task. By this criterion, half the younger children (ages 6 and 8), 80 percent of the older children (ages 10 and 11), and all of the adults can be said to possess an understanding of tonal closure. Thus, the ability may be firmly developed in most children by the age of 10, although closure in melodic contexts may lag behind closure in more complex harmonic contexts.

Subjects who understand tonal closure are often able to articulate their intuitions about why one phrase is finished and the other is not. Their answers to the question, "how do you decide which one is finished?" fell roughly into two categories: those that indicate attention to the tonic and feeling of endedness in the closed phrases and those that indicate attention to the feeling of incompleteness in the open phrases. For example, 10- and 11-year-olds who achieved criterion on the task referred to tonic finality in these explanations:

"Finished ones go all the way down to the bottom note."

"Unfinished cut off on a note. Finished has a low note at the end."

"It sounds like an ending."

Other 10-, 11-, and even some 8-year-olds who succeeded on the task referred to open-endedness:

"It just stops."

"I decide which ones have the trailing note."

"It cuts off when it needs to be going."

"Because it just stops and dies."

"If it's in the middle of the song, then they cut it."

"You can tell if it's going really fast and then stops when it needs to go on."

Rarely did older children give illogical explanations such as the 11-year-old who answered all items correctly and claimed to know because "it sounds like music from *The Champ*."

By contrast, younger children (ages 5, 6, and 8) usually gave explanations that indicated erroneous methods of determining closure that were, in addition, unrelated to the subject's own judgment. What the explanations—and the children's readiness with them—do indicate is that young subjects were attentive to the task and understood its aim. One 5-year-old, as he selected the open (and wrong) phrase said, "This is it because it's more like the end of a song." All the explanations given referred exclusively to musical or metacognitive factors ("I know because I guess") rather than to irrelevant matters, with one 5-year-old exception: "That doll is finished because she needs to rush to work to get money." The most common of the faulty but musical explanations among younger children involved the length or tempo of the phrase. Six young children said they chose whichever was longer; as many said whichever was shorter, one said whichever was faster; but in all cases the reference did not correspond to the child's own judgment, and performance on the task was below criterion.

Five- and 6-year-olds who had a solid understanding of closure were few, but their explanations were either right on target ("I know because the end note is the bottom of the scale") or they declined to elaborate rather than weave a story. One 6-year-old explained, "I just hear it. I can tell," and a 5-year-old, when asked how she happened to answer all items correctly, said simply, "I don't know, but it's easy." These explanations leave little doubt that the children who scored well on the task knew what they were doing and that those who scored poorly nevertheless understood the aim of the task.

Relationship to other variables. The correlation between total closure score and years of musical training, although low, was significant even when age was controlled through partial correlation ($r = .21$, $p < .05$ among children only). We return to the question of the influence of training in a comparison of the present sample with subjects who were undergoing training with the Suzuki method.

There was no correlation between scores on the closure task and scores on the pitch discrimination task ($r = .04$), although it will be recalled that pitch discrimination was significantly correlated with musical training (see chapter 4). In a later section I will argue for the interpretation that skill in discrete pitch discrimination, while it may be one of the consequences of musical training, is not central to music cognition.

With regard to the developmental variables under consideration, success on the closure task was modestly related to raw scores on the Draw-a-Person task even with age controlled through partial correlation (r = .23, p < .03, among children only). Further, success on the closure task was significantly correlated with conservation ability *among the "middle" group of 8-year-olds only* (r = .63, p < .005). Among younger children there was no correlation since there was little variation in either conservation score or closure score or both. (Older children were not given conservation tasks and can all be assumed to be conservers.)

There were no significant gender differences in performance on the closure task in any age group. The overall means for boys (n = 36) and girls (n = 36) were 2.9 and 2.7 respectively for the four-item task.

Comparison to Suzuki subjects. We turn now to a comparison of task performance by the typical or "normal" children described thus far with that of early and/or intensively trained children who have studied violin under the Suzuki method ("Suzuki subjects"). Our task is made difficult by the small numbers of the latter subjects in each age group: The 34 children range in age from 4 to 11. There are only 3 8-year-olds, no 9-year-olds, and 4 11-year-olds, and there are 5 or 6 subjects at each of the remaining age levels.

Figure 5.3 shows the percentage of correct responses given by Suzuki subjects at each age level on item 1 (melodic closure) and on items 2, 3, and 4 combined (harmonic closure). Two results are of interest. First, there is no lag between melodic closure and harmonic closure among Suzuki subjects as there was in the typical or "normal" sample. In fact, 65 percent of the youngest Suzuki subjects (ages 4, 5, and 6) answered correctly on the melodic item and all subjects at age 7 and above answered it correctly. By contrast, subjects in the "normal" sample did not achieve a 100 percent success rate until adulthood and were only roughly at chance prior to that age. One possibility is that the Suzuki subjects' superior performance on this item is a result of their training on the violin, a single-line, melodic instrument. This hypothesis, however, was not borne out in a subsequent analysis of normal subjects who also studied melody-only instruments (brass, woodwinds, and strings) although, of course, their training was not as intensive.

A second result is that, across all items, Suzuki subjects were performing at or close to the 100 percent correct mark by the age of 8. By contrast, "normal" subjects did not reach this level of success until age 10, and even then did so only on harmonic items.

A further comparison may be made by identifying the number of subjects who can be said to possess an understanding of tonal closure, defined as answering correctly three out of four items on the task. Suzuki subjects appear to acquire the understanding earlier than "normal" subjects, but differences between the two groups begin to narrow later on. Among Suzuki subjects, 75 percent of the 6- and 7-year-olds achieved the criterion (and even a third of the 4- and 5-year-olds did so), while only 50 percent of the 6- and 8-year-olds in the normal sample did so. (But see below.) Further, all of the Suzuki subjects at age 8 and above achieved criterion, and although *all* of the normal subjects in an age group did not achieve this criterion under adulthood, the 10- and 11-year-olds in the normal sample had 80 percent of their numbers who did.

It is clear that on the closure task children with early and/or intensive Suzuki training generally have an advantage over the normal sample of

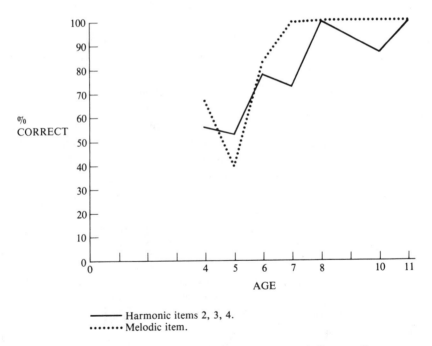

——— Harmonic items 2, 3, 4.
••••••• Melodic item.

Figure 5.3. Closure: Suzuki Subjects Percentage of Correct Responses on Three Harmonic Items and One Melodic Item

mixed trained and untrained children. But the more surprising result is that they do not come by this advantage easily. The analyses below, which compared Suzuki subjects separately against trained and untrained normal subjects, suggest that a considerable degree of training—and consequently age—may be required to effect this advantage and that its longevity may be limited. The small data set allows for only tentative conclusions, which are as follows:

(1) Suzuki subjects demonstrate significantly superior performance over *trained* normal subjects only at age 8 or older, when their training has reached a very advanced level.

(2) However, younger Suzuki subjects with only beginning or intermediate levels of training do not perform significantly better than even *untrained* normal subjects of approximately the same age.

I treat each of these conclusions in turn.

Consider a comparison of all 34 Suzuki subjects and the 35 normal subjects who had received three or more months of formal musical training (labeled "trained" subjects). Figure 5.4 shows the mean closure score (of four items) at each age level. Numerals in the graph indicate the number of subjects represented by that data point.

If the criterion for understanding closure is set at three out of four items correct, then all 12 (100 percent) of the Suzuki subjects at ages 8 to 11 met the criterion. By contrast, only 76 percent of the 29 normal, trained subjects at the same ages met the criterion. This difference in the proportion of subjects who understand closure is significant, so long as the age groups are collapsed to yield a sizable number of subjects (p = .069, Fisher's exact probability test). However, it is clear that the superior performance of Suzuki subjects is due to the wide differences at age 8, differences which appear to narrow later on. Even with very small numbers of subjects, the differences at age 8 begin to approach significance (p = .119, Fisher's test), while the differences at ages 10 and 11 are not significant (p = .31, Fisher's test).[1]

The critical factor here appears to be that 10 of the 12 Suzuki subjects in question (at ages 8, 10, and 11) are at an advanced level of musical ability. That is, they have studied sufficiently to play from memory 10 to

---

[1] Similar results are obtained even when subjects are compared only on the harmonic items (nos. 2, 3, and 4), on which the normal subjects performed better than on the melodic item (no. 1).

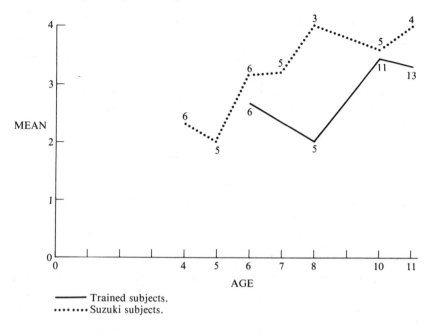

Figure 5.4. Closure: Mean Total Score for Trained Subjects and Suzuki Subjects

15 folk songs and 10 to 30 gavottes, minuets, and other classical pieces, plus one or more concerto movements. Also, 9 of the 12 have studied violin for one and a half to four years and 2 have studied more than four years. That is, 92 percent have somewhere between one and a half to more than four years of training. By contrast, among normal subjects only 45 percent have studied one and a half years or more, and none has studied more than four years. The rest have studied for only three to seventeen months.

In summary, Suzuki subjects do outperform trained, normal subjects, but they do so only at an age and level of training by which they have acquired a very advanced degree of musical skill. Further, it is possible that the difference between Suzuki and trained, normal subjects nevertheless evens out at the later ages.[2]

[2]The critical comparison that needs to be made is that between trained and untrained subjects at ages 10 and 11, but there were too few *untrained* 10- and 11-year-olds in the present sample.

Consider now a comparison involving the 20 Suzuki subjects who were not advanced—that is, the 10 who were at the beginning level (can play a theme and several variations from memory) and the 10 who were at the intermediate level (can play an additional 10 to 15 folk songs from memory). Figure 5.5 compares these subjects to the 37 subjects in the normal sample who had had *no training whatsoever*. (Numerals indicate numbers of subjects, and groups with n < 3 have been omitted from the graph but not from computations.)

The subjects in question are naturally at the younger age levels. The mean age of the Suzuki subjects is 6;5 (s.d. = 2 years; range = 4 to 11), which is not significantly younger than the mean age of 7;3 for normal subjects (s.d. = 2 years; range = 5 to 11), t(55) = 1.54.

It is clear that there was no significant difference between the two samples in performance on the closure task. Across all age groups, the percentage of subjects who met the 3 out of 4 criterion was 55 percent of

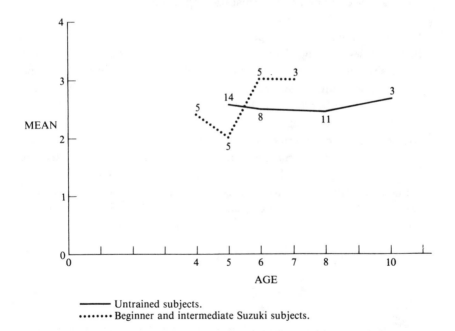

——— Untrained subjects.
••••••• Beginner and intermediate Suzuki subjects.

Figure 5.5. Closure: Mean Total Score for Untrained Subjects and Beginner/Intermediate Suzuki Subjects

the Suzuki subjects and 54 percent of the normal subjects.[3] Further, the mean for Suzuki subjects is 2.7 out of four items (s.d. = 1.1) and the mean for normal subjects is 2.5 (s.d. = 1.2). Moreover, even the means for beginner and intermediate Suzuki subjects are identical (2.7 in each case).

A reasonable interpretation of these and the previous results is that there may be two routes to the acquisition of understanding closure in music. One is to acquire it by late childhood (age 10 or 11) with the minimal amount of formal training common to middle-class children such as those in the present sample. (Perhaps—and in my opinion probably—it would also be acquired later with no training whatsoever.) The other route is to acquire it sooner, by middle childhood (about age 8), with the help of advanced training that has been in progress for a significant amount of time. It is unlikely, however, that most very young children (younger than age 6) would acquire the understanding of closure whether they have been undergoing formal training or not.

Summary. Tonal closure is perhaps the most obvious and ubiquitous of the processes mentioned thus far because, with due respect to modern compositional practice, the vast majority of pieces heard in the West end in the tonal-idiomatic way with a dominant-to-tonic cadence. Thus it is somewhat surprising that the tendency to select the idiomatic ending was not acquired until the age of 10 or 11. At the age of 5, for example, there was no evidence of selecting the idiomatic endings, although task variables inevitably present in a measure such as this one could have masked the ability. Moreover, even the ability to play an instrument was not, at the youngest ages, sufficient to improve task scores over those of *untrained* young children. Rather, only at an advanced level of training (and consequently at older ages) was an advantage for trained subjects seen.

---

[3]When the same comparison is made only for subjects at age 6 and older, 70 percent of the Suzuki subjects achieved criterion, and 48 percent of the untrained, normal subjects achieved criterion. This difference, however, is not significant with the numbers of subjects involved, $\chi^2(1) = 1.56$. In any case, of the 10 Suzuki subjects in question, 8 are at the intermediate level of musical ability and they are being compared to totally untrained subjects.

TRANSFORMATIONS: UNDERSTANDING
SIMILARITY AND DIFFERENCE

The previous sections, with the exception of that on closure, have concerned temporal operations performed on whole, unchanged musical fragments or motives. Much of our discussion has been aimed at fragments strung together (motivic chaining), alternated (patterning), or superimposed on one another simultaneously (motivic synthesis). By contrast the present section and the one that follows it concern the perception of motives that undergo internal change in important ways. For example, we here address the understanding of relationship between two motives when one is a transformation or variation of the other. That is, a motive has been transformed into a similar but different motive by virtue of changes imposed on the original—addition or deletion of tones, expansion, contraction, or inversion of intervals, and revision of harmonic accompaniment. Consider the pair of fragments shown in example 5.2, the original labeled "model" and a transformation of it below.

These two fragments sound undeniably similar, despite the fact that only a single tone occurs in identical positions in each of them (G on beat 1 of bar 2). Their similarity is only in small part due to the fact that they share the same rhythmic pattern which, in the absence of *tonal* similarity, would not be sufficient for them to sound particularly similar. Rather, these fragments sound similar because a relatively small set of specific and musically logical transformations governs the difference between them. One of these transformations is inversion of the broad interval traversed by the tonal movements in each case. For example, the broad outline of the original fragment is a descending fifth to the tonic (first note C to last note F), with passage through the supertonic G (beat 1, bar 2). The transformed fragment, on the other hand, broadly outlines the (tonal) inverse—an ascending fourth to the tonic (first note

Example 5.2

E-flat to last note A-flat), with passage through the leading tone G (beat 1, bar 2). Another and more local transformation is beat 2 of bar 1 in each fragment. Here the sixteenth-note figure maintains the dominant in each case (C or E-flat respectively) with brief ascent to the upper neighbor (D or F) and return. The original fragment uses a step-wise turn figure to accomplish this, however, while the transformed fragment uses interlocking thirds.

Despite such differences, the original form and its transformation sound similar and related. Indeed, we shall see that by the empirical criterion of near-unanimous adult judgment, this pair of melodies and others like it are heard as similar. The question of the present studies is the degree to which children understand a transformation to be similar to its original and hence not as new or unrelated material. Four tasks addressed this question so that the child's understanding could be tapped in a variety of ways.

The first was a matching task (called the Block Task) in which the subject was presented with a melodic fragment, a transformation of that fragment, and an unrelated piece of music. He was asked to find from among the latter two fragments the one that sounded most like the first one. The second task (the Echo Task) compared melody discrimination performance on two types of items: those consisting of new, unfamiliar music and those consisting of transformations of a melody with which the subject had previously become familiar. The assumption was that sensitivity to transformations could be measured by superior performance on the latter type of item. In an identification task (the Bead Task), the subject was first trained to identify each of two melodies as Type A or Type B and then was asked to identify *transformations* of those melodies as Type A or Type B. Finally, the fourth task (the Minuet Task) required the subject to identify occurrences of the Type A melody (from the previous task) as it underwent transformation over the course of a composition.

The subjects were approximately 15 children each at ages 5, 6, 8, 10, and 11 years plus 15 adults (the same subjects who participated in the experiments on simultaneity and closure). In addition, 34 Suzuki-trained children (described in the closure experiment) completed all but the Echo Task. The four tasks were administered consecutively in interviews lasting about twenty minutes.

Experiment 1: Block Task

In this matching task the subject was presented with three fragments of music (see example 5.3): a melody labeled the model, a transformation of the model, and a foil that is unrelated to either. The subject's task was to determine which of the latter two sounded most like the original.

Items 1 and 2 contain transformations that are very similar to their models, involving as they do only transposition (a nonsubstantive change in key) and the addition of one or two tones at the end. Item 3 involves a transformation somewhat more abstract or distant from its model, since it contains an inversion of the melodic figure and the addition of a tone

Example 5.3

at the end. Item 4 (described earlier) is the item that contains the greatest number of alterations—transposition, changes in figuration, and inversion of the broad interval outlined by the melody. As we shall see, the expectation was not borne out that items 1 and 2 would be the easiest to answer correctly, followed by item 3, with item 4 the most difficult. Instead item 3, probably because of its use of an inverted melodic figure, was most difficult.

In order to make such a task accessible to children and to reduce memory demands as much as possible, the task allowed the subject to determine the number and sequence of hearings as he pleased. Three 2-inch wooden cubes (about the size of toy blocks) were arranged so that two of the blocks (X and Y) were set about three inches apart, and a third block (M) was placed equidistant from them about eight inches away. Each block, when lifted off the table, played a musical fragment. This was accomplished by a light-pressure switch installed in the base of each block and connected by an eighteen-inch wire to the remote jack of a tape recorder. When a block was lifted, the tape recorder was activated and a prerecorded musical fragment was heard. The model fragment was heard from block M and the transformation and foil were heard from blocks X and Y respectively (counterbalanced across trials). The subject's task was "to find from these two (X and Y) the one that sounds the most like that one (M)."[4]

Each block was necessarily connected to a different tape recorder (in view of the subject), each of which utilized a high-quality external speaker. Each tape recording contained three repetitions of a fragment, but if a subject so desired the experimenter would rewind the tape to permit additional hearings. An unlimited number of hearings was permitted, and subjects were encouraged to listen and compare as much as possible. We were impressed with how studious even the youngest children were in their approach to this task, although the youngest were also least cognizant of the bases for their choices. (Experimenter: "How do you decide which one to pick?" Six-year-old: "I listen to 'em.") But more than a handful of even the youngest children commented that "this is hard," and many more stared and thought and furrowed the brow in an attempt to hear it better. Two 5-year-olds were dismayed to discover that lifting two blocks at once did not make clearer the choice.

To ensure that younger children understood the task, preparatory training in advance of the task was given to 5-, 6-, and half the 8-year-olds. This consisted of a visual analogue to the task. Three toy animals (birds), two of them similar in appearance and one different, were placed before the child in an arrangement identical to the one to be used for the blocks. The child was asked "to find from those two birds the one that looks the most like that one, or could be that bird's brother, or is in the same family." All children chose the correct one. Then the birds were removed, the musical blocks were arranged, and the child was told that "sometimes things go together because they *sound* the same, not just because they *look* the same. These blocks all look the same, but they each have their own music. Listen to these and then find the one . . . etc." The task was

---

[4]Results from another task had already shown that even the youngest subjects could successfully match similar melodies when presented in this way. See description of practice item under *Abstraction*.

administered without this preparatory training to older subjects—the 10- and 11-year-olds and adults plus the remaining half of the 8-year-olds. There was no significant difference between the performance of 8-year-olds who received training (mean = 2.63 correct out of 4 trials) and those who received no training (mean = 2.78), t(15) = .33.

Results. The results can be phrased briefly as follows: Younger children—5-, 6-, and 8-year-olds—correctly matched the transformation with the model 62 percent of the time, while older children—10- and 11-year-olds—made the correct match 78 percent of the time. As expected, adults had a very high success rate, 95 percent. In addition, there was an increase in the proportion of subjects at each age level who could be said to possess an understanding of transformations as measured by this task. Using the criterion of 3 out of 4 items correct, 44 percent of the 5-year-olds, 64 percent of the 6-year-olds, 59 percent of the 8-year-olds, and 80 percent of the 10-year-olds understood the transformations presented. As in some of the tasks described earlier, the "sixth-grade slump" was in evidence here: only 67 percent of the 11-year-olds meet the criterion. If a more stringent criterion of *all four items correct* is used, only 6 percent of the 5-year-olds, about 20 percent of the 6- and 8-year-olds, and 60 percent of the 10-year-olds meet the criterion. Eleven-year-olds perform at the same level as 6- and 8-year-olds. Using this criterion, 80 percent of adults pass the task, and using the more lenient criterion all of them do.

The following list gives the mean total score (of four items) and the standard deviation for ages 5, 6, 8, 10, and 11 and adults respectively: 2.1 (1.1); 2.7 (1.0); 2.6 (.9); 3.4 (.8); 2.9 (.7); 3.8 (.4). An analysis of variance showed a significant effect of age, $F(5, 86) = 7.25$, p < .01, and post hoc tests (modified LSD at .05) indicated significant differences between adults and the three youngest groups and also between 5- and 10-year-olds.

Two of the above results are worth underscoring at this point. The first is the validity of what we have called the sixth-grade slump. The lower mean in the 11-year-old group cannot be attributed to a handful of subjects who performed poorly, since this group had the lowest standard deviation of all the children's groups. Rather, *many* 11-year-olds performed worse than expected, and they did so while spending *more* time than other groups on repeated hearings of the fragments. As a group, 11-

year-olds listened to the blocks more than any other group except 8-year-olds, who listened the same amount (see below).

Second, it is worth noting that subjects tended either to answer at chance (randomly choosing the transformation and foil on successive items), or they were relatively consistent about choosing the transformation. They did not consistently choose the foil. Only one of the 92 subjects (a 5-year-old) chose the foil on all four items, and only an additional 8 subjects (age 8 and below) chose the foil three times. Across the whole sample, 22 percent of the subjects answered at chance (choosing transformation and foil twice each), 69 percent chose the transformation three or four times and only 10 percent chose the foil three or four times.

The four items did not generate the same patterns of response, however. Item 3 generated fewer transformation choices than did any of the other items. Figure 5.6 shows the percentage of correct responses (transformation choices) on item 3 and on items 1, 2, and 4 combined.

The most probable reason for subjects' greater difficulty on item 3 is

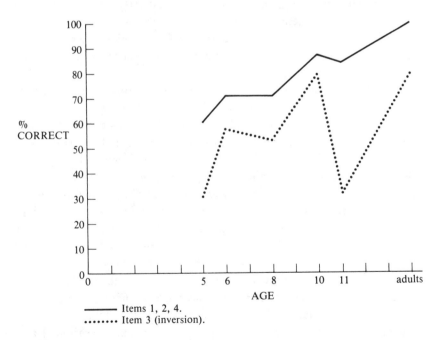

Figure 5.6. Transformations—Block Task: Percentage of Correct Responses

that it is the only transformation to utilize an inverted melodic figure (see example 5.2). Each interval is turned upside-down, as it were; the model contains a descending stepwise figure followed by an upward leap of a fifth, while the transformation contains the inverse: an ascending stepwise figure followed by a descending leap of a fifth. Despite the fact that the model and transformation are in the same key (indeed, they use identical tones), subjects had sufficient difficulty discerning the similarity that they frequently chose the unrelated foil. The inverted melodic figure in item 3 is a more abstract transformation than those utilized in the other items. Items 1 and 2, it will be recalled, use only transposition and the addition of one or two tones at the end. These are minimal changes that leave a transformed melody rather similar to its original. Item 4, although expected to be more difficult, does involve changes that preserve the underlying tonal movement.

Although item 3 contains a more abstract transformation than the other times, 80 percent of the 10-year-olds and adults correctly matched the transformation to its original. On the other hand, 11-year-olds performed very poorly on this item, choosing the transformation only 33 percent of the time, which is roughly the success rate of 5-year-olds. We return later to this phenomenon of the "sixth-grade slump," especially on tasks involving more abstract musical stimuli.

It is obviously of interest how many repeated hearings children gave to the melodies, and whether an increased number of hearings was predictive of success on the task. Generally, older subjects listened more than younger ones, but this fact alone does not account for their greater success. Five- and 6-year-olds listened to each melody only slightly more than once, a mean of 1.3 and 1.4 respectively for each melody. Their success on the task with so few hearings is impressive. Eight- and 11-year-olds listened more than any other group, with a mean of 1.8 hearings per melody, which is significantly more than the 5-year-olds, $F(5,85) = 4.43$, $p < .002$, modified LSD at .05. Ten-year-olds and adults listened to each melody a mean of 1.6 and 1.5 times respectively, before making their choices. In spite of the fact that older children tended to listen more than did younger ones, the number of hearings was not significantly correlated with total task score, $r = .14$, $p > .10$ (for children only). A separate test for the youngest two age groups (5- and 6-year-olds) also showed no correlation between repeated hearings and task success, $r = .16$, $p > .20$.

With regard to relationships between task performance and other variables, there was no correlation between total task score and either the pitch discrimination task (p > .18) or years of musical training (p > .17) when the effects of age were partialled out (for correlations among children only). Likewise conservation of number (p > .12) and weight (p > .28) were not significantly correlated with task score (among subjects in the three youngest age groups) when the effects of age were controlled. Zero order correlations between total task score and all the above variables were positive and significant with the exception of pitch discrimination.

An analysis of variance in children's total scores by gender and age level revealed no significant differences between boys and girls and no significant interaction with age group.

Summary. The Block Task required the subject to match a melodic fragment with its transformation instead of with another, unrelated fragment. Roughly half of the younger children (5- and 6-year-olds), about three-fourths of the older children (10- and 11-year-olds), and all of the adults gave evidence of understanding the similarity inherent in the transformations used in this task. Although the task was designed to eliminate irrelevant memory and task demands as much as possible, younger children's understanding of transformations may have been underestimated here. For the subject must make the relevant comparisons systematically (model M with X and Y) and must remember the result of each comparison in addition to remembering each fragment as it is compared to another. Although an unlimited number of hearings was allowed, a subject would have had to be cognizant of the veracity of his own memory in order to take advantage of repeated hearings. Since young children can be expected to be weaker in these metacognitive and memory skills, the following task attempted to measure the understanding of transformations in a more indirect way.

Experiment II: Echo Task

In this task the experimenter first made the subject familiar with the short melodic fragment shown in example 5.4. The subject was asked to listen to the fragment five times, to sing it aloud or "hum it in your head," and to assure himself that it was the identical melody each time (as, of course, it was). Immediately following this the subject was given an eight-item discrimination task in which he was asked to tell whether pairs of melodic fragments were the same or different. Half the items were transformations of the above familiar melody, and half were new, unrelated material. We assumed that if subjects were sensitive to the similarly inherent in transformations, they would perform better on the former than on the latter type of items.

For younger children (5-, 6-, and half the 8-year-olds) the discrimination task was phrased in terms of the accuracy of a fictitious "echo machine" ("Did the machine play *exactly* the same music?"). Older subjects (the remaining 8-year-olds plus 10- and 11-year-olds and adults) were simply asked whether the fragments were the same or different. The sounds emanated simultaneously from two small audio speakers (approximately 5 by 8 inches) facing each other about twelve inches apart. The one on the right was designated the "echo machine," and the experimenter simply pointed to the left speaker and then to the "echo machine" (right speaker) in turn. As in earlier tasks that used this technique, subjects seemed to have no problem with the illusion of left and right sound sources, although the sounds were not so located spatially.

Example 5.5 shows the items used in the task. Both standard and comparison melodies are shown only for items in which the comparison is different (items 1, 3, 6, and 8). If the comparison is same, only the standard is shown (items 2, 4, 5, and 7).

Different comparisons were generated in each case by interchanging the two medial tones of the standard melody. Each standard melody was tested against both same and different comparisons. Thus, items 4 and 1, 2 and 6, 7 and 3, and 5 and 8 entail same and different comparisons of their respective standard melodies. In addition, half the items on the task involved transformations of the melody with which the subject was familiarized just prior to the task. These transformations appear in items 1 and 4 and items 5 and 8, each pair of items representing a different transformation of the original melody. For example, items 4 and 1 represent a close transformation (similar to the original) insofar as it involves

Example 5.4

Model

changes of interval and key, but no inversions. By contrast, items 5 and 8 are more distant (dissimilar to the original) in that the transformation involves both inversion and expansion of interval size in addition to the insertion of an extra tone. The remaining items (2 and 6, 3 and 7) involve new material unrelated to the familiar melody.

Results. Correct discriminations were scored "1"; incorrect responses were scored zero. Figure 5.7 shows the means, ranging from 0 to 2, for each pair of items that share the same standard. (Transformation items involve variants of the familiar material; new items involve new material.) It is clear that discrimination performance on the *close* transformation items (1 and 4) was superior to that on other items, at every age level

Example 5.5

except among adults, where all discriminations were excellent. By contrast, discrimination performance on the distant transformation items (5 and 8) was no better than it was for new unrelated material (Items 2 and 6; 3 and 7).[5]

These results indicate that children generally showed sensitivity to a transformation, but only in the case of a transformation that is quite similar to the original. This is true for older children more than for younger ones. When each child's performance on the *close* transformation items (1 and 4) was compared to his mean score for the *new* items, the results were as follows. About a third of the youngest children (ages 5 and 6) found discrimination easier on the transformation than on the new-material items. For older children (8-, 10-, and 11-year-olds) the propor-

---

[5]Significant differences were found only among younger children (5-, 6-, and 8-year-olds), where the mean score on items 1 and 4 was significantly greater than the other means *except* that of new items 3 and 7, F(3,135) = 4.83, p < .01, Tukey's HSD at .05. Among older children (ages 10 and 11) there was only a nonsignificant trend for the mean of items 1 and 4 to be higher than one or more of the others, F(3,87) = 2.36, p < .08. (A parenthetical point of interest is the fact that 11-year-olds, as in other tasks, did worse than 10-year-olds on three of the four pairs of items.)

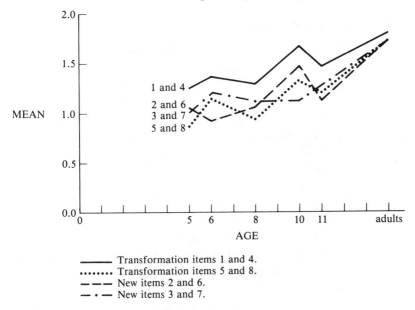

Figure 5.7. Transformations—Echo Task: Means for Transformation and New Items

tion was about 55 percent. (Only about 16 percent of all age groups found transformation items *more* difficult, and the remaining subjects scored equivalently on both types of items.)

Summary. The Echo Task did not reveal a higher proportion of subjects who understood transformations—among either younger or older children—than did the previous Block Task. While the Block Task involved the subject in direct matching of a melodic fragment and its transformation, the Echo Task was an attempt to measure sensitivity to transformations in a less direct way, requiring discrimination skill and minimal memory demands of a long-term sort. By contrast, the following task—called the Bead Task—made the opposite demands on the subject. Here the discrimination skill required was reduced to a minimum because the melodic fragments to be identified were maximally different. However, the long-term memory demands were considerable (especially for younger children), since two different melodies had to be remembered over the course of the task, about 5 minutes.

Experiment III: Bead Task

In this task the subject was first trained to discriminate between two very different melodies, labeled "red" and "green." He was then presented with several transformations of these melodies and was instructed to categorize these new ones as "red" or "green" even though they sounded "slightly different." The question at hand was whether the child would generalize the labels to the transformations or answer at chance, thus treating the transformations as new material.

The task was conducted as follows with only slight modification in instruction for younger and older subjects. The subject was presented with two piles of "beads" (actually round-top, flat-bottom game pieces), eight red ones and eight green ones. He was trained to associate the red and the green respectively with the fragments of music shown in example 5.6. The subject was then told that his task was to listen to a melody, decide whether it was red or green, and drop the appropriate bead into a box. Each subject passed a four-item pretest (two examples of each fragment). The task followed immediately and consisted of ten items, six of which were *transformations* of one of the original melodies (shown in example 5.7) and four of which were *repetitions* of the original melodies ("identity items" 1, 2, 5, and 8, not shown). The purpose of the latter items was to assess subjects' memory for the original melodies during the task. With regard to the transformations, the subject was told that "sometimes the music will sound a little bit different, but you still must choose the red or the green."

Results. Responses were scored 0 (incorrect) and 1 (correct). Table 5.1 shows the mean (range 0 to 6), standard deviation, and percentage of

Example 5.6

Example 5.7

subjects passing at each age level, for the 6 *transformation* items only. The pass criterion was a minimum of 5 out of 6 transformation items correct.

As expected, older subjects—ages 10, 11, and adults—did very well on this task. (Note, however, the sight decrement in performance among 11-year-olds.) Also as expected, subjects who performed well on the trans-

Table 5.1. Bead Task

Age Group	Mean	s.d.	Percent Pass
5-year-olds	2.4	1.4	6%
6-year-olds	4.3	1.4	36%
8-year-olds	4.8	1.3	59%
10-year-olds	5.4	.9	73%
11-year-olds	5.1	1.3	73%
Adults	5.9	.4	100%

formation items also did well on the four identity items intended to measure memory for the original fragment. In fact, among these 45 older subjects (10- and 11-year-olds and adults), all but 4 (9 percent) performed with perfect accuracy on the identity items, and all but one answered at least three of the four identity items correctly.

The results were quite the opposite for the youngest subjects, at age 5. Approximately 94 percent of them failed to meet criterion on the transformation items. It is the performance of these youngest children to which we now turn.

One way to consider the data is to compare performance on identity items with performance on transformation items. Young children might be thought not to possess the concept of melodic transformation if their performance, even on *simple* transformations, is poorer than performance on identity items. For this analysis, item 10 was omitted because it is a more abstract transformation of the "red" melody than any of the others and including it in the total score would underestimate performance on simpler transformations. (In fact, item 10 was very difficult for 5-year-olds, only about one-third of whom answered it correctly. In contrast, about 65 percent to 85 percent of all other age groups answered it correctly.)

Figure 5.8 shows each age group's per item mean (ranging from 0 to 1) for the four identity items and five of the transformation items (excluding item 10). It is clear that the youngest children, at age 5, did more poorly on *transformation* items (mean correct per item, at .40, is below chance) than they did on *identity* items (at .73, better than chance). This difference in performance is significant, $t(15) = 4.64$, $p < .01$. Among 6-year-olds, the performance difference (.69 on transformations vs. .80 on identity items) showed a nonsignificant trend in the same direction, $t(13) = 1.44$, $p < .09$. However, in the older age groups, especially at

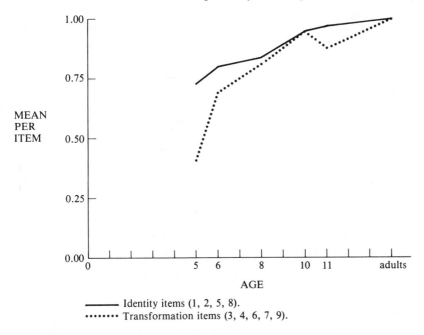

Figure 5.8. Transformations—Bead Task: Mean per Item

age 10 and above, performance on both types of items was roughly comparable and very good.

Another way of looking at the results is to identify subjects whose mean transformation score is *lower than* their mean identity score. Fully 81 percent of the 5-year-olds did more poorly on transformation than on identity items, while the same was true (with one exception) for a steadily decreasing proportion of subjects at each age level: 57 percent, 41 percent, 13 percent, 33 percent, and 0 percent respectively of 6-, 8-, 10-, and 11-year-olds and adults. The exception was the 11-year-old group, whose performance was more similar to that of 8-year-olds than to any other group. Here, as in other tasks, we have evidence of the characteristic performance decrement that we have termed the "sixth-grade-slump."

Although 5-year-olds were better able to identify the *original* melodies (identity items) than transformations, their performance on identity items was nevertheless far from optimal. Only about 73 percent of their responses to identity items were correct. This was confirmed in a follow-up study in which 9 additional 5-year-olds (mean age 5;5), drawn from another school, completed a ten-item task consisting only of *identity items* (no transformations). In this case 67 percent of all responses were correct (or mean correct per item was .67).

In summary, young children generally had difficulty with this task, probably because the demand of remembering and identifying the "red" and "green" melodies over several items was considerable. Still, their performance on transformations was worse than on the original melodies.[6] Older subjects, on the contrary, performed well on both types of items.

The fourth and final task, described below, made two changes in our measurement of the child's understanding of transformations. First, the subject identified transformations over the course of what can genuinely be called a piece of music, making this the most natural listening situation thus far. Second, transformations of only one melody (not two) were used, so that the demands on memory were somewhat reduced.

Experiment IV: Minuet Task

The aim of this task was to determine whether the child recognizes transformations of a familiar melody in its context—that is, in a real piece of music. The subject's task was to listen to a short piano piece and to identify eight occurrences of a target melody by raising his hand on each occurrence. The target melody was the "red bead" song from the immediately preceding task. The specific procedure was as follows: Immediately after the Bead Task the experimenter removed all the beads from the table except one red bead to provide a visual representation of the melody or "song" as it was termed with younger children. The subject was told to "listen for this song [pointing to the red bead] and raise your hand every time you hear it." Two practice trials followed in which the subject heard the target melody alone and raised his hand each time. The experimenter then explained the task: A long piece of music would be heard with the "red bead song hidden in the music." The subject would raise his hand whenever he heard it, even if "sometimes it may sound a little bit different." The subject was not told how many times the target melody would occur. The minuet shown in example 5.8, approximately one minute in duration, was then heard. Asterisks mark occurrences of the target melody.

---

[6]In the previous task, by contrast, their performance on transformations was better than on *new* material.

The first five occurrences of the target melody are tonally and rhythmically identical to the original, except that the underlying harmony is different in each case. In the first occurrence (bar 1) the C major tonic moves to the subdominant; in the second (bar 5) it moves to the dominant after passing through the submediant; and in the third (bar 10) the target melody begins on the dominant. The fourth occurrence (bar 13) also begins on the dominant (of C) but modulates to G major; hence in the next occurrence the target melody features G as the tonic. The remaining occurrences (bars 23, 25, and 28) differ not only in the underlying harmony, but they are melodic transformations corresponding to items 4, 7, and 10 respectively from the Bead Task. (See example 5.7.) Accordingly, the last of the eight occurrences is a difficult and abstract transformation.

It should be noted that the minuet was composed so that the target melody appears at irregular intervals; two, three, four, five, or seven bars

Example 5.8

of material intervene between one occurrence and the next. Thus, a response set on the part of the subject (i.e., automatically raising a hand at a fixed interval) would not result in a high score.

Results. Responses were scored by counting the number of correct and incorrect hand-raises during the piece ("hits" and "false alarms" respectively). Hand-raises that occurred at the onset of, during, or no later than one beat after the target melody were scored as correct. Hand-raises at any other points were incorrect.

The majority of subjects raised their hands at the onset of or during the first occurrence, indicating that they identified the target melody and understood the task. About 50 percent of the 5- and 6-year-olds, 65 percent of the 8-year-olds, and 93 percent of the 10- and 11-year-olds and adults raised their hands on this first occurrence. Performance over the rest of the piece, however, was not up to that standard. Figure 5.9 shows the mean number of correct (hits) and incorrect (false alarms) responses at each age level. It is clear that while older subjects did quite well (at

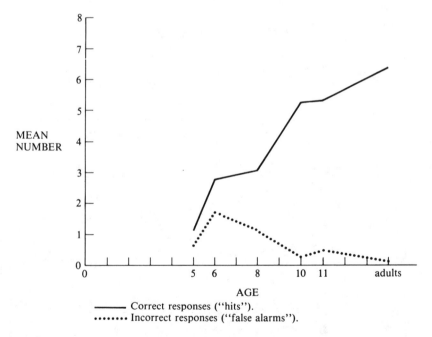

Correct responses ("hits").
.... Incorrect responses ("false alarms").

Figure 5.9. Transformations—Minuet Task: Mean Number of Correct and Incorrect Responses

age 10 and above they identified more than half of the eight target occurrences), younger children did surprisingly worse than might be expected. Five- and 6-year-olds identified only one to three of the target occurrences and their *incorrect* response rate was relatively high—about .6 and 1.7 respectively. It should be noted that too numerous and incorrect hand-raises were, on the whole, rare. Only 4 out of 92 subjects raised a hand 10 or more times, and none exceeded 13 times. (Recall that the target melody occurred eight times.) Across all subjects, only 15 percent of responses were (incorrect) false alarms, and these decreased with age.

Still, when hits were "corrected" by subtracting false alarms, the mean number of target occurrences identified (out of eight) was .5, 1.0, 1.9, 5.0, 4.9, and 6.3 respectively at ages 5, 6, 8, 10, and 11 years, and adults. This shows that, especially by comparison to the dramatic increase in task success at age 10, younger children performed poorly. Seven of the 30 5- and 6-year-olds did not raise a hand *at all*. (One 5-year-old: "I didn't hear it.") An additional 11 of them raised a hand only once, each scoring a hit.

These results were underscored when each subject's task performance was categorized as "pass" (four or more occurrences identified), "partial pass" (two or three occurrences identified), or "fail" (fewer than two identified). Table 5.2 shows the percentage of subjects at each age level who pass and fail; all others were categorized as partial pass. The dramatic increase in performance at age 10 is apparent, as is the lack of success among younger children. Note that there was a slight decrement in performance among 11-year-olds, as on some other tasks.

With regard to performance over the course of the piece, identifying occurrences of the target melody was relatively easy right at the start and more difficult at the middle and end. From 92 subjects there was a mean of 46 hand-raises per occurrence of the target melody. The first and sec-

Table 5.2. Minuet Task

Age Group	Percent Pass	Percent Fail
5-year-olds	7%	87%
6-year-olds	0%	50%
8-year-olds	29%	47%
10-year-olds	73%	7%
11-year-olds	60%	7%
Adults	93%	0%

ond occurrences generated the most hand-raises—68 and 53 respectively—while occurrences that came later and/or involved the melodic *and* harmonic transformations generated fewer: The third, sixth, and seventh occurrences yielded 37, 36, and 33 hand-raises respectively. The eighth and most abstract of the transformations might also have generated fewer responses, but many subjects seemed to raise a hand in the final measures as a last ditch effort to successfully comply with the task, especially if they had had few or no hand-raises up to that point. It is impossible, with this piece as the stimulus, to separate the effects of transformation type from those of location. It seems that both abstract and non-initial occurrences had the fewest responses, and that young children especially were susceptible to losing their way over the course of the piece. One 8-year-old said that the music was "all mixed up like bacon and eggs."

Conclusion and Comparison to Suzuki Subjects

Prior to conducting the experiments, we had anticipated that the understanding of transformations would be among the more difficult for children to acquire. Our expectation was that the temporal tasks, on succession and simultaneity, would generally develop earlier because they involved whole, unchanged melodic fragments acted upon in obvious ways: strung together, alternated in patterns, and so on. Transformations, on the other hand, seemed more difficult and abstract because they involved interior changes in the melody itself.

The expectation that transformations would be a late acquisition was not supported, however. On the Block Task, which required matching a transformation with its original, 44 percent of the 5-year-olds and about 60 percent of the 6- and 8-year-olds gave evidence of understanding the similarity inherent in transformations. Older children did even better, about 67 percent to 80 percent succeeding on the task.

What was difficult for young children, however, was remembering a melody and comparing it to new, incoming material over some period of time, even that required by a short task or piece of music. Thus, young children's performance was quite poor on the Bead Task, where transformations of two previously learned melodies (red and green) had to be compared to their remembered originals, and on the Minuet Task, where new material had to be scanned for the occurrence of a previously learned melody. In tasks such as these, which required substantial memory and comparison skill, we might expect that children intensively trained in the Suzuki method would outperform "normal" subjects (with traditional training or no training) because the Suzuki method involves rigorous musical memory training. Indeed, this expectation was supported, but principally at the younger age levels. Among older children the differences between Suzuki and "normal" subjects begin to even out.

Figure 5.10 shows the means for both groups on the Bead Task, where subjects had to identify six transformed fragments as red or green (thus means range from 0 to 6). Here and elsewhere the small data set from Suzuki subjects (34 across seven age groups) will not permit the traditional analyses, but some aspects of the results are instructive. Figure 5.10 shows that the greatest difference between the two groups was among the youngest children, where Suzuki-trained 4- and 5-year-olds achieved means of 3.2 (n = 6) and 4.6 (n = 5) respectively, while untrained 5-year-olds in the normal sample achieved a lower mean of 2.4.

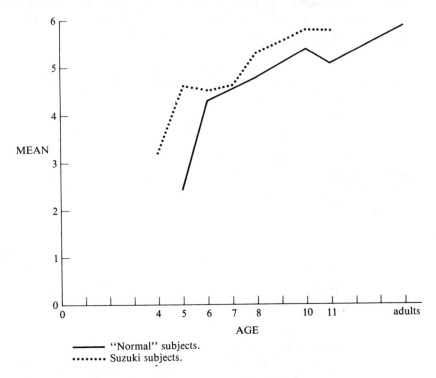

Figure 5.10. Transformations—Bead Task: Means

In a similar way, Suzuki-trained subjects outperformed their contemporaries on the Minuet Task, where occurrences of a target melody were identified. Here the greatest difference between the two groups was at the ages of 6 to 8, since even Suzuki-trained young children (ages 4 and 5) performed poorly on the task, and differences between the two groups seemed to even out at the older ages. Figure 5.11 shows the means for each group on the Minuet Task, where hits have been "corrected" by subtracting false alarms. The graph shows that Suzuki-trained subjects at the age of 6 or older performed about as well as adults.

Intensive training seems to have improved performance, then, on tasks with a substantial memory component. On the other hand, when memory demands are reduced, there are no significant differences between intensively trained and "normal" subjects. The Block Task, where subjects matched a transformation with its original, is a case in point. Here subjects did not have to retain a fragment as long as they did in the other tasks, and an unlimited number of hearings was permitted. Figure 5.12 shows the means (for four items) for each group. It is clear that performances among Suzuki and "normal" subjects were comparable.

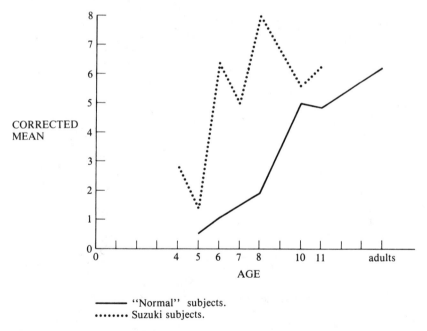

———— "Normal" subjects.
•••••••• Suzuki subjects.

Figure 5.11. Transformations—Minuet Task: Corrected Means

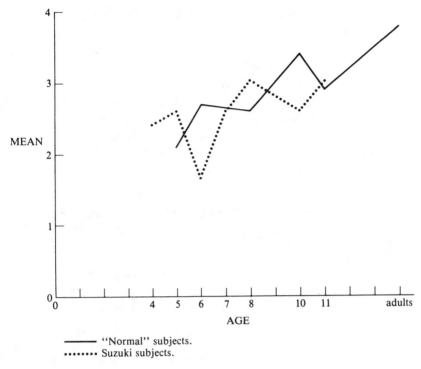

"——— "Normal" subjects.
•••••• Suzuki subjects.

Figure 5.12. Transformations—Block Task: Means

Summary

In summary, the Block Task has provided evidence that, at least to some degree, children understand the similarity inherent in transformations. In this sample the capacity was acquired by most children by the age of 10, by many at 8, and by some even at 5 or 6. The difficulty, however, is that the understanding of transformations may be masked or for all practical purposes rendered ineffective over the course of a composition by the memory skills that must be sustained over time in such a case. It is in the Minuet Task that we have the best evidence of the difference between responding to a task that involves only melodic fragments and responding to one that involves the sustained attention and memory demanded by a whole composition. Training, we have seen, appears to enhance the very memory skills that it takes to sustain attention to whole compositions. On the other hand, training does not appear to make the understanding of transformations itself develop any earlier than it otherwise does.

One question that arises with respect to children's understanding of transformations is the degree to which it may be based on recognition of rhythmic similarity between the original and its transformation, or recognition of some short, interior motive that may be identical in both melodies. I have termed the ability involved *abstraction*; for example, the subject may abstract from a melody the underlying rhythmic pattern and compare it to the rhythmic pattern of the transformation. The following experiments assessed children's ability to abstract in this way.

ABSTRACTION: RECOGNIZING PARTS IN NEW CONTEXTS

Abstraction refers to the ability to recognize some part of a larger unit when it occurs elsewhere in the composition in a new context. I here discuss two types: *motivic abstraction,* recognizing a motive (or part of a melody) when it occurs within an entirely different melody, and *rhythmic abstraction,* recognizing a rhythmic pattern when it occurs in a different melody.

In the experiments reported here, the subjects were approximately 15 children each at ages 5, 6, 8, 10, and 11 years, plus 22 adults. These are the same subjects who completed the tasks on succession described earlier, with the addition of 7 adults who completed only the present abstraction tasks.

Experiment: Motivic Abstraction

The experiment was identical to the Block Task described under Transformations. The subject was presented with three blocks: block M and, about eight inches away, blocks X and Y. Each one, when lifted from the table, played a phrase consisting of an accompanied melody. These were: (1) a phrase labeled the model, M; (2) a related theme (X), that is, a phrase containing a motive that also occurred in the model; and (3) a foil (Y) or phrase that did not contain such a motive and was unrelated to the model. The subject's task was to listen to the model, then select from the other two blocks the one that "goes with" or "sounds the most like" the model. The related theme and foil were counterbalanced across blocks X and Y on successive items. An unlimited number of repeated hearings was allowed. Younger subjects, as described earlier, received pretraining in the form of a visual analogue to the task utilizing toy animals.

A word on the construction of the related theme and foil. Although the original model and related theme did have a motive in common, subjects could, of course, match the two on many other characteristics that might be common between them.[7] Perceived key, contour, mode (major or minor), or general mood (e.g., dramatic or march-like) are a few of the obvious choices. There are two ways of circumventing this problem. One is to use as stimuli either randomly or formula generated tone sequences so that, at least theoretically, neither the related theme nor foil would be more similar to the original model on any grounds other than the common motive in the former. There could be no assurance, of course, that the related theme and foil were not unequally similar to the model. Any piece of music has a mood, no matter how it is generated, and leaving the generation of mood to chance is unlikely to be wholly satisfactory. We rejected this solution on the grounds that the additional drawback of having to use artificial and fundamentally nonmusical stimuli would not solve the problem.

A second route is to intentionally compose the related theme and foil so that they seem equally similar or dissimilar to the model on non-motivic dimensions. (Failing this, the foil could be more similar to the model and thus operate against the hypothesis of motivic matching; however, this would result in underestimating subjects' capacity for motivic abstraction.) This solution also has drawbacks because there are a finite number of factors that can consciously be composed, and elusive characteristics such as mood are not easy to measure and control. We nevertheless opted

[7]To test this assumption we administered two additional items to older subjects (after the initial items) and to as many younger subjects as maintained sufficient attention by that point. The items, not shown in notation here, were similar to the items described above in that an original model and related theme shared a common motive, and a foil did not. However, in one item, the related theme not only shared a motive with the original model but also the same meter (3/4) and a gentle, legato mood. The foil, on the other hand, had a sprightly, staccato mood, contained many skips, and was in 2/4. As expected, 87 percent of the subjects matched the related theme to the model, and even 88 percent of the 5- and 6-year-olds did so. This is a higher success rate than that obtained on any other item. By contrast, another item contained a model and a *foil* that shared the same key as well as the similarity of mood caused by the harmonic device of a Picardy Third at the end. The related theme was also in minor, contained the common motive, but had no Picardy Third. In this case, only 41 percent chose the related theme, which was the lowest success rate of any item. (These were mainly older subjects.)

for this solution and settled on the characteristics of key, mode, and mood as the ones to be controlled in the related theme and foil. Generally allowing for these controls, the principal consideration was creating a model and related theme which, while entirely different, could musically accommodate the same motive.

A total of seven items was used on the task but were not administered to all subjects. A practice item (see example 5.9) was given to all subjects, followed by the two items shown in example 5.10. Five-year-olds were then given two special items (shown in example 5.12) and following this

Example 5.9

as many subjects as were willing in *any* age group completed the two additional items mentioned in note 7. Finally, only older subjects were given the atonal item shown in example 5.11, which was always administered last.

The first item was a practice item intended to ascertain that subjects understood the task and could match similar phrases using the blocks. The model (in A-flat major) and "related theme" (in A minor) were identical except for key and mode (see example 5.9). Among 96 subjects, 90 percent correctly matched the "related theme" to the model. The success rate was 80 percent among 5- and 6-year-olds, 93 percent among 8-, 10-, and 11-year-olds, and 96 percent among adults. Thus, subjects understood the task before them.

Two additional items followed immediately and are shown in example 5.10. In the first item, all three phrases are in 3/4 meter and the major mode, and each is in a different key. Moods vary: the model has an oompah, waltz-like mood; the related theme has a smooth or legato triadic melody; the foil has a militaristic, almost march-like character. The model and related theme, however, share a common motive, the triadic figure of an ascending third followed by a descending fifth. This motive occurs only once in the model (bar 1) and twice in the related theme (bars 1 and 3).

In the second item, all three phrases are in 3/4 meter and the major mode. The related theme and foil are both in the same key (G), which is different from the model (C). Similarly, the related theme and foil are both delicate in mood and contrast equivalently with the dramatic quality of the model. The model and related theme, however, both contain the eight-note turn figure that occurs in bar 1 of the model and bars 1 and 2 of the related theme.

Both of the above items yielded comparable results. Five-, 6- and 8-year-olds answered roughly at chance, since they correctly matched the related theme to the model only 55 percent of the time. Ten-year-olds answered better than chance ($p < .05$), making the correct match 67 percent of the time. Eleven-year-olds and adults performed comparably and much better than chance ($p < .01$), with 84 percent correct responses. This is one of the few tasks in which the "sixth-grade slump" was not in evidence. In fact, 11-year-olds, with a success rate of 87 percent, outperformed all other groups. We shall see in the next experiment, however, that when the more abstract dimension of rhythm was used as the criterion for matching—in an otherwise identical task—a dramatic slump in performance occurred among these very same 11-year-olds.

Older children and adults, then, performed well on a matching task that required the capacity for motivic abstraction. This was further demonstrated by their responses to the atonal item shown in example 5.11. Here all three phrases were written in the contemporary atonal idiom, which was probably unfamiliar to our subjects.

In this item, key and mode in the traditional senses are irrelevant. Both

Example 5.10

the related theme and foil are delicate in mood and contrast with the dramatic quality of the model. The model and related theme share the four-note motive that occurs in bar 1 of the model: a descending seventh followed by a half step descent and rising third. This motive occurs in the related theme three times, in bars 1, 2, and 3.

This item was administered after the initial three items described above and the two items described in note 7. Only older subjects who were unfatigued and willing to continue responded to the item: 22 of the 30 10- and 11-year-olds and 16 of the 22 adults responded. The results were that 73 percent of the 10- and 11-year-olds who responded matched the

Example 5.11

related theme to the model correctly (p < .03). Among adults who re-sponded 94 percent made the correct match (p < .01). Thus, although the subjects willing to respond to this item may represent those of superior attention and ability, it is nevertheless clear that the majority of older subjects responded and did very well. Only rarely did children give evi-dence—and it was always subtle—of paying particular notice to the un-familiar atonal style (e.g., "Who's the pianist?").

On the other hand, we have seen that younger subjects performed poorly on the initial motivic abstraction items, even though those items utilized the familiar tonal idiom. To take a closer look at the capacity of the youngest children, we administered two special items to the 5-year-olds. Thirteen (of 16) 5-year-olds responded to the items shown in example 5.12.

In these items the model is composed of two 1-bar motives; the related theme consists simply of one of those motives (either the first or second) played alone; the foil is unrelated to either. This is perhaps the simplest case of abstraction imaginable, since a nonembedded half of the original model is abstracted, but not relocated to a new context in the normal sense of the term. Instead it is isolated.

Responses to both these items were comparable and very good: 81 percent of the 5-year-olds' responses were correct matches of related theme and model (p < .01). Out of 13 subjects, 9 answered both items correctly and only one child answered both items incorrectly. Sponta-

Example 5.12

neous comments showed that they were certain of their answers: "These two are practically the same music." Regarding a foil: "Uh-oh. This couldn't be it."

In summary, the youngest children matched musical phrases only when a whole chunk or piece of a melody was removed and isolated. On all items, they seemed to work earnestly ("This takes a little concentration"; "This is hard") and to be genuinely engaged by the task ("Hm. *Very* interesting"). But what they were not able to do, and what older children and adults could do, was recognize a chunk that had been removed from the surrounding melody and accompaniment *and placed in a new context.*

An important feature of motivic abstraction in this case is that it involves the abstraction and relocation of a whole "chunk." That is, the chunk consists of the motive's tonal *and* rhythmic pattern, along with the dynamics, phrasing, and articulation that pertain to that motive. In contrast, the following experiment concerns the abstraction and relocation of only a single dimension of a melody and not a whole chunk of it. In this case the rhythmic pattern is removed and superimposed on an entirely different tonal sequence. Intuitively, such a task seems more difficult in the way that recognizing the roundness of both a head and a ball seems more difficult than recognizing a part of a head (e.g., the face) in two locations. A higher order operation seems to be involved when only a single quality or dimension is abstracted, instead of a chunk or piece intact. Nevertheless, we shall see that older children generally did well on such a task.

Experiment: Rhythmic Abstraction

The task was identical to the motivic abstraction task in the previous experiment. To avoid boredom and the possibility that performing one task might influence performance on the other, the two tasks were administered on separate occasions. As described above, the subject was presented with three blocks, each of which played a short, single-line melody (without accompaniment). These were: (1) a melody labeled the model; (2) a melody with the same rhythm but different tonal pattern (in the words of a 10-year-old, "It's the same song, just different notes"); and (3) a foil that was different in both rhythm and tonal pattern. The subject's task was to listen to the model, then select from the other two blocks the one that "goes with" or "sounds the most like" the model.

Locations of the related theme and foil were counterbalanced across successive items. An unlimited number of repeated hearings was allowed.

As before, younger children (ages 5, 6, and about half of the 8-year-olds) were given a pretraining session, which consisted of a visual analogue to the task utilizing toy animals. Older children (10- and 11-year-olds and the remainder of the 8-year-olds) were not given pretraining.

In contrast to other tasks in which the pretraining had no significant effect on 8-year-olds' performance, the present pretraining may have had a beneficial effect. The six 8-year-olds who received pretraining (mean = 3.0 out of 4 items) performed significantly better than the eight 8-year-olds who did not receive pretraining (mean = 2.4), $t(12) = 2.08$, $p < .05$ for a one-tailed test. This result is of minor importance since pretraining at least had no negative effect on the performance of younger subjects.

The main part of the task consisted of the four items shown in example 5.13. Two additional items were subsequently administered and are described later.

The principal consideration in composing the melodies was creating a rhythmic pattern that fit legitimately on two different tonal patterns, meanwhile creating a foil that differed both in rhythm and tonal pattern but not in style and overall mood. An additional consideration was the control of extraneous musical factors (i.e., other than rhythm) on which a subject might match the model with one of the other two melodies. Thus, the three melodies that constituted an item had the same meter,[8] same number of measures and beats, and approximately the same number of tones. Because all three melodies were played at the tempo of one beat per second, they were all of the same duration. With singular exceptions,[9] all three melodies were in the same mode (usually major), each was in a different key, and they were either in the same general register or the model was equally different from each of the other two. The few exceptions favored the foil's similarity to the model. In addition, the overall pitch distance traversed was comparable in each melody, or the model was approximately different on this dimension from each of the other two (no more than six half steps or a minor third). *Pitch distance traversed*

[8]In item 2, the 6/8 meter of the model may be considered a duple meter like the 2/4 of the foil. Even assuming the contrary, and hence a foil less similar to the model, this may be balanced by the factors mentioned in footnote 9.

[9]In item 2, key and register favor the foil's similarity to the model; in item 4, use of the major mode favors the foil.

refers to the total number of half steps traversed over the successive intervals of the entire melody and may be considered a measure of the
balance between stasis and pitch movement in a melody. For example, a
rising fifth followed by a descending major second covers a total pitch
distance of nine half steps. In each item on the task the model, melody
with same rhythm, and foil were controlled for overall pitch movement.

Results. Figure 5.13 shows the percentage of correct responses at each
age level on each item. Although there was some variability across items,
young children (ages 5 and 6) generally answered near chance, while older
children (at age 10) did considerably better than chance.

Example 5.13

Table 5.3 shows for each age level the mean total score (for four items), standard deviation, and percentage of subjects who passed the task when the pass criterion was three out of four items correct. There was a clear age trend, with significant differences between 5- and 10-year-olds and between the two youngest age groups and adults, $F(5,90)$ = 9.42, $p < .001$, Scheffé test at .05. The tendency to match on the basis of an abstracted rhythmic pattern increased at each age level with the dramatic exception of the decline at age 11. Eleven-year-olds did not perform significantly better than even the youngest children, despite the fact that they voluntarily availed themselves of more repeated hearings of the melodies than did any other age group. That is, 11-year-olds listened to each melody a mean of 1.8 times, which is significantly more than the mean for 5- and 6-year-olds (only 1.2 times) and for 8-year-olds (1.3 times),

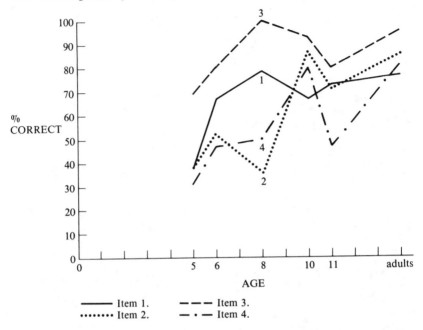

Figure 5.13. Rhythmic Abstraction: Percentage of Correct Responses

Table 5.3. Rhythmic Abstraction Task

Age Group	Mean	s.d.	Percent Pass
5-year-olds	1.8	.8	19%
6-year-olds	2.5	.7	47%
8-year-olds	2.6	1.0	57%
10-year-olds	3.3	.7	87%
11-year-olds	2.6	1.0	57%
Adults	3.4	.7	91%

$F(5,89) = 5.49$, $p < .001$, Scheffé test at .05. The 10-year-olds and adults listened to each melody a mean of 1.5 and 1.6 times respectively. Thus, the "sixth-grade slump" was in evidence in this task, with 11-year-olds seeming to try harder but perform no better than the youngest children. In any event the number of repeated hearings of the melodies did not account for success on the task, since total task score and number of repeated hearings were not significantly correlated ($r = .17$, $p > .07$ for children only).

With regard to the relationship between task success and other variables, there were no significant correlations between total task score and amount of musical training or score on the pitch discrimination, Draw-a-Person, or conservation tasks, when age was controlled through partial correlation. (The factor of age was the best predictor of task success, r = .39 for children only.) In an analysis of variance of total scores by age group and gender, the factor of gender and the age by gender interaction were not significant.

In summary, older subjects (about 90 percent of the 10-year-olds and adults) generally matched melodies on the basis of a shared rhythmic pattern, while the majority of the youngest subjects (age 5) generally did not. Older children were often able to make their matching criteria explicit, as several made spontaneous comments to the effect that "I go by rhythm," "these are alike in beat," and "these two go in step." It must be pointed out that the operation involved here is a sophisticated one: The model and melody with same rhythm do not really sound alike, and they are quite different in melodic flow. They are related only if one abstracts the rhythmic pattern from each, and it is precisely this that the older children did so well. An exception to this generalization was the performance of 11-year-olds, only about half of whom matched on the basis of rhythm, or approximately the same proportion as the 6- and 8-year-olds who did so. The *non*-rhythmic matching criteria that may have been employed by the other younger children remains unclear ("These are both tall sounds"), although they often seemed unnervingly sure of their choices ("You can absolutely tell").

With the possibility that younger children would match on the basis of an abstracted property *other* than rhythm, two additional items were administered immediately to those subjects who maintained sufficient energy and attention. Eleven 5-year-olds, 10 6-year-olds, and nearly all of the subjects in the remaining age groups completed these items. On these items, the model could be matched with *either* of the other two melodies depending on whether *rhythmic pattern* or *texture* was the criterion. The property of texture was chosen as the alternative matching criterion because it seemed like an immediately accessible property. The two conditions of texture were simply the presence and absence of accompaniment for the melody.

The items are shown in example 5.14. The model is an accompanied

Example 5.14

melody; the melody with the same rhythm is *unaccompanied*; and the foil is an accompanied melody like the model but with a maximally different rhythmic pattern. To ensure this, the meter is different as well.

Because the model can be matched legitimately with either of the other two melodies, a 50/50 split in subjects' responses might be expected. The results, however, were as follows. The youngest children, at age 5, matched on the basis of *texture* 78 percent of the time (p < .003). Subjects from age 6 to adulthood, on the contrary, matched on the basis of *rhythm* 57 percent of the time. This latter proportion of responses is only slightly more than the expected 50 percent, but it is nevertheless significant (p < .05).

It is worth noting that the proportion of rhythm-matches for 10- and 11-year-olds and adults, which was about 60 percent for each group, represents something of a decline for 10-year-olds and adults compared to their performance on the previous four items. On the previous four items, 10-year-olds and adults matched on the basis of rhythm 82 percent and 85 percent of the time respectively, while the proportion for 11-year-olds was only 68 percent. This means that although a "slump" in performance from age 10 to 11 was not observed in the two rhythm-versus-texture items described here, the reason is that 10-year-olds (and even adults) declined to approximately the level of rhythm-matching that the 11-year-olds had earlier employed.

With regard to consistency of responses, about 50 percent to 73 percent of the subjects at each age level were consistent in their matching criteria, using either rhythm *or* texture for both items. Among younger subjects at ages 5, 6, and 8 who matched consistently (n = 20), 60 percent used the criterion of texture. However, among older subjects at ages 10, 11, and adulthood who matched consistently (n = 35), 63 percent used the criterion of rhythm. This relationship between age group (younger/older) and the criterion used was significant, $\chi^2 = 5.18$, p < .03.

As might be expected, subjects (at ages 8, 10, 11, and adulthood) who consistently matched on the basis of rhythm also had higher scores on the first four (rhythm abstraction) items on the task. Their mean (3.52 of four items) was significantly higher than that of subjects who consistently matched on the basis of texture (mean = 2.71) or who matched inconsistently on the two rhythm/texture items (mean = 3.00), $F(2,61) = 4.79$, p < .05, Scheffé test at .05.

Conclusion

The results of both the motivic and rhythmic abstraction tasks raise the need to make distinctions between the sorts of abstracting operations that may be called upon in each case. In the case of motivic abstraction we have seen that younger children were capable of recognizing a whole, intact chunk of a melody when it was removed and isolated. Only older subjects, however, consistently recognized a motive in what is surely the more common case in real compositions—i.e., when a motive is removed from both its surrounding melody and accompaniment and is placed in a new context.

The results of the rhythmic abstraction task, on the other hand, raise the need for a distinction between the types of musical properties that may be abstracted and recognized in musical compositions. One type of property may be termed *global* and includes texture (e.g., few or many instruments, presence or absence of accompaniment), tempo (e.g., fast or slow), dynamics (loud or soft), and the timbre or tone color of a musical passage. These qualities permeate a musical passage in a general way and can be characterized in one- or two-word descriptions. We speak of a thin texture, a brisk tempo, a bright tone color, and so on. Another category may be termed *formal* and includes the properties of pitch sequence, rhythm, and meter. These properties are also present throughout a musical passage, but they are amenable to analysis (even informal analysis on the part of novices or nonmusicians) and can be formalized in writing with considerable specificity. A pitch sequence or rhythmic pattern, for example, can be quite precisely specified in the notation of lines and dots; its ongoing pattern on a moment-by-moment basis, from one impulse to the next, can be conceived (or monitored) and formalized in a way that the more global properties of texture, timbre, or tempo are not. It remains unclear, of course, whether the latter, global properties could be made amenable to the formal, analytic conception that characterizes pitch and rhythm. What seems to be clear, however, is that young children can abstract and match on the basis of a global property like texture, but not on the basis of a formal, analytic one like rhythm. Moreover, the slump in performance that occurred between the ages of 10 and 11 was evidenced in the former but not in the latter case.

HIERARCHIC LEVELS: UNDERSTANDING
MUSICAL STRUCTURE

As described earlier, the concept of hierarchic levels as representative of the structure of music has been well demonstrated through the analysis of compositions. What has not been well demonstrated is the cognitive reality of hierarchic levels, and particularly their development in childhood. The data reported here are suggestive but not definitive. In contrast to the results from tasks reported earlier, only adults and not older children were unequivocally successful on the task, and even then adult performance was not as good as it was on the other tasks. This may indicate that the understanding of musical structure is a more advanced process that requires formal knowledge. Further, the age trends showed some regressions not found on any other tasks, and for this reason I report the results separately for individual items.

The subjects were the same as those who completed the tasks on simultaneity, closure, and transformations: that is, approximately 15 children each at ages 5, 6, 8, 10, and 11 years, and 15 adults, plus the 34 Suzuki-trained children described earlier. In addition, 86 adults completed one of the items reported here as part of another experiment.

Experiment: Hierarchic Levels

The task was identical to the Block Task described under Transformation and Abstraction. The subject was presented with three wood blocks, each of which, when lifted from the table, played a musical phrase. The three phrases were: (1) a phrase labeled the model; (2) a reduction, that is, a phrase consisting of tones that represented the underlying structure of the model; and (3) a foil, that is, a phrase consisting of tones that did not represent the structure of the model. The subject's task was to listen to the model, then select from the reduction and foil the one that "goes with" or "sounds the most like" the model. Although this instruction does not do justice to the concept of structure (as an underlying skeleton, not just a simple similarity as implied here), we opted for this instruction on the grounds that it was more accessible to younger children and that the instruction should be consistent across age groups. Thus, correct matches of the model and reduction are assumed to be based on the understanding of structure only because the concept of structure best describes the relationship of the reduction and the model. The concept is not, of course, necessarily available to the subject's conscious awareness.

There were four items, with the reduction and foil counterbalanced across different blocks. An unlimited number of repeated hearings was allowed. Younger children at ages 5 and 6 listened to each phrase a mean of 1.4 times while older children and adults listened 1.6 times. This is comparable to the number of hearings subjects had on the other block tasks. There was no correlation between number of repeated hearings and total task score, which indicates that subjects who listened more were not significantly more successful on the task.

As before, younger children (5- and 6-year-olds plus half the 8-year-olds) were given pretraining in the form of a visual analogue to the task utilizing toy animals. ("Find the bird over here that's similar to that one, or goes with that one, or is in the same family or could be that bird's brother.") Older children (10- and 11-year-olds plus the remaining half of the 8-year-olds) and adults were given no pretraining. There was no significant difference in total score between 8-year-olds who received pretraining (mean = 2.63 out of 4 items) and those who did not (mean = 3.00), $t(15) = .60$.

Results. Example 5.15 shows the model, reduction, and foil for the first two items on the task, where a short, unaccompanied melody constituted the model. In item 1, the reduction represents the underlying structure of the model melody because it consists only of the principal or most important tones of that melody. In bar 1, those principal tones are the first tone, "f" (the tonic occurring on a strong beat) and the fourth tone, "e," which also occurs on a strong beat and functions as a stepwise passing tone to the strong-beat "d" in the next bar. Hence "f" and "e" are the first two tones of the reduction. The four additional tones in bar 1 of the model have the function of embellishing or circumscribing the "f" and the "e" and of providing rhythmic movement and interest. They occur on weak rather than strong beats. Similarly, in bar 2, the principal tones are the "d" (including its repetition) and the "c." The structure of the melody, therefore, consists of the smooth, stepwise descent shown as f-e-d-c in the reduction. The foil, on the other hand, consists of tones that do not represent this structure and that occur on unaccented or weak beats. A less analytic way of describing the structure here is to say that experiencing the model melody involves experiencing a tonal descent from

Example 5.15

the tonic down a perfect fourth to the dominant, as shown in the reduction, rather than experiencing the disjunct line made by unaccented tones, as shown in the foil.

The reader can easily verify that, similarly in item 2, the reduction shows the structure of a melody that basically moves from the third of the scale (on the first tone) to the tonic (on the last tone). The foil, on the other hand, is entirely unrelated to this structure.

It is important to point out that the foils in each case consist of tones that *do* occur in the model melody (or their octave equivalents) and that the foils make just as much melodic sense, on their own, as do the reductions. In other words, neither the reduction nor foil sounds like a "wrong" or impossible melody (or structure). The difference is that the reduction sequences the principal or structural tones of the model and the foil the nonprincipal ones.

For both of these items, subjects confirmed this assertion. The results for both items were comparable: Among adults, 83 percent of the responses were correct matches of the model and its reduction (p < .002). Among older children at ages 8, 10, and 11, 70 percent of responses were correct matches (p < .003).[10] Among younger children at ages 5 and 6, the results were at chance, with exactly half the responses favoring the reduction and half the foil. Figure 5.14 shows the age trend, where the results for both items are combined.

It is interesting to note that most adults, although they seemed confident of their choices, could not explain how they decided on an answer:

"I don't know, but something in there is alike."

"I use a sort of mood decision making."

"I go by how much movement, how many voices."

Only two adults approached a description of the idea of structure, one describing the reduction as "the same tune, only more drawn out" and another describing the model as "an embellished version" of the reduction.

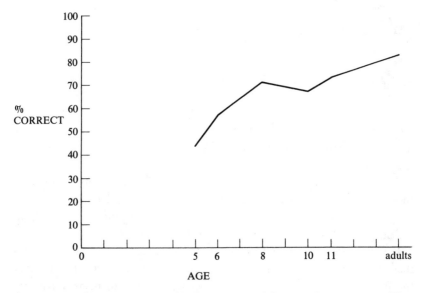

Figure 5.14. Hierarchic Levels: Percentage of Correct Responses on Two Melodic Items

[10]Here and elsewhere, of course, the results for several age groups are collapsed only when the percentages were comparable for each group.

Similarly, older children who answered correctly seemed confident of their choices, and they did give explanations, however improbable, for their answers. Several mentioned focusing on just the beginning or ending of a phrase, and several claimed to focus on pitch or rhythm:

"I know because the front sounds the same."

"I compare the endings or just one section of the song."

"Because the bounce in both is at a higher pitch."

"I decide by the rising and fallings of the pitch."

"High on one, high on another, and low on the wrong one."

"It goes down, then up."

"By the same beat."

Others wisely declined to explain and said simply, "I just listen" or "It just sounds like it."

Fewer of the younger children gave explanations of a kind other than "I use my ears," "I just know," or "I just guess." But what is striking about the few quasi-explanations is how much they reveal a 5- or 6-year-old trying hard to make *musical* sense out of the task. None of the explanations was nonmusical, as would be the case with references to the wood blocks, the experimenter, some magical figure, and so forth. One child explained an answer by describing the model and its match thus: "One is on the big black notes and one is on the little white notes." Another was clearly aware of how different the model was from the other two: "I like the first ones best" (that is, the models). One child tried to lift two blocks at once in order to compare them simultaneously. One recalled the pretraining in an explanation: "It's because these two songs are brothers." One child felt a sure-fire recognition for item number 3 described below: "I can tell this is *Chopsticks*."

The third item on the task is shown in example 5.16. In contrast to the unaccompanied melodies in items 1 and 2, this item uses a melody with chordal accompaniment that emphasizes tonic and dominant harmony. The reduction, then, presents both the melodic and harmonic structure. The foil, on the other hand, is maximally different from the model, since its melody goes in the opposite direction (ascending rather than descending), it repeatedly emphasizes higher pitches, such as "b," "c," and "d," that hardly occur in the model (only once in bar 1), and it modulates to an entirely different key.

The results from this item were somewhat perplexing, however. Although both adults and 8-year-olds responded, as expected, by choosing the reduction (73 percent and 71 percent in each case, which is marginally significant at $p < .06$ and $p < .08$ respectively), older children at ages 10 and 11 most often chose the *foil*. Fully 67 percent of the 10- and 11-year-olds matched the foil to the model, which is significant at $p < .05$. Younger children at ages 5 and 6 responded at chance as expected (55 percent chose the reduction).

Example 5.16

We have no ready explanation for the reversal at ages 10 and 11. This is the only item on any of the tasks in the entire battery with a significant effect in favor of the "wrong" answer. Possibly the novelty of the foil's modulation made it especially interesting or attractive to older children, who might be more likely than 8-year-olds to focus on a change in harmony. Adults, on the other hand, although they might notice a modulation, would be less likely to choose on that basis given the instruction to match on similarity. In any case, only subjects older and younger than 10- and 11-year-olds correctly chose the reduction. (It may also be noted that 10- and 11-year-old Suzuki-trained children (n = 9), who otherwise did very well on the Hierarchic Levels task, performed more poorly on this item than on any of the others. They performed at chance, with 5 (55 percent) choosing the reduction.)

Somewhat similar results were found in the final item on the task, shown in example 5.17. This is an example of a compound melody, described earlier, in which a single-line melody is thought to have a two-component structure. The two components are the upper and lower melodies shown in the reduction.

In contrast to the previous item, the reduction and foil in this case sound similar to one another, and consequently we expected this to be a very difficult item. The reduction and foil are identical in texture and very similar in rhythm and harmonic movement. In fact, they reflect the rhythmic structure and underlying harmony of the model almost equally well (although the reduction is somewhat superior). The principal difference between them is that the pattern of individual melody tones is different—although not radically so—in each case. In bars 2, 3, and 4, for example, the reduction shows the principal tones of the model while the foil contains tones that do not even occur in the model in those measures. But the differences are subtle: in bars 5 and 6, for example, the reduction shows in the upper melody line the sequence e–d–c, while the foil shows e–c–d. The latter sequence is not, by itself, wrong-sounding, but it is simply less representative of the melodic activity in the model at that point. Thus, a subject who extracts only *harmonic* information from the model would not be more likely to select the reduction over the foil, since both are similar on that dimension. Rather, the correct match would seem to require extracting information about the compound melodic structure.

The results were somewhat equivocal, but nevertheless suggestive. The present sample of adults responded at chance, with only 57 percent cor-

Example 5.17

rectly choosing the reduction. However, when the item was administered to a larger group of adults as part of another experiment (n = 86), there was a significant proportion of correct responses, 64 percent (p < .006). Older children at ages 8 and 10 also performed better than chance, with 72 percent of them correctly choosing the reduction (p < .01). It is worth noting that Suzuki-trained children at approximately this same age also made a significant proportion of correct responses. Among the 17 Suzuki-trained 7-, 8-, 10- and 11-year-olds, 82 percent chose the reduction (p < .006). The anomaly was that 11-year-old "normal" (not Suzuki) subjects performed at chance level (54 percent chose the reduction); although this proportion is not significantly lower than that of the 8- and 10-year-olds (Fisher's Exact Test, p > .06), the possibility remains that this is related to the general decline in performance at age 11 observed on many of the other tasks. The youngest subjects at ages 5 and 6, as expected, also performed no better than chance (63 percent chose the reduction).

A summary of the age trends for items 3 and 4, respectively the melody with harmonic accompaniment and the compound melody, is shown in figure 5.15. (The adult rate shown for item 4 is the 64 percent from the larger sample.) Here the decline in reduction choices at age 10 or 11 is clear, although the only significant difference is that on item 3 between the 8-year-olds' performance (71 percent correct) and the 10-year-olds' performance (27 percent correct), $\chi^2 = 4.52$, $p < .05$.

With regard to relationships with other variables, success on the hierarchic levels task was uncorrelated with both musical training and score on the pitch discrimination task when age was controlled through partial correlation. There were no significant gender differences across the whole sample or in any age group.

There was some evidence, however, that Suzuki-trained children in the older age groups outperformed the "normal" (or not Suzuki-trained) children at the same age. Figure 5.16 shows the mean total score for all four items on the task for both groups of subjects.

In contrast to the results for the closure and transformation tasks, where

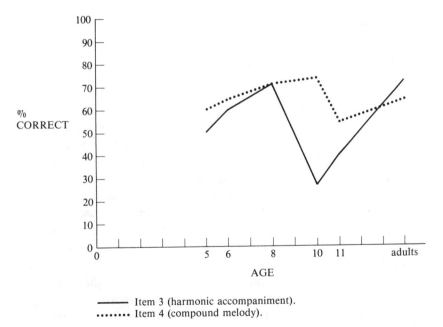

——— Item 3 (harmonic accompaniment).
••••••• Item 4 (compound melody).

Figure 5.15. Hierarchic Levels: Percentage of Correct Responses on Items 3 and 4

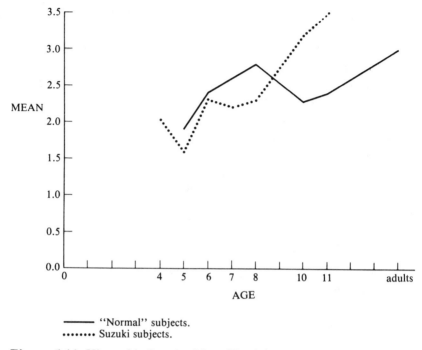

——— "Normal" subjects.
•••••••• Suzuki subjects.

Figure 5.16. Hierarchic Levels: Mean Total Score

differences at the younger ages were seen to even out in late childhood, the results here showed the opposite pattern: There were no significant differences at the younger ages, but among older children, Suzuki subjects outperformed their agemates in the normal sample. The mean score for the nine Suzuki subjects at ages 10 and 11 (3.3) was significantly higher than that of "normal" subjects the same age (2.4), $t(35) = 2.49$, $p < .02$. This may indicate that intensive, formal training plays an important role in developing the understanding of musical structure—at least the sort of hierarchic structure described here. Whether this understanding can also come about as part of normal development and experience—with minimal or no formal training—is not conclusively demonstrated here. The results for short, unaccompanied melodies gave evidence that simple underlying structures were accessible to subjects at age 8 and above, but examples of the more complicated structures involved in harmony and compound melody yielded equivocal findings.

CHAPTER 6

Conclusions

A major aim of this book has been to argue that music is most usefully regarded as a universal acquisition; that is, it is acquired by all persons with normal experience and exposure to music and is not simply possessed by the few with relevant traits (such as talent) or by those with formal musical training. In focusing on those aspects of music that are universally acquired, I have argued for a specific set of cognitive processes that meet two conditions. First, they likely underlie all three of the activities associated with music-making, that is, composing, performing, and listening; and second, they can be observed across many different types or styles of music. In making this argument I have avoided two of the more traditional emphases: (1) the notion that veridical perception—as defined by acuity or discrimination—is a central process in musical understanding; and (2) the tendency to describe musical understanding in terms of music's supposed elements—that is, pitches, chords, melody, harmony, rhythm, and meter. Indeed, I have argued that such elements may be useful and necessary to formal reflection, but they are not necessarily descriptive of cognitive reality.

Moreover, in addressing this nonelemental level of cognitive processing, I have insisted on a distinction between style-specific and generic cognitive processes. This grows out of the observation that there are many types or styles of music, associated with various cultures or communities, that sound different from one another because different rules or organizational principles are employed for the composing and hearing of each of them. These rules represent style-specific cognitive processes. But there cannot be an infinite number of such rules, and in any case people can certainly understand more than a single style. Thus there must exist some higher-level, pan-stylistic cognitive processes, and I have referred to these as "generic." I have described two categories: temporal processes (succession and simultaneity) and nontemporal processes (closure, transformation, abstraction, and hierarchic levels).

The main findings that emerge from experiments on these processes are the following. First, the processes do "exist" insofar as the tasks designed to measure them are valid. Moreover, the processes are generally well in place in human cognition by the age of 10 or 11 years, are *not* strongly in evidence earlier at around 5 years of age, and are not dependent on intensive formal tuition in the interim. Developmental trends for most of the tasks would seem to indicate a rapid period of growth in musical understanding between the ages of 8 and 10 or 11 years. Finally, and contrary to expectation, temporal processes appear to develop *after* rather than before nontemporal ones. I consider these points below.

DEVELOPMENTAL TRENDS

Late Childhood

Ten- and 11-year-olds appear to be in possession of most of the temporal and nontemporal processes, with one special qualification. Roughly two-thirds to three-fourths of the 10- and 11-year-olds in the present sample succeeded on the tasks presented. In the successive dimension, these older children understand that motives chained together constitute longer melodies (motivic chaining); that patterns result from repetition and alternation; and that longer passages of music—even asymmetrical ones—can be divided into subgroupings or phrases. Most important, children at this age have a notion of what constitutes a coherent motive or unit, at least as it is defined in the tonal idiom. Similarly the simultaneous dimension is clear to children at this age. They understand that two timbres or two motives may be combined to produce a single, simultaneous unit, and yet the components retain for the child enough of their original identity that they can still be discriminated.

A limitation on ability in the simultaneous dimension, however, is that 10- and 11-year-olds have difficulty identifying the number of simultaneous parts that constitute a complex texture, especially if there are more than one or two parts. Only half of the 11-year-olds were successful on the Textural Abstraction task; in the present sample a high rate of success was not found until adulthood.

In the nontemporal domain, 10- and 11-year-olds have no trouble grasping the idea of closure in music, and they can reliably determine which of two phrases closes with the conventional dominant-to-tonic finish. In a number of tasks they demonstrated an understanding of melodic transformations: They can match two fragments, where one is a transformation of the other, and they can identify transformations as being derived from one or another initially heard original (as in the Bead Task). They can also identify transformations over the course of a longer composition, such as that heard in the Minuet Task. In these latter two tasks, 10- and 11-year-olds gave no evidence of memory problems that might impede the grasp of transformations.

Underlying the understanding of transformations is the ability to abstract similar features from two different phrases of music. Ten- and 11-year-olds can match disparate phrases of music that share only a common melodic motive or, seemingly more difficult, that share only a common rhythmic pattern when all the tones are different.

Finally, 10- and 11-year-olds show evidence of perceiving hierarchic levels in music, at least in simple, single-line melodies. They readily match a melody with a representation of its structure as opposed to a musically similar but nonstructural representation. In more complex music, however, including accompanied and compound melodies, the evidence regarding older children's perception of hierarchic structure is equivocal.

An important qualification on the impressive facility of 10- and 11-year-olds is that several tasks showed an unexpected *decline* at age 11. Although it can be argued that some of the decrements at age 11 were not statistically significant by comparison to 10-year-olds, nevertheless even a slight decrement is important because what is *expected* is an increase in performance. Also, similarly consistent declines did not occur at any other age level in these tasks. The decrement at age 11 warrants further research, and there are no immediately obvious causes for it in the present data, since the decline cannot be attributed to differences between 10- and 11-year-olds in intelligence, degree of musical training, or gender. More specifically, mean normal scores for 10- and 11-year-olds on the Draw-a-Person test, which provides a measure of intellectual maturity, were 107.1 and 107.5 respectively. (Like IQ tests, the Draw-a-Person test is standardized with a mean of 100 and a standard deviation of 15.) As expected, 11-year-olds had slightly more musical training than did 10-year-olds (the older a group, the longer they are likely to have studied). That is, 43 percent of the 11-year-olds had studied an instrument for three to seventeen months, while an additional 40 percent of them had studied for one and a half to four years. The comparable figures for 10-year-olds are 47 percent and 37 percent respectively. To be sure, such differences between the two groups are either inconsequential or a slight advantage to 11-year-olds. Further, the "slump" in task performance at age 11 occurred in both of the subsamples used as subjects. It will be recalled that girls predominated in one of the 11-year-old subsamples (which took half the tasks) and that boys predominated in the other half (which took the remaining tasks). Yet both subsamples showed the "slump" on some of the tasks.

The tasks that showed the greatest performance decrements at age 11 were as follows:

(1) The Pitch Discrimination task (taken by both subsamples);
(2) The Idiomatic Construction task, which measured sensitivity to coherence in melodic units, and the Rhythmic Abstraction task, which measured the ability to abstract a common rhythmic pattern from different tonal sequences (taken by one of the subsamples);
(3) The Motivic Synthesis task, which measured the awareness that two motives can be combined to create a simultaneous unit, and the discrimination of melodies on the Echo Task of the Transformation series (taken by the other subsample). Note that 11-year-olds showed no significant decrement in the understanding of transformations *per se,* but they did perform more poorly than 10-year-olds on the melodic discrimination required in that task.

One hypothesis that emerges with regard to the performance decrement at age 11 is that it occurs in two sorts of tasks: (1) those that require an especially acute, analytic skill in the auditory domain (such as that required for pitch discrimination, rhythmic abstraction, motivic synthesis, and melody discrimination); and (2) those that require sensitivity to conventional or cultural musical rules such as those embodied in the tonal idiom and measured by the Idiomatic Construction task. (It is worth noting that the Closure task, which also measures sensitivity to the tonal idiom, showed a slight decline at age 11.)

It is possible that decrements in some areas of music cognition are necessary for other gains to be made, perhaps in areas not measured by the present studies. A confirmation of the decline at age 11 and a fuller investigation of it awaits additional research.

Middle Childhood

Although the majority of the cognitive processes are not in evidence until age 10 or 11, a few are apparent earlier, at age 8. Perhaps most important is the fact that 8-year-olds gave evidence of perceiving hierarchic levels in simple melodies. Their correct response rate on this task (about 70 percent) was comparable to that of the older children. This is the only one of the nontemporal tasks on which 8-year-olds performed as well as did older children. In addition, 8-year-olds did very well (100 percent passed) on the simultaneity task involving timbre. That is, they easily identified simultaneous combinations of timbres, although they were not as successful when the components combined were melodic motives. Finally, it will be recalled that 8-year-olds did as well as older children and even adults on the discrimination of random melodies (on the Idiomatic Construction task), although *unlike* older groups they did no better on coherent melodies constructed in accordance with the tonal idiom.

Although hierarchic levels, timbre synthesis, and the discrimination of random melodies exhausts the list of tasks on which most 8-year-olds performed as well as older children, there are a few additional processes which some 8-year-olds gave evidence of possessing. About half of them showed facility with melodic motives in both the successive and simultaneous domains, since they correctly identified two motives strung together (motivic chaining) or played simultaneously (motivic synthesis). Slightly more than half of them passed the Rhythmic Abstraction task; that is, they correctly matched disparate phrases that shared only a common rhythm. In addition, about 60 percent of the 8-year-olds passed two of the Transformation tasks (Block and Bead tasks), although only a very few were successful when transformations had to be identified over the course of a longer composition (Minuet Task). Despite such successes, the majority of the 8-year-olds had difficulty with most other tasks, such as those that concerned tonal closure at the ends of phrases and the repetition and alternation inherent in patterns.

Early Childhood

Based on the present subject sample and series of tasks, the years from 8 to 10 represent a period of rapid growth in music cognition. This conclusion is derived in part from the unexpected result that 10- and 11-year-olds showed evidence of possessing nearly all the processes, while 5- and 6-year-olds, equally unexpectedly, showed evidence of possessing almost none of them. By and large children in the youngest age groups had trouble with both the temporal and nontemporal processes. They did not correctly identify either successive or simultaneous combinations of motives or even combinations of timbres. They were insensitive to repetition and alternation in the Patterning task and performed very poorly—that is, underestimating—when asked to determine the number of simultaneous parts in a particular texture.

Young children do, however, show signs of an emerging understanding of the successive and simultaneous dimensions. In the present sample the youngest subjects were able to divide an in-progress piece of music into two phrases when the division point was obviously marked harmonically and rhythmically. In addition, although they were unable to identify the number of simultaneous parts in a texture, they did mistake rhythmic complexity for an increased number of parts. This is a sign that some attempt to decipher the texture, to read it as thick or thin, complex or simple, is being made.

Five- and 6-year-olds also showed signs of early skill in the nontemporal processes. Although they were not successful on the closure, motivic abstraction, and hierarchic levels tasks, about half of the youngest children were successful in matching transformations (Block Task) and about a fifth were successful on the Rhythmic Abstraction task. These successes indicate that, especially in a matching task provided by the block apparatus, some young children show signs of sensitivity to the subtle features of musical passages, such as transformations and abstracted rhythmic patterns.

THE ROLE OF FORMAL TRAINING AND PITCH DISCRIMINATION

For the majority of the generic processes investigated here, subjects with instrumental training did not perform better than subjects without training, with the factor of age controlled. Only two tasks—closure and motivic chaining—showed significant correlations with training, and these correlations were low. In addition, pitch discrimination was correlated with instrumental training, but pitch discrimination itself was generally uncorrelated with success on the tasks. Although the possibility cannot be ruled out that the absence of significant correlations is only an artifact of the tasks and subject sample employed, the conclusion seems inescapable that, at the least, formal instrumental training is neither necessary nor sufficient for the development of the generic processes. Rather, with age as the principal predictor of success on the tasks, the more potent factors may be general (nonmusical) cognitive growth and normal, everyday musical experience.

This is not to say that educational experiences do not contribute. Indeed, typical school experiences with music may well be part of the normal, everyday experiences that contribute to the acquisition of the processes in question. But traditional instrumental training does not appear to be necessary to that acquisition, and in the present sample neither did it seem to enhance it.

A somewhat different issue, however, is whether the acquisition can be enhanced by extremely intensive and/or very early instrumental training, such as that provided by the Suzuki method. Although the present research was limited in a number of ways and cannot be considered definitive, a summary of the results concerning children with Suzuki training may be suggestive. First, Suzuki-trained children were superior to the "normal" sample in three ways:

(1) They achieved higher scores on the Closure task, that is, on a task requiring implicit knowledge of the conventional tonal idiom.
(2) They achieved higher scores on the Hierarchic Levels task, which is the most formal and abstract of the nontemporal processes.
(3) At the younger ages, they achieved higher scores on tasks with a heavy memory demand—that is, the Bead and Minuet tasks in the Transformations series—although these differences evened out at the older ages.

It is important to point out that Suzuki-trained subjects were not superior in the understanding of transformations per se. Indeed, when memory demands were reduced (in the Block Task), Suzuki and "normal" children performed comparably across the age span investigated.

A second point is that Suzuki training was effective in the case of closure and hierarchic levels only after a substantial amount of training had taken place. It will be recalled that, on the Closure task, advanced Suzuki subjects did better than their agemates, but intermediate and beginning Suzuki subjects did no better than untrained children of the same age. On the Hierarchic Levels task, differences between the two groups widened rather than narrowed at the older ages, when more training had taken place. Thus, instrumental training may indeed have a facilitative effect on some of the generic processes, but the training must be extremely intensive, as it is in the Suzuki method, and long-term, as it was in the case of the older and more advanced subjects here.

With regard to the role of pitch discrimination, we have seen that the ability to determine whether two pitches are the same or different did not emerge as a good predictor of success for the majority of the tasks. Among the nontemporal tasks—closure, transformations, abstraction, and hierarchic levels—there were no significant correlations with pitch discrimination, except for the two transformation tasks with heavy memory demand (Bead and Minuet tasks). These latter two tasks were correlated with pitch discrimination, although the Block Task of the Transformation series, which reduced memory demands, was not.

In contrast to the results for nontemporal tasks, some of the temporal tasks *were* significantly correlated with pitch discrimination. Three of the simultaneity tasks—Textural Abstraction, Motivic Synthesis, and Timbre Synthesis—and one of the succession tasks (Motivic Chaining) were so correlated.[1]

These results may be interpreted as indicating that pitch discrimination is not highly related to higher-level cognitive processes in music. What it may represent, however, is a kind of analytic auditory acuity that is most similar to the cognitive skill required in the temporal tasks and tasks requiring a heavy memory load.

Taken together, the evidence regarding formal training and pitch discrimination calls to mind Piaget's distinction between the figurative and operative domains in cognition. Figurative skills are those that involve accurately perceiving and remembering a particular stimulus. Operative skills are those that involve the performing of mental operations or manipulations on the material at hand. In the standard conservation task, for example, it is important to distinguish between the figurative skills of seeing and remembering the pouring of liquid into a new container and the operative skill of compensating the different heights and widths to render a conservation judgment. Tentatively, then, the results of the present studies may indicate that formal training enhances two sorts of skills:

---

[1]Some of these tasks—textural abstraction, timbre synthesis, and motivic chaining—were also correlated with conservation skill in 5-, 6-, and 8-year-olds.

(1) figurative skills (e.g., pitch discrimination and memory skills demanded by the Bead and Minuet tasks); and (2) knowledge of the conventional tonal idiom, such as that required in the Closure task. (This latter is reasonable because knowledge of culturally specific conventions would seem to be learned.) Training may not, however, affect the operative skills presumably represented in the majority of the (other) tasks. In any case, it is worth pointing out that differences between intensively trained and "normal" subjects evened out at later ages in the Bead, Minuet, and Closure tasks.

The exception to this general conclusion—that musical training affects figurative but not operative skills—was the Hierarchic Levels task. Here the training effect *widened* rather than narrowed with age. Thus, there seem to be two hypotheses in need of further testing. Either my conclusion is in error and training does indeed affect the operative skills called upon in this task, or the Hierarchic Levels task is perhaps more bound up with cultural or style-specific knowledge than I had originally proposed. This latter is certainly a possibility since all four items on the task exemplify the tonal idiom and their underlying structure emphasizes tonic-dominant relations. On the other hand, the mental "reduction" of a series of tones into their underlying structure, as is presumably demanded by this task, would seem to be a sophisticated mental operation.

Thus, the distinction between figurative and operative skills in music cognition needs further investigation. But it is instructive to note that not only the training data but also the "sixth-grade slump" points to this distinction. That is, the performance decrements observed at age 11 tended also to occur on the more figurative tasks (such as pitch discrimination) and on tasks that required knowledge of the tonal idiom.

TEMPORAL AND NONTEMPORAL PROCESSES

The distinction between temporal and nontemporal generic processes is a critical one. Temporal processes concern the obvious fact that musical events always stand in some temporal relation to one another. One event is obviously before or after another (succession) or occurs at the same time (simultaneity). Whether the events in question are construed to be longer melodies succeeding one another (phrasing) or are shorter motives or simultaneous timbres (motivic chaining or timbre synthesis), the understanding of temporal relations seems to be an obvious necessity in listening to music.

Nontemporal processes, on the other hand, concern the internal, abstract, and formal properties of musical passages and are not tied to temporal relations per se. The notion of hierarchic levels, for example, describes not the temporal relationship between two passages but rather how a single passage is structured from within. Similarly, closure concerns how a passage is finished, transformation describes how a passage bears a similarity relation—not temporal relation—to some other passage, and abstraction concerns some commonality of rhythm or motive that is unrelated to the temporal order of the passages themselves.

Nontemporal processes are formal in the sense that formal reflection—music analysis—is employed to articulate or discover them. Hierarchic levels, closure, transformation, and abstraction of the sort I have described are all processes that derive from an analytic stance being taken toward some (many) pieces of music—that is, from the *notation* of pieces of music. Not so with temporal processes. Little time and scholarly energy are required to determine whether two passages within a composition follow or occur simultaneously with one another. Yet it is precisely such seemingly obvious temporal relations that take time to develop in childhood.

Given this characterization of temporal and nontemporal processes, a somewhat counterintuitive result in the present sample is that *non*temporal, formal, and abstract processes (with the exception of closure) seemed to develop earlier, and in the present sample were easier for young children, than were the seemingly obvious temporal processes. For example, half the 5- and 6-year-olds passed the Transformations (Block) task, and about a fifth of the 5-year-olds and half the 6-year-olds passed the Rhythmic Abstraction task. Among 8-year-olds, about 60 passed both of the aforementioned tasks, and they did as well as older children on the Hierarchic Levels items that involved single-line melodies. By contrast, the vast majority of 5- and 6-year-olds performed badly on temporal tasks for motivic chaining and synthesis, textural abstraction, patterning, and even on timbre synthesis, seemingly the easiest of the temporal tasks. Although the 8-year-olds passed the Timbre Synthesis task, only half passed motivic chaining and synthesis, and the majority failed on patterning and textural abstraction.

Although task effects may account for some of the differences between success rates on temporal and nontemporal tasks, a conceivable interpretation is that the child first makes sense of music out of its global features and only later develops temporal ideas. The temporal processes are certainly more difficult in that they require what may be characterized as constant analytic monitoring. For example, on the Patterning task one must attend continuously to each motive, monitoring the changes and picking up the pattern of alternation. Similarly on motivic chaining one must attend carefully to determine when one motive ends and another begins. By contrast, although the nontemporal tasks involve sophisticated (even if implicit) knowledge, they depend on a more global and less analytic strategy and do not require continuous, almost note-by-note attention. Rather, this sort of analytic strategy (which, it will be recalled, was more frequently correlated with both pitch discrimination and conservation) seems to be a later developing ability.

CONCLUSION

Two themes have been with us through the opening arguments and experimental demonstrations in this book. The principal one is a definition of music as cognition, in which the artform is not considered a clearly specified external object, but rather an internal, subjective entity springing from mental operations. The fact that musical understanding changes from childhood to adulthood was interpreted as evidence for this view. For the child possesses no deficiencies in *hearing* that make his understanding of succession, simultaneity, transformation, and so on dissimilar to that of the adult. Rather, it is a difference in cognition that distinguishes how different a composition is for the child and for the adult.

The theme of music as cognition was elaborated here into a set of cognitive processes—transformation, hierarchic levels, etc.—thought to form a core of understanding common to composing, performing, and listening. Evidence of the existence of such processes is in large part the evidence in compositions themselves. Hence formal analysis—of the kind denoted by the term music theory—is thought to play a critical role in describing cognitive reality. The dangers of misinterpreting the results of music theory notwithstanding (particularly in the style-specific rather than generic aspects of music), formal analysis is a necessary route to discovering how internal, cognitive-musical processes become externalized in compositions.

Yet another offshoot of the theme of music as cognition, and the specification of the processes, is the calling into question of the notion that music perception and understanding arise principally from *auditory acuity*. For example, the ability to discriminate small differences in pitch—say, differences smaller than those used in the style—is here taken to be irrelevant to music perception and understanding. It will be recalled that correlations between the pitch discrimination task and the musical-cognitive tasks were few; those that did occur were interpreted as evidence of a common analytic strategy that underlies pitch discrimination, certain of the temporal tasks, and perhaps even conservation.

A second theme that permeated our discussions was the theme of universal acquisition. Broadly speaking, there are two kinds of human abilities in every domain: those that are universal, common to everyone (e.g., walking, language) and those that are traditionally called "individual differences" and are acquired by some people but not others (e.g., athletic ability and talent in poetry). My aim has been to delineate those aspects of music that are universally acquired. I have argued that not only "enjoyment" or "preference" or "perception" are universals in music, but that specific processes form the core of understanding common to members of a musical community. In my view, such processes are analogous to acquisitions such as language and concepts of space, time, number, and so on, rather than to special, individual talents found in devotees of sport or poetry.

Two additional points are related to the theme of universal acquisition. One is that music cognition is not a *trait* (acquired either environmentally or as a result of heredity). The other is that music cognition results from normal cognitive growth and everyday experience with music, and not from learning in the narrow sense. At the least, musical understanding as described here does not grow out of the ability to perform learned music on an instrument. The task performance of trained and untrained subjects of different ages was interpreted here as evidence that instrumental training is neither necessary nor sufficient for music cognition. Although it may facilitate some aspects of the processes, it is fair to say that it is probably a much less potent predictor of musical understanding than might be expected. In that regard, the image of the youngest intensively trained subjects, who could perform in concert a theme with variations and perhaps additional pieces from memory, yet who could not pass the closure or transformation tasks conducted here, is particularly striking.

Philosophers and psychologists have long been careful about the distinction between sensation and perception on the one hand—that is, the intake and interpretation of a stimulus through one of the five senses—and cognition on the other—that is, the having of thoughts or ideas. Put simply, one of the enduring debates is which domain exerts the greater influence over the other: whether what we perceive is the source of what and how we think, or whether what we think is the determiner of what we will perceive. I have argued the latter viewpoint here: that the state of a child's cognitive mechanisms, the availability of particular processes, is the surest determiner of what he will perceive.

The more important point to emphasize in these closing pages, however, is that the distinction between sensation/perception on the one hand and cognition on the other—in tandem with the definition of music as cognition—has important implications for a theory of music and even more generally for what we consider an art. *For the principal criterion of goodness in the domain of sensation is ultimately pleasure or beauty, while the principal criterion of goodness in cognition is organization.* (Only paradoxically do we say of something that is logical, coherent, or well-organized that it "makes sense.")

This point about the criterion of goodness is made dramatically clear when we consider the difference between what I shall call the formal arts—music, art, and dance[2]—and other practices which have long-standing traditions in our culture and which are sometimes colloquially referred to as arts—for example cuisine, vintnery, tea-blending, perfumery, and the creation of colors for paint or textiles. These latter domains have everything to do with sensation and little to do with cognition, for we say of a fine tea that it tastes good, and not in the least that it makes sense. But what distinguishes music from these sensory practices, I have argued, is that it belongs to the realm of cognition, where the understanding of organization is the defining characteristic. I believe that a similar argument could be made for visual art and dance.

Experimental cognitive psychologists have implicitly acknowledged this distinction in that they do not confuse the results of stimulus perception

[2] I omit poetry, drama, and fiction from my list of considerations here because their dependence on ordinary language seems to require a category separate from that of music, art, and dance.

experiments with cognitive activities that are also interesting to study. For example, they have studied cognitive activities such as logical reasoning (e.g., understanding syllogisms), map reading, chess playing, and narrative story understanding, but they do not begin their work by raising questions about the visual perception of letters, words, and spaces in a logical statement, or the sensory detection of colors and shapes on a map or chessboard. Rather, although they acknowledge that sensation and perception are the necessary companions of all waking human activity, they do not search in those domains for the explanation of how logic, complex games, and narration occur; instead, it is in the domain of cognitions that arise *in addition to* sensations and perceptions that an account of the phenomenon at hand is sought.

But in music, I have argued, it is precisely this sort of confusion between lower-level perception and higher-order cognitions that has caused so much trouble. Searching vainly in the domain of pitch perception for an explanation of music is the result of falsely supposing that music belongs principally to the domain of sensation and perception rather than to the domain of cognition. To do this is to mis-categorize music with tea-blending and perfumery.

In part this confusion stems from early aesthetic theories that promoted beauty and pleasure as the principal criteria for art. Thus psychologists at least since Helmholtz' time have been fascinated with what accounts for *acoustic* consonance and dissonance—that is, why some sounds are harmonious and others harsh. This question, while important to the domain of sensation (as is, what makes something taste bad?) cannot give rise to a theory of music any more than shape detection can give rise to a theory of chess. What I have tried to argue in this book is that the aim of music, while the art need not be unpleasant or unbeautiful, is more than simply to sound good.

References

Bach, C. P. E. 1949. *Essay on the True Art of Playing Keyboard Instruments*. W. Mitchell, tr. New York: Norton.

Balzano, G. 1977. "Chronometric Studies of the Musical Interval Sense." Ph.D. dissertation, Stanford University, 1977. *Dissertation Abstracts International*, 36:2898B.

Bamberger, J. S. and H. Brofsky. 1975. *The Art of Listening*. 3d ed. New York: Harper and Row.

Benade, A. H. 1960. *Horns, Strings, and Harmony*. Garden City, N.Y.: Doubleday-Anchor.

Bentley, A. 1966. *Measures of Musical Ability*. New York: October House.

Berry, W. 1976. *Structural Functions in Music*. Englewood Cliffs, N.J.: Prentice-Hall.

Berry, W. 1980. "On Structural Levels in Music." *Music Theory Spectrum*, 2:19–45.

Blechner, M. 1978. "Musical Skill and the Categorical Perception of Harmonic Mode." Ph.D. dissertation, Yale University, 1977. *Dissertation Abstracts International*, 39:1931B.

Burns, E. M. and W. D. Ward. 1982. "Intervals, Scales, and Tuning." In D. Deutsch, ed., *The Psychology of Music*. New York: Academic Press.

Carpenter, P. 1967. "The Musical Object." *Current Musicology*, 5:56–87.

Cogan, R. and P. Escot. 1976. *Sonic Design*. Englewood Cliffs, N.J.: Prentice-Hall.

Collier, G. 1975. *Jazz*. London: Cambridge University Press.

Colwell, R. 1970. *Music Achievement Tests*. Chicago: Follett Educational.

Cooper, G. and L. B. Meyer. 1960. *The Rhythmic Structure of Music*. Chicago: University of Chicago Press.

Crocker, R. L. and A. P. Basart. 1971. *Listening to Music*. New York: McGraw-Hill.

Deutsch, D. 1972. "Octave Generalization and Tune Recognition." *Perception and Psychophysics*, 11:411–412.

Dowling, W. J. 1971. "Recognition of Inversions of Melodies and Melodic Contours." *Perception and Psychophysics*, 9:348–349.

Dowling, W. J. 1972. "Recognition of Melodic Transformations: Inversion, Retrograde, and Retrograde Inversion." *Perception and Psychophysics,* 12:417–421.

Dowling, W. J. 1978. "Scale and Contour: Two Components of a Theory of Memory for Melodies." *Psychological Review,* 85:341–354.

Dowling, W. J. and A. W. Hollombe. 1977. "The Perception of Melodies Distorted by Splitting into Several Octaves: Effects of Increasing Proximity and Melodic Contour." *Perception and Psychophysics,* 21:60–64.

Drake, R. 1957. *Drake Musical Aptitude Tests.* Chicago: Science Research Associates.

Flanagan, O. J. 1984. *The Science of Mind.* Cambridge: MIT Press.

Forte, A. 1955. *Contemporary Tone-structures.* New York: Bureau of Publications, Teachers College, Columbia University.

Forte, A. 1973. *The Structure of Atonal Music.* New Haven: Yale University Press.

Forte, A. 1974. *Tonal Harmony in Concept and Practice.* 2d ed. New York: Holt, Rinehart, and Winston.

Forte, A. 1980. "Aspects of Rhythm in Webern's Atonal Music." *Music Theory Spectrum,* 2:90–109.

Frauenfelder, U., J. Segui, and J. Mehler. 1980. "Monitoring Around the Relative Clause." *Journal of Verbal Learning and Verbal Behavior,* 19:328–337.

Fux, J. S. 1943. *Steps to Parnasus: The Study of Counterpoint.* A. Mann, tr. New York: Norton.

Gaston, E. T. 1958. *Gaston Test of Musicality.* 4th ed. Lawrence, Kan.: Odell's Instrument Co.

Gordon, E. E. 1965. *Musical Aptitude Profile.* Boston: Houghton Mifflin.

Grout, D. J. 1973. *A History of Western Music.* 2d ed. New York: Norton.

Guntharp, M. G. 1980. *Learning the Fiddler's Ways.* University Park: Pennsylvania State University Press.

Harris, D. B. 1963. *Children's Drawings as Measures of Intellectual Maturity.* New York: Harcourt, Brace, and World.

Harwood, D. L. 1976. "Universals in Music: A Perspective from Cognitive Psychology." *Ethnomusicology,* 20:521–533.

Healy, A. F. and J. E. Cutting. 1976. "Units of Speech Perception: Phoneme and Syllable." *Journal of Verbal Learning and Verbal Behavior,* 15:73–83.

Helmholtz, H. 1954. *On the Sensations of Tone* (1877). New York: Dover.

Hindemith, P. 1942. *The Craft of Musical Composition.* 2d ed. A. Mendel, tr. New York: Associated Music Publishers.

Jeppesen, K. 1939. *Counterpoint: The Polyphonic Vocal Style of the Sixteenth Century.* G. Haydon, tr. New York: Prentice-Hall.

Kivy, P. 1980. *The Corded Shell: Reflections on Musical Expression.* Princeton, N.J.: Princeton University Press.

Kowalcyk, R. M. 1976. "The Associative Relation Between Triadic Musical Chords and Color." Ph.D. dissertation, Fordham University, 1976. *Dissertation Abstracts International,* 37:2545B.

Krumhansl, C. L. 1979. "The Psychological Representation of Musical Pitch in a Tonal Context." *Cognitive Psychology*, 11:346–374.

Kwalwasser, J. and P. Dykema. 1930. *K-D Music Tests*. New York: Carl Fischer.

Langer, S. K. 1953. *Feeling and Form*. New York: Scribner's.

Lowry, R. 1982. *The Evolution of Psychological Theory*. 2d ed. New York: Aldine.

Lundin, R. W. 1967. *An Objective Psychology of Music*. 2d ed. New York: Wiley.

Lundin, R. W. 1949. "The Development and Validation of a Set of Musical Ability Tests." *Psychological Monographs*, 63:1–35.

Madsen, C. K., R. D. Greer, and C. H. Madsen, eds. 1975. *Research in Music Behavior: Modifying Music Behavior in the Classroom*. New York: Teacher's College Press, Columbia University.

Madsen, C. K. and T. L. Kuhn. 1978. *Contemporary Music Education*. Arlington Heights, Ill: AHM Publishing.

Maher, T. 1976. "Need for Resolution Ratings of Harmonic Musical Intervals: A Comparison Between Indians and Canadians." *Journal of Cross Cultural Psychology*, 7:259–276.

Mainwaring, J. 1931. "Tests of Musical Ability." *British Journal of Educational Psychology*, 1:313–321.

McNeill, D. and K. Lindig. 1973. "The Perceptual Reality of Phonemes, Syllables, Words, and Sentences." *Journal of Verbal Learning and Verbal Behavior*, 9:295–302.

Mellers, W. H. 1973. *Twilight of the Gods: The Beatles in Retrospect*. London: Faber and Faber.

Merriam, A. 1964. *The Anthropology of Music*. Evanston, Ill.: Northwestern University Press.

Meyer, L. B. 1956. *Emotion and Meaning in Music*. Chicago: University of Chicago Press.

Meyer, L. B. 1967. *Music, the Arts, and Ideas*. Chicago: University of Chicago Press.

Meyer, L. B. 1973. *Explaining Music*. Berkeley: University of California Press.

Miller, G. H. 1956. "The Magic Number Seven, Plus or Minus Two." *Psychological Review*, 63:81–97.

Mills, E. and T. C. Murphy, eds. 1973. *The Suzuki Conception: An Introduction to a Successful Method for Early Music Education*. Berkeley, Calif.: Diablo Press.

Mitchell, W. J. 1948. *Elementary Harmony*. 2d ed. New York: Prentice-Hall.

Mozart, L. 1948. *Treatise on the Fundamentals of Violin Playing*. E. Knocker, tr. New York: Oxford University Press.

Mursell, J. L. 1937. *The Psychology of Music*. New York: Norton.

Narmour, E. 1977. *Beyond Schenkerism*. Chicago: University of Chicago Press.

Nettl, B. 1956a. *Music in Primitive Culture*. Cambridge: Harvard University Press.

Nettl, B. 1956b. "Unifying Factors in Folk and Primitive Music." *Journal of the American Musicological Society*, 9:196–201.

Nettl, B. 1973. *Folk and Traditional Music of the Western Continents.* 2d ed. Englewood Cliffs, N.J.: Prentice-Hall.

Palisca, C. 1961. "Scientific Empiricism in Musical Thought." In H. H. Rhys, ed., *Seventeenth-Century Science and the Arts.* Princeton, N.J.: Princeton University Press.

Parry, C. H. H. 1896. *The Evolution of the Art of Music.* New York: Appleton.

Pederson, P. 1975. "The Perception of Octave Equivalence in 12-tone Rows." *Psychology of Music,* 3:3–8.

Pflederer, M. R. 1966. "How Children Conceptually Organize Musical Sounds." *Bulletin of the Council for Research in Music Education,* 7:1–12.

Piston, W. 1962. *Harmony.* 3d ed. New York: Norton.

Rakowski, A. 1979. "The Magic Number Two: Seven Examples of Binary Apposition in Pitch Theory." *Humanities Association Review,* 30:24–45.

Russo, W. 1968. *Jazz Composition and Orchestration.* Chicago: University of Chicago Press.

Salzer, F. 1952. *Structural Hearing.* New York: Boni.

Salzer, F. and C. Schachter. 1969. *Counterpoint in Composition.* New York: McGraw-Hill.

Savin, H. B. and T. G. Bever. 1970. "The Non-Perceptual Reality of the Phoneme." *Journal of Verbal Learning and Verbal Behavior,* 9:295–302.

Schenker, H. 1954. *Harmony* (1906). E. M. Borgese, tr., O. Jonas, ed. Chicago: University of Chicago Press.

Schenker, H. 1979. *Free Composition* (1935). E. Oster, tr. New York: Longman.

Searle, C. L. 1979. "Analysis of Music from an Auditory Perspective." *Humanities Association Review,* 30:93–103.

Seashore, C. E. 1938. *The Psychology of Music.* New York: McGraw-Hill.

Seashore, C. E., D. Lewis, and J. Saetveit. 1960. *Measures of Musical Talents* (1919, 1930). New York: Psychological Corp.

Serafine, M. L. 1986. "Music." In R. F. Dillon and R. J. Sternberg, eds., *Cognition and Instruction.* New York: Academic Press.

Serafine, M. L. 1981. "Musical Timbre Imagery in Young Children." *Journal of Genetic Psychology,* 139:97–108.

Serafine, M. L. 1979. "A Measure of Meter Conservation in Music, Based on Piaget's Theory." *Genetic Psychology Monographs,* 99:185–229.

Shepard, J., P. Virden, G. Vulliamy, and T. Wishart. 1977. *Whose Music? A Sociology of Musical Languages.* New Brunswick, N.J.: Transaction Books.

Shuter, R. 1968. *The Psychology of Musical Ability.* London: Methuen.

Shuter-Dyson, R. and C. Gabriel. 1981. *The Psychology of Musical Ability.* 2d ed. London: Methuen.

Siegel, J. and W. Siegel. 1977a. "Absolute Identification of Notes and Intervals by Musicians." *Perception and Psychophysics,* 21:143–152.

Seigel, J. and W. Siegel. 1977b. "Categorical Perception of Tonal Intervals: Musicians Can't Tell Sharp from Flat." *Perception and Psychophysics,* 21:399–407.

Smith, K. U. 1984. "'Facedness' and Its Relation to Musical Talent." *Journal of the Acoustical Society of America,* 75:1907–1908.

Strunk, O., ed. 1950. *Source Readings in Music History.* New York: Norton.

Strunk, S. 1979. "The Harmony of Early Bop: A Layered Approach." *Journal of Jazz Studies* (Fall/Winter), pp. 4–21.

Thurlow, W. R. and W. P. Erchul. "Judged Similarity in Pitch of Octave Multiples." *Perception and Psychophysics,* 22:177–182.

Tolstoy, L. 1955. *What Is Art?* A. Maude, tr. London: Oxford University Press. (See also J. Stolnitz, ed., *Aesthetics.* New York: Macmillan, 1967.)

Treitler, L. 1974. "Homer and Gregory: The Transmission of Epic Poetry and Plainchant." *Musical Quarterly,* 60:333–372.

Wing, H. 1961. *Standardized Tests of Musical Intelligence* (1930). London: National Foundation for Educational Research.

Wing, H. D. 1948. "Test of Musical Ability and Appreciation." *British Journal of Psychology Monograph Supplement,* Vol. 8.

Wink, R. L. and L. G. Williams. 1976. *Invitation to Listening.* 2d ed. Boston: Houghton Mifflin.

Yeston, M. 1976. *The Stratification of Musical Rhythm.* New Haven: Yale University Press.

Yeston, M. 1975. "Rubato and the Middleground." *Journal of Music Theory,* 19:286–301.

Zenatti, A. 1975. "Melodic Memory Tests: A Comparison of Normal Children and Mental Defectives." *Journal of Research in Music Education,* 23:41–52.

Zenatti, A. 1976. "Children's Aesthetic Judgment About Music Consonance, Tonality, and Isochronism of the Rhythmic Beat." *Psychologie Française,* 21:175–184 (abstract).

Index

Ability, *see* Music tests; Trait theory
Abstraction, 83–85
Abstraction experiments, 196–212
Acculturation to tonal idiom, 130–34
Acoustics, 18–22, 236
Acquisition, 5, 234; *see also* Development
Acuity, 11, 77, 233–34
Aleatoric music, 70
Analysis, 20, 25–26, 35–39, 51–64; *see also* Music theory
Antimentalism, *see* Behaviorism
Aptitude, *see* Music tests; Trait theory
Aron, P., 47
Artifacts of analysis, 20–22, 52–64
Atonal music, 34, 50; *see also* Twentieth-century music

Bach, C. 39
Bach, J. S., *English Suite,* 85
Balzano, G., 56
Bamberger and Brofsky, 39
Basilar membrane, 20, 58–59
Behavior, *see* Composing
Behaviorism, 16–18, 104
Benade, A., 23
Bentley, A., 9–10
Berg, A., 34
Berry, W., 51, 85
Birdcalls, 70
Blechner, M., 63
Boethius, 45–46

Catholic church, 43
Cerebral dominance, 11
Change, 4–5, 17, 31–33, 51–52
Child development, *see* Development

Chords, 24, 46–50, 77; historical development of, 47–50; derivation of, 53–55; role in perception, 55–60; use in research, 56–60; *see also* Harmony
"Chunks," *see* Phrasing
Classical music: compared to folk, rock, jazz, 40–42
Closure, 80
Closure experiment, 157–70
Cogan and Escot, 39
Cognitive processes, *see* Processes
Cognitive stage of younger subjects, *see* Conservation
Cognitive structures, *see* Structures
Collier, G., 76, 82, 84
Colwell, R., 9
Communication, 6, 12–16
Communities, *see* Musical communities
Composers: number in U.S., 5n
Composing: nature of, 55, 61; relationship to performing and listening, 6, 33, 67, 71–72
Composition: idea of, 36
Compound melody, 87–88
Con junto music, 31
Conservation, 90, 97, 102–3; and motivic chaining, 120–22; and idiomatic construction, 134; and textural abstraction, 138; and motivic synthesis, 150; and closure, 165; and transformations, 179; and rhythmic abstraction, 209
Consonance and dissonance, 44, 46–48, 52, 236
Constructivism, 7, 67, 70
Cooper and Meyer, 51
Counterpoint, 46–48; as texture, 78–79

Crocker and Bassart, 39
Cross-cultural evidence, 59
Culture, 33–35

Darwin, C., 8
"Dawg" music, 31
Debussy, C., 50
Decrement in performance by 11-year-olds, *see* "Sixth grade slump"
Deutsch, D., 52, 57
Development: questions concerning, 76, 79
Developmentalism, 88–93, 233–34
Developmental trends in music cognition, 224–28
Discrete pitches, 24–27; historical origin of, 60–64; role in perception, 62–64; *see also* Pitch discrimination
Diversity, 4, 17
Divine inspiration, 18–19, 52
Dowling, W., 52, 57, 58, 83
Dowling and Hollombe, 57
Drake, R., 9
Draw-a-Person test, 97; and motivic chaining, 121–22; and textural abstraction, 138–39; and motivic synthesis, 150; and closure, 165; and rhythmic abstraction, 209
Durations: as units of rhythm, 60
Dykema, P., *see* Kwalwasser and Dykema

Early childhood: music cognition in, 227–28
Early music, 32
Elements of music, 7, 25–26
Elements of perception, 60–64
Emotions, 12–16
Epistemology: aims of developmentalism, 88–93
Evolutionary forces, 18, 23
Expectation, 14–16, 76

Figurative skills, 154–55; compared to operative skills, 230–31
Figure *versus* ground, 78–79
Fixed pitches, *see* Discrete pitches
Folk music, 40, 75, 76, 79, 80, 82, 84, 85
Formal *versus* global properties, 212
Forte, A., 39, 50, 51, 85
Frauenfelder, Segui, and Mehler, 64
Fugue, 78–79

Fux, J., 48

Gabriel, C., *see* Shuter-Dyson and Gabriel
Galton, F., 8
Gaston, E., 9
Gender differences, 101–2, 150, 154, 179, 209, 221
Generic processes, 6, 30, 39–40, 52, 62, 73–88; *see also* Nontemporal processes; Style-specific processes; Temporal processes
Glarean, H., 48
Global *versus* formal properties, 212
Goodenough-Harris Draw-a-Person test, *see* Draw-a-Person test
Goodman, B., 85
Goodness in music, 235–36
Gordon, E., 9
Gregorian chant, 42–46, 61–62
Grisman, D., 31
Grout, D., 43, 45, 62
Guido of Arezzo, 43, 46
Guntharp, M., 82

Harmony, 47–50; *see also* Simultaneity
Harris, D., 97
Healy and Cutting, 63
Helmholtz, H., 53, 236
Hierarchic levels, 85–88
Hierarchic levels experiment, 213–22
Homophony, 78–79
Horizontal style, *see* Counterpoint
Human figure drawing, *see* Draw-a-Person test

Idiomatic construction, 74–75; and motivic chaining, 133–34
Idiomatic construction experiment, 110–17
Implication-realization model, 14–16
Individual differences, 234; *see also* Trait theory
Information processing, 26
Intellecltual maturity, *see* Draw-a-Person test
Intelligence tests, 8
Intervals, 18–22, 44, 46, 57
Inversion, 83

Jazz, 35, 40, 75, 76, 79, 82, 83, 84

Jeppesen, K., 39, 48
Jimenez, F., 31

Keys, *see* Scales
Kivy, P., 13
Kowalcyk, R., 56
Krumhansl, C., 56
Kwalwasser and Dykema, 8–9, 63

Langer, S., 14
Late childhood, music cognition in, 224–26
Learning theory, *see* Behaviorism; Training
Listening, *see* Composing
Lundin, R., 9, 63

McNeil and Lindig, 63
Mainwaring, J., 9
Mathematical order, 18, 23, 45–46, 52
Medieval theory, 44–46
Mellers, W., 41
Melody, *see* Counterpoint
Melody and accompaniment textures, 78–79
Melody discrimination, *see* Idiomatic construction experiment; Transformation experiments
Mentalism, 17
Merriam, A., 36
Meyer, L., 14–15, 51
Middle childhood: music cognition in, 227
Miller, G., 19, 57
Mills and Murphy, 103
Mitchell, W., 39, 49
Modes, 45, 46–48; *see also* Scales
Motivic abstraction, 83
Motivic abstraction experiment, 196–204
Motivic chaining, 75–76
Motivic chaining experiment, 117–23
Motivic synthesis, 78
Motivic synthesis experiment, 145–50
Mozart, L., 39
Mursell, J., 10
Music: definition of, 64–67, 69–73; *see also* Behaviorism; Communication; Nature theories of music; Sound; Trait theory
Musical ability, *see* Music tests; Trait theory
Musical change, *see* Change
Musical communication, *see* Communication

Musical communities, 33–35
Musicality, *see* Music tests; Trait theory
Musical style, *see* Style
Musical talent, *see* Music tests; Trait theory
Musical training, *see* Training
Music analysis, *see* Analysis; Music theory
Music as object, 64–67
Music cognition: assumptions regarding, 6–7
Music tests, 7–12, 56; critique of, 10–12; *see also* Trait theory
Music theory, 20, 27; aims of, 6; *see also* Analysis

Nature theories of music, 18–23, 57–60
Nettl, B., 76, 79, 80, 82, 84, 85
New music: writing of, 5
Nonaural activities, 70–72
Nonmusical activities, 70–72
Nontemporal processes, 79–88; *see also* Abstraction; Closure; Hierarchic levels; Temporal processes; Transformations
Notation, 22, 37, 51–52, 61–62; development of, 42–44
Numerology, *see* Mathematical order

Objective definition of music, 64–67
Octave equivalence, 57
Odo of Cluny, 43
Older children's musical cognition, 224–26
Operative *versus* figurative skills, 230–31
Ornamentation, 38, 82
Overtones, 18–22, 50

Palestrina, G., 48
Parry, H., 23
Patterning, 76
Patterning experiment, 112–17
Pedagogy, 22, 37–39, 45, 52; *see also* Training
Pederson, P., 57
Perception: elements of, 55; contrasted with cognition, 27, 90–91, 154–55, 233–34; *see also* Acuity; Music tests
Perfumery: music compared to, 235
Performance decrement in 11-year-olds, *see* "Sixth grade slump"
Performance practice, 32, 37–39
Performing, *see* Composing

Pflederer, M., 84
Phoneme class, analogy to discrete pitches, 60*n*, 63–64
Phrasing, 76–77
Phrasing experiment, 108–12
Piaget, J., 90, 230
Piston, W., 39, 49
Pitch discrimination, 62–64, 230–31; ability of subjects in, 100–1; and musical training, 101; and idiomatic construction, 134; and textural abstraction, 138; and motivic synthesis, 150; and closure, 164; and transformation, 179; and rhythmic abstraction, 209; and hierarchic levels, 221
Pitches, *see* Discrete pitches; Music tests; Trait theory
Polyphony, 78–79
Porter, C., 85
Procedure: for experiments, 95–98
Processes, 18, 29–30, 39–40, 73–88, 233–34; *see also* Generic processes; Nontemporal processes; Style-specific processes; Temporal processes
Property abstraction, 83–84
Psychology of music: aims, 1–7, 27; critique of, 52–64
Pythagoras, 23

Qualitative developmental changes: vs. quantitative, 89, 122–23, 133

Rakowski, A., 56, 57
Rameau, J., 23, 45, 47–50
Ratios, 18–19
Reflection on music, 35–37, 42–64; *see also* Analysis; Music theory
Reinforcement, *see* Behaviorism
Repeated hearing of music, 32
Repetition, 81
Response bias in young children, 128–29, 148, 161–62
Retrograde, 83
Retrograde inversion, 83
Rhythm, theories of, 51
Rhythmic abstraction, 83–84
Rhythmic abstraction experiment, 204–12
Rhythmic complexity, sensitivity in young children, 139–42
Rock music, 31, 35, 40, 75

Russo, W., 79, 83

Salzer, F., 39, 48, 50
Savin and Bever, 63
Scales, 18–22, 46–48, 49; derivation of, 53–60; role in perception, 56–60
Schachter, C., 39, 48
Schenker, H., 22, 45, 49, 50, 85
Schoenberg, A., 34
Searle, C., 58
Seashore, C., 8, 10, 63
Serafine, M., ix, 10, 78, 88*n*, 155
Serialism, 70
Sex differences, *see* Gender differences
Shepard, R., 53, 59
Shuter-Dyson and Gabriel, 10, 77
Siegal, J., 53
Siegel and Siegel, 63
Similarity and difference, *see* Transformation
Simultaneity, 77–79; *see also* Motivic synthesis; Textural abstraction; Timbre synthesis
"Sixth-grade slump," 132, 138, 225–26, 231; in pitch discrimination, 100–1; in patterning experiment, 113, 116; in motivic synthesis, 148–49; in closure experiment, 161–62; in transformation experiment, 176, 191; absence in motivic abstraction, 199, 211; in rhythmic abstraction, 207–8
Smith, K., 11
Sound: music defined as, 24–27, 64–67, 69–70; *see also* Trait theory
Speech perception: analogy to music perception, 60*n*, 63–64
Structures, 18; "Golden section," 22; *Urform*, 22; hierarchic, 85–88
Strunk, S., 85
Style, 4–5, 29–30, 33–35, 51–52
Style blends, 31
Style change, *see* Change
Style diversity, *see* Diversity
Style-specific processes, 6, 29–30, 73; *see also* Generic processes
Subject-object relations, 69
Subjects: in all studies, 98–99
Substantive transformation, 82

Succession, 74–77; *see also* Idiomatic construction; Motivic chaining; Patterning; Phrasing
Suzuki, S., 103
Suzuki subjects' performance: on conservation, 106; on Draw-a-Person test, 106; on closure task, 165–70; on transformation tasks, 192–96; on hierarchic levels task, 219, 221–22
Suzuki training, 103–6; effects of, 229–31

Talent, *see* Music tests; Trait theory
Task construction, 92–93, 232
Temporality, 25, 36, 69, 72, 74–79
Temporal processes: vs. nontemporal processes, 231, 232; *see also* Simultaneity; Succession
Tests, *see* Music tests
Textural abstraction, 78–79
Textural abstraction experiment, 135–45
Theories of music, *see* Behaviorism; Communication; Music theory; Nature theories of music; Sound
Theory: lack of, 26
Thurlow and Erchul, 57
Timbre synthesis, 77–78
Timbre synthesis experiment, 151–55
Time, *see* Temporality
Tolstoy, L., 12
Tonal closure, *see* Closure
Tonal idiom, 19–22, 46–50, 59, 76; role in motivic chaining, 122–34; *see also* Idiomatic construction; Closure
Tones, *see* Discrete pitches; Music tests; Trait theory
Tonic cadences, 46–48; *see also* Closure

Training: aims of studying, 90–91; levels of subjects, 99; and pitch discrimination, 101; and motivic chaining, 120–22; and idiomatic construction, 134; and textural abstraction, 138–39; and closure, 164; and transformations, 179; and rhythmic abstraction, 209; and hierarchic levels task, 221; effects of, 228–31; *see also* Suzuki subjects' performance; Suzuki training
Trait theory, 7–12, 234
Transformation, 30, 40, 80–83
Transformation experiments, 171–96
Transposition, 57
Treitler, L., 62
Twelve-tone technique, 34, 50; *see also* Serialism
Twentieth-century music, 50–51, 59

Universality, 1–4
Universals, *see* Generic processes

Webern, A., 34
Western music, *see* Tonal idiom
Wing, H., 9, 77
Wink and Williams, 39

Yeston, M., 51, 84
Young children, 78; response bias in, 128–29, 148, 161–62; sensitivity to rhythmic complexity, 139–42; perception and memory, 154–55
Young children's musical cognition, 227–28

Zarlino, G., 48–49
Zenatti, A., 57